Escudo (shield) of Fuentesaúco

SILVÁN LEAVES

Out on a Limb

Patricia Ruiz Steele

Book Two of the Spanish Pearls Series

AMERICA DISPLACED THE NAMES OF MEN AND
SWALLOWED THE NAMES OF WOMEN

"If you don't know history, you don't know anything. You are a
leaf that doesn't know it is part of a tree."
-- Michael Crichton

SILVÁN LEAVES
Out on a Limb

Copyright @ 2014 by Patricia Ruiz Steele
Plumeria Press
Casa Grande, Arizona, USA

ISBN: 978-0-9890013-1-1
Library of Congress Control Number: Pending

Cover artwork by Chris Howard, at Blondesign

Visit author's website: www.patriciabbsteele.com

Also by Patricia Steele ~
"Living with Cystic Fibrosis" in *Your Health Magazine*
Shoot the Moon, a romantic mystery novel
Mooning over a Drug Card, (an eBook of Shoot the Moon)
A Roundabout Passage to Venice, a humorous travel log
Cooking DRUNK (and wine tasting 101), a cookbook
 Goodbye Balloon, a children's story

Spanish Pearls Series:
Book One: The Girl Immigrant – Their immigration story
Book Two: Silván Leaves– Biographies, Documents and Photos

In Progress:
Book Three: Ruiz Legacies – Biographies, Documents and Photos

OUR *SILVAN* LEAVES

Patricia Ruiz Steele

A Spanish Heritage
2014

This book follows' *The Girl Immigrant*; these are the leaves flowing from the SILVAN family tree honoring their history

Inside Story: Silvan photos, biographies and history

It was the story about our family tree and the leaves that followed from Fuentesauco, Spain to America by the roundabout way of Hawaii and the sugar cane fields. It was the story of the exhilaration of endless expectations as our ancestor's world opened up from a stagnant economy after the offer of a life in Hawaii shifted their spirits. It was the story that was being lived as the ink was drying on their commitment contracts. It was the story of their lives in the agricultural industry of Hawaii and their love of the Hawaiian music and flowers. This story began in 1911 as they were introduced to sugar fields, swinging palms, banana plants, the ukulele and island music in the shifting tropical winds. It was the story of their ethnic communities where they met and married Spaniards and Portuguese. It was the story of the history of their lives and passing the torch onto their children and their children's children.

As our ancestors began their trek creating lives we enjoy through the telling, their names fleshed out into the real people only some of us remember. We are bound to them. Though we cannot look into their eyes or hear their voices, we honor their history and cherish their lives. For all the leaves that come after us, we know they will smile and so will we.

Fuentesauco, Villaescusa, Villamor de Escuderos and Toro, Zamora, Spain

FELIPE
AGAPITA
MATIAS
VICTORINO
EDMUNDO
ANGEL
JUAN FRANCISCO
GERONIMO
LORENZO
CRESCENCIA
AGUSTIN

SILVAN

The descendents that follow...

With the help of many family members, I have been able to sort, organize, clarify and add factual family information through stories, pictures and documents. If there are any errors in the information forthwith, I take full responsibility. I have worked diligently to clarify and confirm names, dates, places, children and overall history.

I have enjoyed getting to know the past familial connections and delighted in meeting the long-lost cousins from all the limbs of our Silvan tree.

Therefore, my next book will include the Ruiz family, the other half of my Silvan-Ruiz tree.

I encourage our family members to send me any information, stories, documents and pictures in your attics, basements, files, boxes or your treasured places so the Ruiz family's book will be as golden as this one.

Book One, THE GIRL IMMIGRANT, tells the Silvan's 1911-1920 immigration story.

SILVÁN Descendant leaves have budded and bloomed

Celestino Pedro SILVÁN Dovales
Agustina Hernández Martín

Other things may change us,
but we start and end with the family.

SPANNING DECADES AND UNITING GENERATIONS

Table of Contents

Acknowledgements
Introduction
Family Tree

Part 1 19
Spain: SILVÁN foundation family at a glance

Part 2 37
Spain: Spanish Homeland SILVÁNS

Part 3 69
Immigrant SILVÁNS from Spain to Hawaii and into America

Part 4...…....……155
First Generation of SILVÁN Descendants in America

Part 5 370
The Other SILVÁN Family

The Silván Family Reunion......................................382

ACKNOWLEDGEMENTS

In contemplating the many people who contribute to a work such as this, one recognizes how deeply she is influenced, supported, and assisted by others. First and foremost, I acknowledge that this book would not have been written without the eager and consistent support from the many Silván descendants; some I have never met.

Thanks to the many contributions from new friends, my distant cousins, in California, Oregon, Michigan, Hawaii, Colorado, Texas, Montana and the Diocese of Spain in the Province of Zamora, with the help of José Carlos de Lera as well as Cristóbal Navas Pérez, a conscientious and diligent researcher who studied at the Universidad de Málaga, now in Barcelona, Spain.

J. Robert Ruiz and Jeffrey Cortopassi gave me the skeleton basics of family tree information. Without their research and listening to family history from my Silvan aunts and uncles, I might still be twisting in the wind.

And I thank abuelita Manuela Silván Trascasas and my father, Michael Silván Ruiz, for the family stories, documents and the burning desire to "meet" my ancestors.

I saw a photo of an empty bench before a peaceful bay with trees above and flowers around me with a note, "if you could have just one hour with someone who is no longer in your life, who would you choose." My immediate thought was my daughter, Christina Marie, who died in 1978 from Cystic Fibrosis but I knew I could not get past the lump in my throat to do so.

Then, I chose my father, Michael Silván Ruiz, who was the first in our immediate family to investigate the Silván family tree. He asked questions. He found documents. He walked on Spanish soil in Fuentesaúco. Over the years, he shared family history. I barely remember. Now he is gone. All his documents and genealogical information disappeared with him. Nobody knows where his briefcase ended up. Yes, one hour to ask my father some questions and see his face fill with pride as he hears that I have walked in his footsteps and found our family. I wish…......

I want to especially thank my brother, Steven Ruiz Bettencourt, who was my translator, driver and research companion during my trip to Spain. He drove through villages, inspected cemeteries, drank Spanish wine and shared our contentment and pride of being Spanish. Without him, I certainly could not have traced those ancestral footsteps nor could I have understood the language swirling around me. And… without his knowledge, friends and contacts in southern Spain, I would have missed a stunning paella dinner. A Spanish friend's outside grill, his table under a portico, sipping red wine and later hearing him play the guitar and his simplistic view of the world. "One needs good wine, good friends and less war." Steven translated so softly I thought I understood the man's Spanish in my head. Magic.

Special thanks to cousins, strangers, who shared documents, photographs, stories and their homes during this research and interview process. I've learned to love these people, sincerely overwhelmed by their generosity. Their excitement has fueled my insatiable need to share this work so they can hold in their hands, their own, very personal Spanish **SILVÁN LEAVES ~ Out on a Limb**.

INTRODUCTION

SILVÁN LEAVES is a familial biographical history of the Silván family tree that germinated and grew out of Fuentesaúco, in the Province of Zamora, Spain based on long hours of research stemming from family stories, photographs, ancestral documents, www.ancestry.com sources, personal visits, phone conversations and memories. It encompasses the Silván siblings beginning with Felípe, Agapita, Matías, Victorino Luciano, Edmundo, Angel, Juan Francisco, Gerónimo, Lorenzo, Crescéncia and Agustín Silván Hernández with extensions from the family that came before them. Perhaps the beauty and mystic of working backwards into the villages of Spain was the capacity to flesh out our ancestors with the help of so many descendants that popped out of the fabric of America to act as puzzle pieces full of imagination and mystery.

"Every family has its ups and downs, and there are certain people who get along well and a few who clash," says author, William H. Gass, in which he raises questions about how biographers distinguish "relevant" from "irrelevant" material when assessing their subjects' characters.

He continues, "What are the data that determine any person's life? Of the things we desire, do, see, think or feel, what should be discarded like spoiled paper, and what should be retained? How shall the residue be weighed? How shall these elements be joined to one another? And why should we really bother putting the puzzle together at all, at such expense of time and reflection?"

My focus is getting to know the family member, not gossiping about their shortfalls of character. Noting some flaws in their lives makes them real. It doesn't make them less of who they were to themselves or to their children and grandchildren. They were real life people who were loved for who they were to the many who remember them. If I have offended anyone in my delivery of their family's biography, I apologize before you turn the first page. It was not my intent.

This book is the second in my Spanish Pearls Series, a genealogy summary penned after the story of the Silván's trek from Spain, their forty-eight days in February 1911 that sailed the immigrants to Hawaii and the sugar plantations before saving enough money to continue on to California where most of their descendants remain. The first book, *The Girl Immigrant*, was published after my trip to their Spanish villages, where I concluded my findings after walking along Calle San Salvador, poking into the Fuentesaúco Cementerio and standing on the stone steps of the Santa Maria Church. It was their immigration story. This book is who they were.

Many of the following biographies describe some family members in rich detail, while others briefly touch on other member's lives. The reason for the short biographies can reasonably be explained because many descendants were ever so willing to share information; others were disinterested, cautious to share or could not be found.

The inspiration to gallop through the family tree with wild abandon began too late to question either my father or my abuelita, Manuela Silván Trascasas. Sorrowfully, during their lives, their stories bounced around inside my head without substance. I neglected to write down the names, places, people or stories. With the help of many good aunts, uncles and cousins, I have found new family to share with those I have known all my life and enriched all of us by extending the family tree beyond the tiny world we believed held the only Silván people left behind. It is with great excitement that brings the Silván biographies to so many family members who also thought their line had become extinct. Not so!

I will begin in the middle with the family in Fuentesaúco and move in both directions; those who remained, those who were already long gone and the descendants that keep their memory alive in so many ways. Creating these biographies from all my research notes brings them into focus for me and I hope they will for other descendants of these proud people from Spain.

The beginning of the story

In 1898, the United States annexed Hawaii and in 1900 the Territory of Hawaii was established. The first successful Hawaiian sugar cane plantation was started in Koloa, Kauai in 1835 and by 1898 the industry was booming and the plantation owners soon had a shortage of workers. Most of the workers were Asian, primarily Japanese who were starting to strike for better wages and conditions by 1900. As they tried to organize unions, the plantation owners tried to stop it by looking elsewhere, looking for workers who would not understand the union organizers and therefore work in their plantations and be happy to do so. They had to devise an enticing lure.

In 1905, as part of a plan to encourage new workers to work in their sugar plantations, the Hawaiian Board of Immigration adopted a policy to bring to Hawaii persons who would be eligible for American Citizenship. They targeted Spain and Portugal because they grew sugar cane; they were hardworking and familiar with harvesting techniques.

To encourage the immigration of workers, The Hawaiian Sugar Plantation Association promised to provide families from Spain and Portugal an acre of land, a house, free schooling for their children, guaranteed work and free passage to the Hawaiian Islands financed by contributions from sugar plantations and agencies. Posters would be distributed throughout Spain and Portugal announcing the program with the hopes of enticing them to their sugar cane fields.

In the winter of 1906, representatives of Hawaii's sugar industry arrived in the seaport of Málaga on the southern tip of Spain. Bulletins (broadsheets) were posted in plazas, shops and given to local citizens saying, *"Emigracion Con Pasaje Gratuito Al Estado de Hawaii"* (emigrate with free passage to the State of

Hawaii. The first voyage was scheduled for 1907 and many of the younger men jumped at the invitation.

Our Silván ancestors from the small village of Fuentesaúco, about 100 miles northwest of Madrid in the Province of Zamora, saw the poster. Some villagers met with the alcalde but in the end their fears stopped them; nobody from Fuentesaúco left the village on that first voyage.

A few years later, with political unrest becoming worse and the military conscription causing havoc, they began to listen and ponder the possibility and by the end of 1910, it was decided. Between four Silván siblings, there were nine children aged 10 months to 12 years. José, Agustín, Alejandro, Jacinto, Celestino, Juanitco, Felisa, Manuela and Teodora. When it was time to leave, each family gathered their belongings into the one trunk they were each allowed. Geronimo and Agustín carted it and the children to the train station where they went from rail to boat to trail. The train took them over the mountains to Seville where they boarded a boat headed for Sanlúcar sailing down the Guadalquivir River to the ocean. The twelve-days of walking, camping, working and tedious travel took them to La Línea at the border of Spain and Gibraltar where the ship, SS Orteric would be their watery home for some weeks.

They knew that once they arrived, they must dispose of the cart and donkey and haul out the trunks and children. They had no trouble selling as there were those waiting at the border to purchase the immigrant's carts and discarded possessions at a fraction of their worth.

Our family crossed the border to a dock clogged with immigrants waiting to board the Orteric. Once their documents were inspected and approved, they departed on February 24, 1911. Everyone in the Silván family sailed except Lorenzo Silván, who was turned away for poor health; he chose to follow others to Cuba. The siblings were devastated but logic and practicality dictated and our families saw Spain drop into the ocean as they sailed away.

The Orteric's maiden voyage was launched at Greenock, Scotland on January 28, 1911. She was capable of 12-13 knots an hour at 3,000 hp. There were a total of 1,451 passengers; 547 men, 373 women and 531 children. The ship sailed past the northwest coast of Africa and then crossed the Atlantic Ocean to South America. From there it proceeded down the east coast of South America through the Strait of Magellan, making a coal refueling stop at Punta Arenas, Chile and finally heading northwest on the Pacific Ocean to Hawaii.

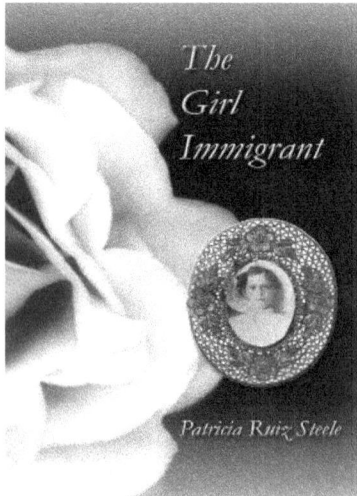

This book is about the Silvan family tree; I retell their immigration story in brief capsules from the first book of the Spanish Pearls Series, *The Girl Immigrant*. I hope these memories of shadow grandparents will brush warmth over living Silvan hearts.

The Girl Immigrant is Book One In the *Spanish Pearls Series*

Books can be purchased at www.patriciabbsteele.com or by contacting the author at patricia@patriciabbsteele.com.

The book is also available at www.amazon.com
And ordered from Barnes & Noble bookstores

Familia de SILVÁN Tree[1]

Ángel SILVÁN Martin *(1820-1870)*
+ María DOVALES Alejo *(1825-1870)*
Their son: *Celestino Pedro SILVÁN Dovales (1850-¿)*

Miguel HERNÁNDEZ Hernández
+ Margarita MARTIN Rodríguez
Their daughter: *Agustina Hernández Martin (d. after 1911)*

Celestino Pedro SILVÁN Dovales
+ Agustina HERNÁNDEZ Martin

Felípe SILVÁN Hernández (1859 – Unknown)
Matías SILVÁN Hernández (1867 – Unknown)
Victorino Luciano SILVÁN Hernández (1868-1925)
Edmundo SILVÁN Hernández (1870 – Unknown)
Ángel SILVÁN Hernández (1873 – Unknown)
Agapita SILVÁN Hernández (1874 – Unknown)
Juan Francisco SILVÁN Hernández (1875 – 1945)
Gerónimo SILVÁN Hernández 1877 – unknown)
Lorenzo SILVÁN Hernández (1880 – unknown)
Crescéncia SILVÁN Hernández (1884 – 1946)
Agustín SILVÁN Hernández (1887 – unknown)

---

[1] This is the earliest Silván ancestor I could find as of this publication

JUAN SILVAN

VICTORINO SILVAN
· RAMONA MARTIN LORENZO

Felisa
(Seraphin
Madeira)
· Jerome
· Melvin

Manuela
(Bernardo Ruiz)
· Frank
· John
· Rose
· Bernardo
· Michael
· Gloria
· Jose
· Dolores
· Delia

María (Frank Cuellar)
· Frank · Rose
· Fred · Helen

CHRISTINA SILVAN

J. FELIX GONZALES

Jacinta

Celestino

Theodora (John Sousa)
· Josephine   · Dorothy
· Victor   · Lillian
· Alfred   · Robert
· George   · Jerome

Agustina
(María Fernandez)
· John
(Ruby Clinton)

José
(Carola Ayus)
· Job

Ramona

Alejandro (Lena Fernandez)
· Telo   · Zena Flint
· Christine   · Zena
· Herman   · Long
· Celestino   · Ralph · Zena
· Felix   · Zelare · John
               · Gwel Anna

Tohue

Cletel (Robinson)
· Barbara
· Jim
· Gordon

C. Sarcinella
(Alice Huckaby)
· Christine
· Alice
· Felix

Victorina (Elvin
· Ramona Viner)
· Sally

María (Orville Miller)
· Christopha · John
· Orville   · James

Agustina (Robert
· Judy   Coombs)

Alfred (Estella Lewis)
· Theresa (Sarah Browne)
· Alicia
· Theresa (Basil Sackett)
· Gwel
· Chester

Eusebio (Phyllis Yankee)
· Linda
· Patricia
· Philip

ANGEL SILVAN

GERARDO SILVAN

LORENZO SILVAN

AGUSTÍN SILVAN

FELIPE SILVAN   EDMUNDO SILVAN   MATIAS SILVAN

AGUSTINA SILVAN

SILVAN HERNANDEZ

SILVÁN DONALES — AGUSTINA HERNÁNDEZ MARTÍ
CELESTINO PEDRO

Descendants of Angel SILVAN Martin
Generation 1

1. ANGEL[1] SILVAN MARTIN was born about 1820 in Villaescusa, Zamora, Castilla-Leon, Spain. He died between1867-1870. He married MARIA DOVALES ALEJO, daughter of Dovales and Alejo. She was born about 1825 in Fuentesauco, Zamora, Spain. She died between1867-1870.

Angel SILVAN Martin and Maria DOVALES Alejo had the following child:

2.   i. CELESTINO PEDRO[2] SILVAN DOVALES (son of Angel SILVAN Martin and Maria DOVALES Alejo) was born about 1842 in Fuentesauco, Zamora, Spain. He died in Spain. He married AGUSTINA HERNANDEZ MARTIN, daughter of Miguel Hernandez Hernandez and Margarita MARTIN Rodriguez. She was born about 1850 in Villamor de los Escuderos, Province of Zamora, Spain. She died in Fuentesauco, Province of Zamora, Spain.

Generation 2

2. CELESTINO PEDRO[2] SILVAN DOVALES (Angel[1] SILVAN Martin) was born about 1842 in Fuentesauco, Zamora, Spain. He died in Spain. He married AGUSTINA HERNANDEZ MARTIN, daughter of Miguel Hernandez Hernandez and Margarita MARTIN Rodriguez. She was born about 1850 in Villamor de los Escuderos, Province of Zamora, Spain. She died in Fuentesauco, Province of Zamora, Spain.

Celestino Pedro SILVAN Dovales and Agustina Hernandez Martin had the following children:

FELIPE SILVAN[3] HERNANDEZ (son of Celestino Pedro SILVAN Dovales and Agustina Hernandez Martin) was born about 1859 in Fuentesauco, Zamora, Spain.

MATÍAS SILVAN HERNANDEZ (son of Celestino Pedro SILVAN Dovales and Agustina Hernandez Martin) was born on 24 Feb 1867 in Fuentesauco, Zamora, Spain.

VICTORINO (VITORINO) LUCIANO SILVAN HERNANDEZ (son of Celestino Pedro SILVAN Dovales and Agustina Hernandez Martin) was born on 21 Jul 1868 in Fuentesauco, Province of Zamora, Spain. He died on 15 Dec 1925 in San Leandro, Alameda, California (Victorino lived at 214 Dabner St., Oakland, CA. He married ROMANA MARTINEZ LORENZO, daughter of Pedro Martin and Sabina Lorenzo. She was born on 09 Aug 1874 in Fuentesauco, Zamora, Spain. She died on 29 Mar 1955 in San Leandro, Alameda, California USA (Ramona died from cerebral vascular disease. At the time of her death, she lived at 877 Joaquin in San Leandro and was buried at St. Mary's in a shared grave with Victorino.).

EDMUNDO (MUNDO) SILVAN HERNANDEZ (son of Celestino Pedro SILVAN Dovales and Agustina Hernandez Martin) was born on 16 Nov 1870 in Fuentesauco, Zamora, Spain.

ANGEL SILVAN HERNANDEZ (son of Celestino Pedro SILVAN Dovales and Agustina Hernandez Martin) was born on 01 Oct 1873 in Fuentesauco, Zamora, Spain.

AGAPITA SILVAN HERNANDEZ (daughter of Celestino Pedro SILVAN Dovales and Agustina Hernandez Martin) was born on 14 Sep 1874 in Fuentesauco, Zamora, Spain.

JUAN FRANCISCO SILVAN HERNANDEZ (son of Celestino Pedro SILVAN Dovales and Agustina Hernandez Martin) was born on 16 Aug 1875 in Fuentesauco, Province of Zamora, Spain. He died on 05 May 1945 in Benicia, Solano, California, USA. He married EUSTOQUIA RITA TRASCASAS MARZO on 23 Apr 1900 in Fuentesauco, Zamora, Spain, daughter of Manuel Trascasas Alonso and Manuela MARZO García. She was born on 28 Sep 1880 in Toro, Province of Zamora, Spain. She died on 13 Jun 1953 in Woodland, Yolo, California, United States (Age: 72).

GERONIMO (JERONIMO) SILVAN HERNANDEZ (son of Celestino Pedro SILVAN Dovales and Agustina Hernandez Martin) was born on 30 Sep 1877 in Fuentesauco, Province of Zamora, Spain. He died about 1945 in Fuentesauco, Province of Zamora, Spain. He married JOAQUINA BRAGADO VICENTE on 30 Aug 1919 in Parroquia de Arcenillas, Spain. She was born about 1876 in Spain. She died about 1950 in Fuentesauco, Zamora, Spain.

LORENZO SILVAN HERNANDEZ (son of Celestino Pedro SILVAN Dovales and Agustina Hernandez Martin) was born on 05 Sep 1880 in Fuentesauco, Zamora, Spain.

CRESCENCIA SILVAN HERNANDEZ (daughter of Celestino Pedro SILVAN Dovales and Agustina Hernández Martin) wasHernandez Martin) was born on 15 Jun 1884 in Fuentesauco, Zamora, Castilla-Leon, Spain. She died on 24 Oct 1946 in Winters, Yolo Co., California, USA (Age: 62). She married FELIX HERNANDEZ GONZALES on 06 May 1906 in Fuentesauco, Province of Zamora, Spain. He died on 27 Dec 1963 in Winters, Yolo, California, USA (Age at Death: 82).

AGUSTIN SILVAN HERNANDEZ (son of Celestino Pedro SILVAN Dovales and Agustina Hernandez Martin) was born about 1887 in Fuentesauco, Province of Zamora, Spain.

PART 1

Spain:
SILVÁN Foundation Family at a Glance

Province of Zamora, Spain

Ángel Silván Martin, Villaescusa

María Dovales Alejo, Fuentesaúco

Miguel Hernández Hernández, Villamor de los Escuderos

Margarita Martin Rodríguez, Villaescusa

Celestino Silván Dovales, Fuentesaúco

Agustina Hernández Martin of Villamor de los Escuderos

Silván Family Map Site Areas

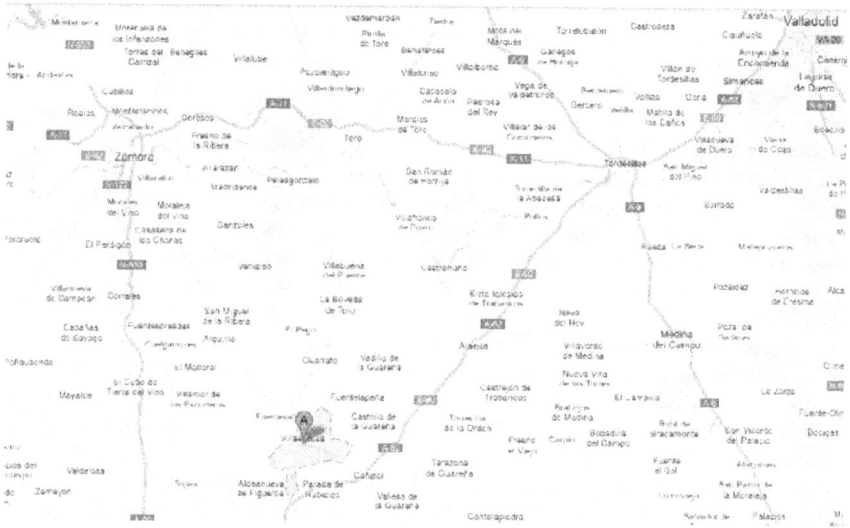

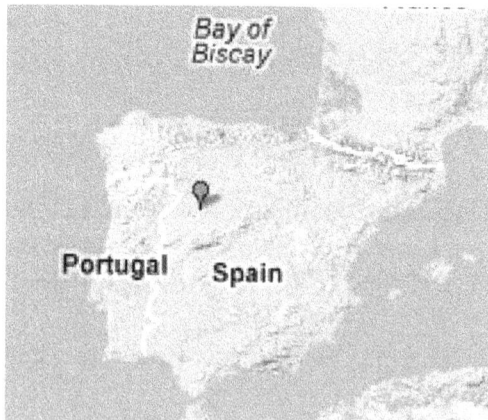

Zamora is a richly diverse province in the region of Castile-Leon, one of Spain's best kept secrets still awaiting discovery by the masses to learn of its history and charm.

Fuentesaúco is located in the province of Zamora, Castile and León, Spain. It is also the county seat for nearby villages. Fuentesaúco's name stems from the Plaza with its "fuente" (fountain) of water amid ceramic swans that spout water and saúco (elderberry) trees. This is the home village of the Silván siblings as well as their father, Celestino Pedro Silván Dovales and his mother, Maria Dovales Alejo. The village is 110 miles southwest of Madrid and a center point from each of the smaller ancestral villages. The area is about 26 square miles and 2,638 feet above sea level. Current population is about 1800. There were ninety seven Fuentesaúco immigrants who left Fuentesaúco and sailed on the SS Orteric in 1911.

Villaescusa is a Spanish village in the province of Zamora, Castile and León, Spain. This is the home village to Margarita Martin, mother of Agustina Hernández Martin, who was the mother to the Silván siblings in our family. This village is about 19 miles southeast of Fuentesaúco, 17 square miles in area and 2,700 feet above sea level. There are currently just over 300 people living in the village.

Vista aérea de la iglesia de Villaescusa

Villamor de los Escuderos, Zamora, Spain - a municipality located in the Province of Zamora, Castile and León, Spain. This is the home village to Miguel Hernández Hernández, father of Agustina Hernández (mother to the Silván siblings in our family). It is about twenty five miles northwest of

Vista aérea de Villamor de los Escuderos

Fuentesaúco, 22 square miles in area and 2,743 feet above sea level. Currently just over 600 people living in the village, 2012.

A street in Toro with the Torre del Reloj at background.

Toro, Zamora, Spain – Toro, a town and municipality in the province of Zamora, part of the autonomous community of Castile and León, Spain; the home of Eustoquia Rita Trascasas Marzo and her parents, Miguel Trascasas Alonso and Manuela Marzo Garcia. It is located on a fertile high plain, northwest of Madrid and almost directly north of Fuentesaúco, about twenty four miles. Toro has been long famous for its wine and is known as a center of Mudéjar art. It is located on the Duero River roughly half way between Zamora and the province of Valladolid.

ÁNGEL SILVÁN MARTIN
Villaescusa, Province of Zamora, Spain

Villaescusa is a tiny village located in Zamora, Castile and Leon with 321 inhabitants (c. 2012), a few miles from Fuentesaúco. Born in this village was Angel Silván Martin who married María Dovales Alejo, parents of Celestino Pedro Silván Dovales.

Also Margarita Martin Rodriguez, mother of Agustina Hernandez Martin. The Martin and Alejo families were also ancestors to the Martin cousins (San Leandro and Hayward, California) through Romana Martinez Lorenzo (wife of Victorino Silván Hernández).

Proven document lists:
Ángel Silván. Natural de Fuentesaúco ¿antes de 1800? Jornalero. Fallecido antes de 1884. Casado con María Dovales, natural de Fuentesaúco, fallecida antes de 1884[2].

---

[2] Ángel Silván, Natural of Fuentesaúco, born about 1800, an orchardist, who died before 1884. He married María Dovales, natural of Fuentesaúco, who died before 1884.

MARÍA DOVALES ALEJO
Fuentesaúco, Province of Zamora, Spain

Maria Dovales Alejo is listed on Juan Francisco Silván Hernández' birth document as *Nieto por linea paterna de Ángel Silvan, jornalero y del María Dovales naturales de esta villa difunto.* (Paternal grandson of Ángel Silvan paternal line, day laborer and of María Dovales originally of this town (Fuentesaúco), deceased).

Fuentesaúco is the village where the Silván family's emigration from Spain began in 1911. My Silván soul lead me through the small village where tall, swaying trees amid the gentle whisperings of my ancestors lined small plazas. Time stood still.

Initially, I felt panicky. Should we find Santa María church first? The plaza mayor? The ayuntamiento? Would we knock on doors asking if anyone remembered the Silván family? Were Silvan descendants still living in the village? We drove through narrow streets while creening our necks looking for the tall spires of the church. And then sat in awe when it stood before us. But to our dismay, it was locked tight; doves had taken over doorways, window ledges and across the wide steps and portico. Bird poop littered every inch surrounding the church and my hope of speaking with a priest to look at church records flew off with the birds. We took photos from every angle, touched the gigantic stone squares and smiled to remember a cousin before us, Eusebio (Sab) Gonzales had chunks of the stone from the church's renovation some years before. For us, no memorial chunks, but we smiled as our hands touched the doors, the hardware, the stones.

Fuentesauco is a maze of streets as if the connected houses were tossed about like dice, smoothed into lined abodes and then whitewashed. The village streets were laid out like a wagon wheel all leading toward the plaza mayor and pointing to smaller plazas.

There were dogs running everywhere and men lingering in the shade for their afternoon chats. Women gathered in doorways trying to outshout one another and children raced around them. The memory is forever etched in my mind.

Then time stand still; we found the Silván residence at 6 Calle San Salvador listed in the birth documents.

The cemetery was slightly outside the village branched off on its own long avenue. A small sign hung above a doorway leading inside stating *Este trista mansion recuerda nuestro fin preparate. Oh mortal! Queesforzoso morir*[3]. Stepping inside, a shadowy, cool foyer greeted us.

I couldn't have imagined the sight that met us as we entered the cemetery grounds, hot sunshine bouncing off marble. A long center walkway split the grounds in half and headstones, body-sized stones and trinkets shocked our senses. Not just a bit daunted, my brother went left and I went right. The walkway slanted up a gentle hill surrounded by stone walls on three sides. Then we began exploring. We wanted to find stones etched with Silván, Alejo, Hernández, Martin, Dovales and Gonzales. Our eyes picked apart every gravestone, some so tightly wedged beside another, I could not slip my foot between them. Walking, stooping, reading against the glaring sun and snapping photos of names that sounded familiar, we trudged on.

With a pounding heart, I stared and stopped. The grave was lined with a simple stone edge and flowers adorned the lettered base spelling *Familia Hernández Martin*. A few graves away, I found

---

[3] It is difficult to translate but may be words of peace to remember the final preparation for the mansion in heaven?

the *Familia Hernández Hernández*. Smooth marble laid flat, some standing higher than I could reach, some in alcoves, others splayed across the ground. I was giddy and took more photos, waving to get my brother's attention and later caressed the ancestral stones.

No stones for Silván or Gonzales could be found but assessing the time and place, we knew where they must be settled. The poor side of the cemetery. Next to the hundreds of beautiful stones etched lovingly and covered with vases and other symbols of love, stood a huge, barren area of land littered with crosses, statues, rocks and weeds. We knew they were there and looked for them. I picked up stones as mementos. I knew my aunt Millie would value the simple rocks as would I. Without her jump starting my research by giving me documents from her mother's belongings, I would not be on the quest. I owed her especially and tucked the stones into my bag.

On the way out of the cemetery, we walked slowly and glanced again at the disproportionate difference between one side and the other. Near the door, a cemetery worker saw the camera in my hand. He kindly told us, … no photos. We smiled and nodded. I'd snapped so many photos my fingers ached. Holding my camera to my chest and the stolen memory rocks, we slipped out, breathed deeply and agreed the ancestral village would never be forgotten.

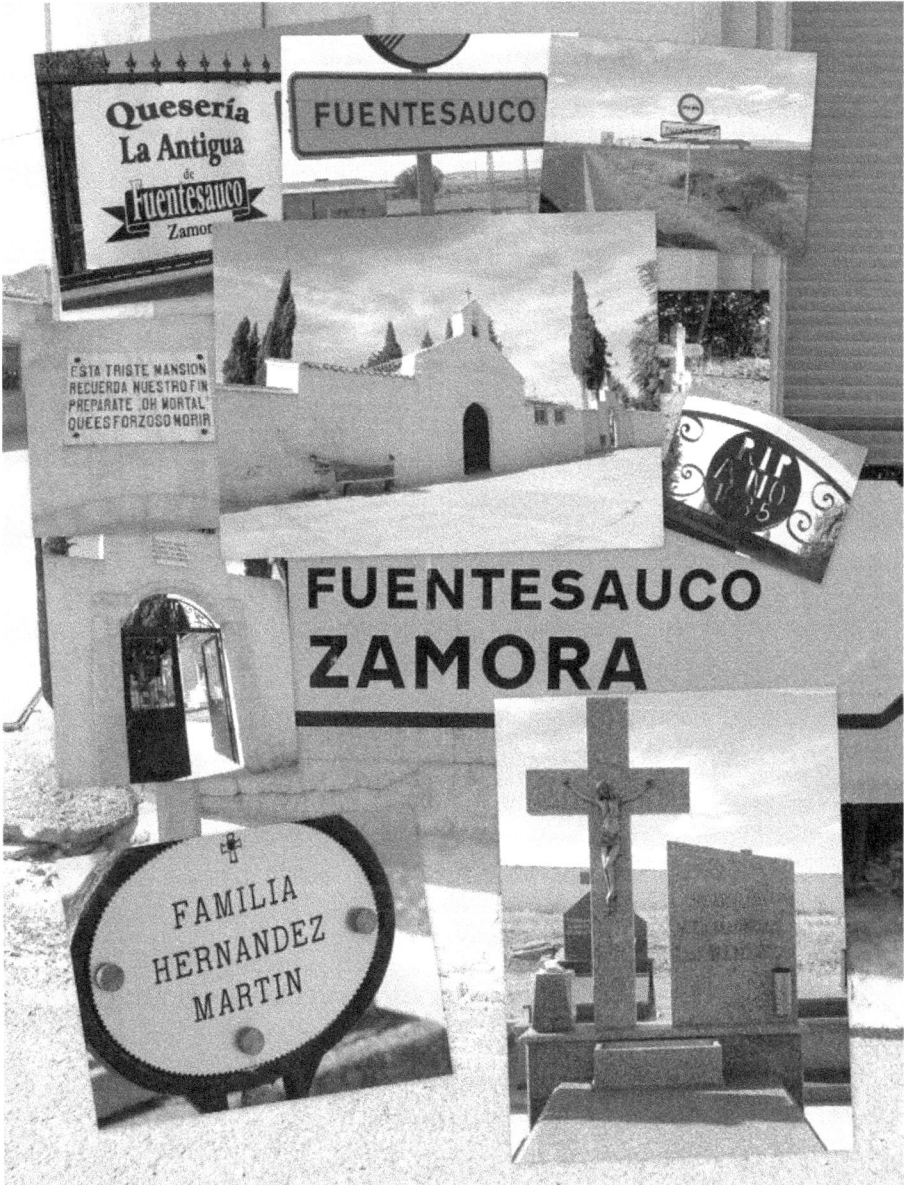

MIGUEL HERNÁNDEZ HERNÁNDEZ

Villamor de los Escuderos, Province of Zamora, Spain
Born: unknown; Died before 1884

    Villamor de los Escuderos lies west of Fuentesaúco past the bullring and across farmland where trees line some areas as if wedged into a crossword puzzle. The village is small, poor and a little decrepit, but charming, welcoming. Many stone buildings are falling down around themselves but others are carefully bordered with beautiful stonework, colorful picture tiles and pots of brightly-colored flowers. Along the streets you can see many *se vende* (for sale) signs above doorways and plastered along sides of buildings. I felt the depression of low employment, the dust along the streets and a swirling sadness the signs portrayed.

    When we drove into the village, our goal was to find the cemetery. We wanted to find the ancient gravestone for Miguel Hernández Hernández, the father of Agustina Hernández Martin. She was the mother to the Silván siblings, Victorino, Juan Francisco and Crescencia whose American descendants became Silván, Souza, Medeiros and Gonzales.

Following the steeple, we found the old church and then the cemetery. A locked gate didn't deter us; within minutes we were inside its stone walls and walking among the stones; we knew family members were buried nearby, but found no stones for Hernández Hernández. Too poor or etchings dissolved over time? Taking a moment, we inhaled the peace surrounding the tiny area amid   ghosts   of   the   past   and   the   quiet   streets.

uentespreadas   El Pego

    Cuelgamures   Argujillo

                           Guarrate

      El Maderal

ibo de
del Vino   Villamor de   Fuer
       los Escuderos

                  Fuentesauco

                Villaescusa

MARGARITA MARTIN RODRIGUEZ
Villaescusa, Province of Zamora, Spain
Born: unknown; Died before 1884

        The road to Villaescusa is six miles east of Fuentesaúco. After turning at the Villaescusa signpost, the road initially framed beautiful houses before the road narrowed to guide us into the main part of the village. At that junxture, everything changed. First a road and then a cluster of houses appeared like a mirage; one could almost imagine the wavering edges, blurry and hidden as we nosed our car through its strangely-laid grid of streets toward the village center. Houses were older, smaller, sitting back and mostly connected on dead end streets that snarled and twisted in several directions. There was an old woman in a flowered dress hanging laundry above us from a brightly-tiled balcony. Dogs barked on the street below. Then the ayuntamiento suddenly rose above us, flags thrust outward above its doors. The plaza mayor in Villaescusa was encircled by small round tables with chairs near the entrance where about ten Spaniards sat smoking and stared at us with undisguised interest.

        Ángel Silván Martin was born and probably buried in this village. He was the father of Celestino Pedro Silván Dovales, who was the father to Victorino, Juan Francisco and Crescensia Silván Hernández. ALSO born in Villaescusa was Margarita Martin

Rodriguez, the mother of Agustina Hernández Martin, the wife of Ángel Silván.

Many village cemeteries are near a church. Once past the plaza and interested men before the ayuntamiento, we found the white-washed church where stork nests were stacked on its roof. We followed a tree-lined dirt lane to the outskirts of the village. A chapel, a memorial bench and a peaceful vista greeted us as we neared the Iglesia Ermita del Olmo.

The gated cemetery hugged the right side of the church amid trees and stones. The gate didn't budge without a little muscle; I jiggled the handle loose, lifted the wooden door and we slid in. Steven snickered at my cleverness. The small cemetery grounds were crammed with shrines; we split up and meticulously read each stone. Hard stones marked many graves, some had brick "headboards" and metal fences bordered others. We peeked at each stone looking for the names of Silván, Martin, Alejo, Dovales and Rodriguez. We knew they were buried there but found none. We saw no other (poor) section within the stone walls; many gravestones spilled over one another, clearly in disrepair. They stood in loosely-structured rows, some old and weathered, spotted white, their etching long-smoothed away; some leaned and some had fallen in pieces altogether from age.

Leaving quietly after jiggling the lopsided gate back into place, we felt the family's aura around us as we stepped away toward the chapel's entrance. We found a massive, ancient (dead) tree stump with its limbs chopped off, a sign screwed to its trunk. The stump stood as a haven to a framed poem encased in plastic. Steven read the Spanish aloud, and then translated it into words sweeter than I can describe. It attested to a community of loving memories.

ÁRBOL CENTENARIO ~ CENTENNIAL TREE at Ermita del Olmo

Centennial tree
Alongside the road
you have room
for the pilgrim.

A few peasants
In your cool shade
they stop to eat
they have a smoke
and sleep the siesta.

Centennial tree
you are most honored
more faithful and silent
than any human.

Conversations
You guard in your
leaves
of children that run
of the tired elderly
of young men and women.

In your branches nest
ants in your trunk
at your feet worms
that tickle you

You stand for everything
And nothing angers you
To the rhythm of the wind
You dance la jota.

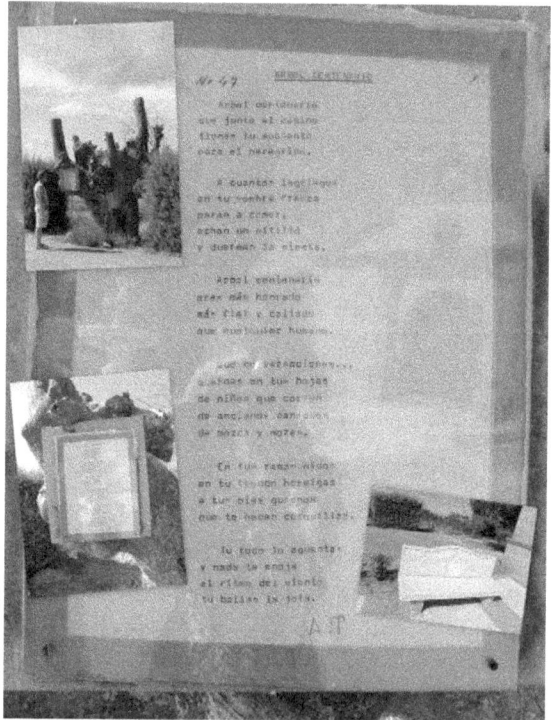

CELESTINO PEDRO SILVÁN DOVALES
Birth: 1822 / Death: between 1889 - 1911

Proven document from Spain lists *Celestino Silván, Natural de Fuentesaúco, en 1822. Jornalero. Casado con Agustina Hernández, natural de Villamor, hija de Miguel Hernández, natural de Villamor, jornalero, fallecido antes de 1884, y Margarita Martín, natural de Villaescusa (Zamora), fallecida antes de 1884.*

Celestino Pedro Silván Dovales, native of Fuentesaúco born in 1822. Laborer. Married with Agustina Hernández Martin, a native of Villamor, daughter of Miguel Hernandez, a native of Villamor, laborer, died before 1884, and Margaret Martin, a native of Villaescusa (Zamora), died before 1884.

His last child was born when he was 67, which should have been 1889, but ship records indicate Agustín was born in 1887. We know he was already gone by February 1911 when his sons boarded the SS Orteric ship because they list their living relative as "Agustina Hernández, mother, Fuentesaúco, Spain."

He was the patriarch of the Silván family as far back into the pedigree tree that I was able to find. There is a marked resemblance from this man to his many sons. Although I found documents relating to his children, the Spanish records were not as available for the older generation.

It is amazing that we have a photograph of Celestino Silván Dovales. Manuela Silván Trascasas (Ruiz) kept an old photo album and her daughter, Manuela (Millie) gifted the album to me. It was an honor to receive these ancestral photos; the photograph album was deep in the shadowy confines of an old trunk in her garage. Aunt Millie hugged it and said, "I want you to have these pictures because you are the one who cares so much about finding our family with all your research." Then she hugged me. I tingled with excitement thinking of the secrets the album might hold. My genealogical-addicted brain went into overdrive. She knew I would share everything I found and the bits and pieces begin with this man as you turn the following pages. You will see all the photos and documents for the Silván link to our family tree.

AGUSTINA HERNÁNDEZ MARTIN
Villamor de los Escuderos, Province of Zamora, Spain
Unknown date of birth – death after 1911

Agustina Hernandez Martin was born in Villamor de los Escuderos, a village northwest of Fuentesaúco by just a few miles. Her father, Miguel Hernandez Hernández was also from Villamor de los Escuderos but her mother, Margarita Martin, was from Villaescusa, a village a few miles on the other side of Fuentesaúco.

Records indicate Agustina was some years younger than her husband, Celestino Silván Dovales. When her last child, Agustín, was born in 1887, Celestino was 67 years old. Since Agustina was within child-bearing age, she may have been nearly twenty years younger than her husband but in those days, that was not a rarity.

I try to imagine the matriarch of the Silván family. She probably cooked a lot of garbanzo beans since that was a staple and Fuentesaúco's biggest crop. I imagine reddish hair and blue eyes, eyes that have been genetically shared with many of the Silván descendants. Her daughter, Crescéncia, resembled her mother as did her granddaughter, Manuela, the daughter of her son, Juan Francisco. In this photo, her hand holds a tiny purse. She has three rings on her fingers as well as beautiful dangling earrings. The dress appears cool, crisp and the rattan chair and linoleum makes me curious about where she sat for this photo. On Sundays she probably wore a mantilla to the Iglesia del Santa María Castillo.[4] I wish I had known her.

She was still alive when she watched four of her children leave Fuentesaúco in February of 1911. I could not find records of her death but believe she is buried in the family plots in Fuentesaúco among the *Hernandez Martin* graves. Surrounded by stones, sparse trees and marble-etched headstones, the sun warms the area with a golden aura of reverence within its stone walls.

---

[4] The *mantilla* (shawl) is draped over the *peineta* (comb) that typically has five teeth to anchor it to the woman's hair. One can also slip the mantilla through the teeth of the *peineta* before it is anchored to the hair. Before animal rights issues, the combs were made of Tortoise shell; now other substances are used.

PART 2

Spain: Spanish Homeland SILVÁNS

Felípe Silván Hernández
Matías Silván Hernández
Edmundo Silván Hernández
Ángel Silván Hernández
Agapita Silván Hernández
Gerónimo Silván Hernández
Lorenzo Silván Hernández
Agustín Silván Hernández

Supporting Documents and Sources
Santa María del Castillo Iglesia en Fuentesaúco, Zamora, Spain

FELÍPE SILVÁN HERNÁNDEZ
About 1858 – Unknown

Martín, que lo es de Villaescusa. Fue su padrino Felipe
Silván Hernández, casado, hermano consanguíneo del
bautizado y natural como los abuelos paternos de esta
misma villa, al que advertí el parentesco espiritual y
consiguientes obligaciones.

Felipe may have been the first child born to Celestino Pedro Silván Dovales and Agustina Hernandez Martin. He is clearly listed on the baptismal document as the brother and godfather to Geronimo (aka Jeronimo) Silván Hernandez. Calculations from the dates on the baptismal certificate shows Felipe would have been about nineteen years old and married. Despite, working with the Diocese of Zamora to obtain baptismal certificates, there was nothing received for Felipe. I was told many certificates were held at the church, some burned during the inquisition and many were not indexed or detailed before 1860.

Regardless, even though I have only a name, he is included in our Silván ancestral biographies because we know he was part of this family tree.

MATÍAS SILVÁN HERNÁNDEZ
24 February 1867 - Unknown

ARCHIVO HISTÓRICO DIOCESANO

CERTIFICACIÓN LITERAL DE PARTIDA DE BAUTISMO

Parroquia Santa María del Castillo

Diócesis Zamora

Provincia Zamora

Código 120.2

Libro 10

Folio 290v

Núm.

Notas marginales

No tiene

Don José Ángel Rivera de las Heras, Encargado del Archivo Parroquial de Santa María del Castillo en depósito en el Archivo Diocesano, Diócesis de Zamora, Provincia de Zamora,

CERTIFICA: Que el acta al margen reseñada, correspondiente al Libro de bautizados donde se asienta la partida de Matías Silván Hernández, y literalmente dice así:

" En la iglesia parroquial de Santa María del Castillo de esta villa de Fuentesaúco, diócesis y provincia de Zamora, y día veintisiete de febrero de mi ochocientos sesenta y siete, yo el infrascrito párroco de ella bauticé solemnemente un niño que había nacido el día veinticuatro del mismo a las tres de la mañana, a quien puse por nombre Matías. Es hijo legítimo de Celestino Silván, de esta parroquia, y Agustina Hernández de Villamor. Abuelos paternos Ángel y María Dobales; maternos Miguel, de Villamor y Margarita Martín, de Villaescusa, difunta. Padrino el abuelo paterno a quien advertí lo necesario.

Y lo firmo

Juan Antonio Álvarez (rubricado)".

Zamora, a 9 de marzo de 2012

Obispado de Zamora
V.º B.º:
El Vicario General,

TRANSLATION OF BAPTISMAL DOCUMENT FOR MATÍAS SILVÁN

Don Jose Ángel Rivera de las Heras, responsible for the parochial file of Santa Maria del Castillo inside the Archive Diocese File of Zamora, Province of Zamora.

CERTIFY: That the actual margin and correspondence of the baptismal book where Matías Silván Hernández is listed is literal to say:

"In the parroquial church of St. Mary of the Castle of this village of Fuentesaúco, diocese and province of Zamora, and the 17th day of February of 1867, I, the signer of this solemn baptism of a boy born the 24th day of the same year at 3:00 a.m., to whom I put the name Matías. He is the legitimate son of Celestino Silván, of this parish and Agustina Hernández of Villamor. Paternal grandparents are Ángel and Maria Dobales; Maternal grandparents are Miguel of Villamor and Margarita Martin of Villaescusa, dead. Godfather is the paternal grandfather to whom I notified was necessary. And I sign, Juan Antonio Alvarez (endorsed)

Santa Maria del Castillo, Diocese & Province of Zamora
Codigo 120.2, Book 10, Page 290v
There are no notes in the margin

Archivo Historico Diocesano, Zamora

EDMUNDO "Mundo" SILVÁN HERNÁNDEZ

16 November 1870 – Unknown

m. Pilar Juanez Alonso

CERTIFICACIÓN LITERAL DE PARTIDA DE BAUTISMO

Parroquia Santa María del Castillo

Diócesis Zamora

Provincia Zamora

Código 120.2

Libro 11

Folio 29v

Núm.

Notas marginales

No tiene

Don José Ángel Rivera de las Heras, Encargado del Archivo Parroquial de Santa María del Castillo en depósito en el Archivo Diocesano, Diócesis de Zamora, Provincia de Zamora,

CERTIFICA: Que el acta al margen reseñada, correspondiente al Libro de bautizados donde se asienta la partida de Edmundo Silván Hernández, y literalmente dice así:

" En la iglesia parroquial de Santa María del Castillo de esta villa de Fuentesaúco, diócesis y provincia de Zamora, a veinte de noviembre de mi ochocientos setenta, yo el licenciado Don Calixto García, cura ecónomo de la misma, bauticé solemnemente un niño que había nacido el día diez y seis, a las tres de la mañana, al que puse por nombre Edmundo. Hijo legítimo de Celestino Silván Hernández *(sic)*, de oficio jornalero, natural de esta villa, y Agustina Hernández de Villamor de los Escuderos. Abuelos paternos Ángel y María Adovales Alejo, ya difuntos, naturales de esta villa; maternos Miguel, natural de dicho Villamor, y Margarita Martín Rodríguez, de Villaescusa. Fueron sus padrinos Felipe Silván y Lorenza Lorenzo, que no tocó a la criatura y a quienes advertí lo necesario; siendo testigos Tomás Alonso, Cipriano Lorenzo, y otros varios.

Y lo firmo.

Calixto García (rubricado)".

Zamora, a 9 de marzo de 2012

Obispado de Zamora
V.º B.º:
El Vicario General,

TRANSLATION OF BAPTISMAL DOCUMENT FOR EDMUNDO SILVÁN HERNÁNDEZ

Don Jose Ángel Rivera de las Heras, responsible for the parochial file of Santa Maria del Castillo inside the Archive Diocese File of Zamora, Province of Zamora.

CERTIFY: That the actual margin and correspondence of the baptismal book where Edmundo Silván Hernández is listed is literal to say:

"In the parroquial church of St. Mary of the Castle of this village of Fuentesaúco, diocese and province of Zamora, and the 20th day of November, 1870, I, the licensed priest, Don Calixto Garcia signer and priest of the solemn baptism of a boy born the 16th day at 3:00 a.m., to whom I put the name Edmundo. He is the legitimate son of Celestino Silván Hernández, a workman and native of this village and Agustina Hernández of Villamor de los Escuderos. Paternal grandparents are Ángel and Maria Adovales Alejo both dead, natives of this village; Maternal grandparents are Miguel native of said Villamor and Margarita Martin Rodriguez, of Villaescusa. They were the godparents, Felípe Silván and Lorenza Lorenzo, though they were not there to touch the child, to whom I notified was necessary. Being witnesses were Tomas Alonso, Cipriano Lorenzo and various others And I sign, Calixto Garcia(endorsed)

Santa Maria del Castillo, Diocese & Province of Zamora
Codigo 120.2, Book 11, Page 107v
There are no notes in the margin

Archivo Historico Diocesano, Zamora
Family oral history implies that "Mundo" went to South America.

Being mostly poor and rural, the ease of obtaining work permits along with the same language and previous Spanish colonialism of South America made it very attractive to the Spaniards.

So, Uncle Mundo was lost in the family history.

Before I found the Sao Paulo Public Archives, we did not know where he landed, when he left Spain, if he married and/or had children or whether he died once he landed on those foreign shores.   We do know, through the various family stories that nobody heard from him after he left Spain.

http://www.arquivoestado.sp.gov.br/livros_estrangeiros_descricao.php?fam=46840&liv=077&pag=170&tipo=Desembarque%20com%20base%20nos%20Livros (Public Archives of Sao Paulo)

With help from a descendant of the Boiza family in Brazil, I found "Asmundo Silván Hernández" on a ship named SS Aquitaine that sailed from Spain the summer before the first immigrant ship left Spain for Hawaii.

Data Certificate

Name:	Asmundo	Surname:	SILVAN HERNANDEZ	Kinship:	BOSS
No. of Page:	170	No. of Book:	077	Family:	46840
Nationality:	HESPANHOLA	Age:	37	Civil Est:	MARRIED
Sex:	M	Religion:	CATH.	Provenance:	SANTOS VALENCIA
DOB.:	/ /	Profession:	FARMER	Destination:	BENT
Steam:	Aquitaine	Departure:	/ /	Arrival	16/06/1906

Disclaimer:

I declare to be aware of the restrictions of Law Archives - arts. 4 and 6 of Law 8159/91, of the arts. 138-145 of the Penal Code which provides for the crimes of slander, libel and slander, as well as the ban, resulting from art. 5, X, of the Federal Constitution, to disseminate information obtained which, although associated with collective interest or collective interest me or my particular interest, relating to privacy, honor, and the image of others. I assume, therefore, full and sole responsibility in civil and criminal matters, by material or moral damage that can generate using the requested document and the information contained therein, dismissing therefore any liability for the PUBLIC FILE THE STATE OF SÃO PAULO and their agents, by their usage.

Arquivo Público
do Estado de São Paulo

Home | Servicing | Contact Us | SAESP | Public Memory | Informative

Share

Quick access: ▼

O Acervo
Guia do Acervo
Catálogos
Acervo digitalizado

Books of Registration Lodge Immigrant Records relating

Book	Page	Family	Arrival	Surname	Name	Age	Sex	Kinship	Nationality	Steam	Est.Civil	
077	170	46840	16/06/1906	SILVAN HERNANDEZ	Asmundo	37	M	BOSS	HESPANHOLA	Aquitaine	MARRIED	Send Certificate
077	170	46840	16/06/1906	JUANEZ ALONSO	PILAR	38	F	WER	HESPANHOLA	Aquitaine	MARRIED	Send Certificate

I found this especially interesting because a 1907 document showed his brother, Juan Francisco Silván Hernández, prepared to sail on the Heliopolis, which was the first ship that carried Spanish and Portuguese immigrants to Hawaii. Juan delayed until 1911.

Was it Edmundo who actually started the exodus? He arrived in Brazil on June 16, 1906. He is shown with his wife, Pilar Juanez Alonso. As an additional note, I read on Edmundo's baptismal certificate on the previous page that one of the witnesses at his baptism was named Tomas Alonso. Could Pilar have been related to Tomas? A father? An arranged marriage?

ÁNGEL SILVÁN HERNÁNDEZ
1 October 1873 - Unknown

CERTIFICACIÓN LITERAL DE PARTIDA DE BAUTISMO

Parroquia Santa María del Castillo. Fuentesaúco

Diócesis Zamora

Provincia Zamora

Código 120.2

Libro 11

Folio 84v

Núm.

Notas marginales

No tiene

Obispado de Zamora
V.º B.º:
El Vicario General,

Don José Ángel Rivera de las Heras, Encargado del Archivo Parroquial de Santa María del Castillo de Fuentesaúco en depósito en el Archivo Diocesano, Diócesis de Zamora, Provincia de Zamora,

CERTIFICA: Que el acta al margen reseñada, correspondiente al Libro de bautizados donde se asienta la partida de Ángel Silván Hernández, y literalmente dice así:

" En la iglesia parroquial de Santa María del Castillo de la villa de Fuentesaúco, obispado de Zamora, y en el día cinco de octubre de mil ochocientos setenta y tres, yo el presbítero don Miguel Hernández, coadjutor de la misma, en ausencia de su cura ecónomo, bauticé solemnemente a un niño, hijo legítimo de Celestino Silván, de oficio jornalero, natural de esta villa, y de Agustina Hernández, natural de Villamor de los Escuderos, y feligreses de ésta de Santa María. Nació el día primero de este mes sobre las diez de su mañana y le impuse el nombre de Ángel. Son sus abuelos paternos Ángel Silván y María Dobales, ya difuntos y naturales de esta villa; y maternos Miguel Hernández, del referido Villamor, y Margarita Martín de Villascusa, ya difunta. Fue su padrino Pablo Torrecilla, soltero y natural de esta villa, al que advertí el parentesco espiritual y obligaciones que el Ritual previene.

Y para que conste lo firmo, fecha ut supra

Daniel Carrascal (rubricado), Miguel Hernández (rubricado)".

Zamora, a 9 de marzo de 2012

TRANSLATION OF BAPTISMAL DOCUMENT FOR ÁNGEL SILVÁN HERNANDEZ

Don Jose Angel Rivera of Heras, charged with the
Parish Archive of Santa Maria del Castillo on deposit in the Diocesan Archive, Diocese of Zamora, Zamora province,

Certifies: that the certificate profiled in the margin, corresponds to the Book of Baptisms where
is found the certificate of Angel Silvan Hernandez and literally says the following:

"In the parish church of Santa Maria del Castillo
of the town of Fuentesauco, bishopric of Zamora, on the fifth day of October of eighteen hundred seventy three, I the priest don Miguel Hernandez, warden of the same, in absence of the treasurer priest, solemnly baptize a boy legitimate son of Celestino Silvan Hernandez, day laborer, originally of this town, and Agustina Hernandez originally from Villamor de los Escuderos, parishioners of this Santa Maria. Born the first day of this month about ten in the morning and was given the name Angel. His paternal grandparents are Angel Silvan and Maria Dosales, deceased, originally of this town; Maternal grandparents Miguel Hernandez of the referenced Villamor, and Margarita Martin of Villaescusa deceased. Present was his godfather Pablo Torrecilla, unmarried and originally from this town, who I advised of his parental and spiritual obligations required by the ritual.

And for the record I sign it, date as above [in Latin]
Daniel Carrascal (with flourishes), Miguel Hernández (with flourishes)"
Santa Maria del Castillo, Diocese & Province of Zamora
Codigo 120.2, Book 11, Page 84v
There are no notes in the margin

AGAPITA SILVÁN HERNÁNDEZ
14 September, 1874 - Unknown

ARCHIVO HISTÓRICO DIOCESANO

CERTIFICACIÓN LITERAL DE PARTIDA DE BAUTISMO

Parroquia Santa María del Castillo. Fuentesaúco

Diócesis Zamora

Provincia Zamora

Código 120.2

Libro 10

Folio 255r

Núm.

Notas marginales

No tiene

Don José Ángel Rivera de las Heras, Encargado del Archivo Parroquial de Santa María del Castillo de Fuenesaúco en depósito en el Archivo Diocesano, Diócesis de Zamora, Provincia de Zamora,

CERTIFICA: Que el acta al margen reseñada, correspondiente al Libro de bautizados donde se asienta la partida de Agapita Silván Hernández, y literalmente dice así:

" En la villa de Fuentesaúco, diócesis y provincia de Zamora, a diez y ocho de setiembre de mil ochocientos sesenta y cuatro, yo don Manuel Fernández Castañera, presbítero coadjutor de Santa María del Castillo con anuencia del párroco don Juan Antonio Álvarez, bauticé solemnemente a una niña que había nacido el catorce, a quien puse por nombre Agapita. Es hija legítima de Celestino Silván y Agustina Hernández, aquel natural de esta, y esta de Villamor de los Escuderos, y feligreses de esta de Santa María. Abuelos paternos Ángel Silván y María Novales, ya difuntos, y vecinos que fueron de esta villa; Maternos Miguel Hernández y Margarita Martín, ya difunta y vecina de Villamor. Fue su padrino Agapito Lamera a quien advertí lo necesario. Fueron testigos Juan Santos Zambrano y Juan Álvarez, de esta vecindad.

Y por verdad lo firmo, fecha ut supra.

Juan Antonio Álvarez (rubricado) Manuel Fernández Castañera (rubricado)".

Zamora, a 9 de marzo de 2012

Obispado de Zamora
V.º B.º:
El Vicario General,

TRANSLATION OF BAPTISMAL DOCUMENT FOR AGAPITA
SILVÁN HERNANDEZ

Don Jose Angel Rivera of Heras, charged with the
Parish Archive of Santa Maria del Castillo on deposit in the
Diocesan Archive, Diocese of Zamora, Zamora province,

Certifies: that the certificate profiled in the margin, corresponds to
the Book of Baptisms where
is found the certificate of Agapita Silvan Hernandez and literally
says the following:

"In the town of Fuentesauco, diocese and province of Zamora, on
the eighteenth day of September of eighteen hundred seventy four,
I don Manuel Fernandez Castanera, priest curate of Santa Maria del
Castillo with the authority of parish priest don Juan Antonio
Alvarez, solemnly baptize a girl that was born the fourteenth, who
was given the name of Agapita. She is the legitimate daughter of
Celestino Silvan and Agustina Hernandez, he from this town and
she from Villamor de los Escuderos, parishioners of this Santa
Maria. Paternal grandparents Angel Silvan and Maria Dosales,
deceased, from this town; Maternal grandparents Miguel
Hernandez and Margarita Martin, she is deceased he of Villamor.
Present was his godfather Agapito Lamera who I advised that
which is necessary. Witnesses present Juan Santos Zambrano and
Juan Alvarez

Truthfully I sign it, date as above [in latin]
Juan Antonio Alvarez (with flourishes), Manuel Fernandez Castanera
(with flourishes)"

Santa Maria del Castillo, Diocese & Province of Zamora
Codigo 120.2, Book 10, Page 255r
There are no notes in the margin

GERÓNIMO SILVÁN HERNÁNDEZ
30 September 1877 - Unknown
m. Joaquina Bragado Vicente

Jerónimo (aka Geronimo) Silván Hernández was born in Fuentesaúco, Province of Zamora, Spain to Celestino Silván Dovales and Agustina Hernández Martin in the fall of 1877. His paternal grandparents were Ángel Silván Martin and Maria Dovales Alejo. His maternal grandparents were Miguel Hernández Hernández of Villamor de los Escuderos and Margarita Martin of Villaescusa.

Jerónimo was baptized on October 4, 1877 in Santa Maria del Castillo Church in Fuentesaúco and his godfather was his older brother, Felípe Silván Hernández.

He stood 5' 9" tall, the tallest of the Silván brothers that we know of. He married a woman from Arcenillas, Spain named Joaquina Bragado Vicente on August 30, 1919. She was 5' 4" tall, a widow with at least one child named Felicidada.

OBISPADO de ZAMORA
ARCHIVO HISTÓRICO DIOCESANO

CERTIFICACIÓN LITERAL DE PARTIDA DE BAUTISMO

Parroquia Santa María del Castillo. Fuentesaúco

Diócesis Zamora

Provincia Zamora

Código 120.2

Libro 12

Folio 52v

Núm. 207

Notas marginales
"Contrajo matrimonio canónico con doña Joaquina Bragado Vicente en la parroquia de Arcenillas, el día 30 de agosto de mil novecientos diez y nueve
De que certifico.
El párroco, Barba (rubricado)".

Obispado de Zamora
V.º B.º.
El Vicario General,
José - F. Matilla

Don José Ángel Rivera de las Heras, Encargado del Archivo Parroquial de Santa María del Castillo de Fuentesaúco en depósito en el Archivo Diocesano, Diócesis de Zamora, Provincia de Zamora,

CERTIFICA: Que el acta al margen reseñada, correspondiente al libro de bautizados se asienta la partida de Jerónimo Silván Hernández, y literalmente dice así:

"En la iglesia parroquial de Santa María del Castillo de la villa de Fuentesaúco, obispado de Zamora, y en el día cuatro de octubre de mil ochocientos setenta y siete, Yo el infrascrito cura ecónomo de la misma bauticé solemnemente un niño, hijo legítimo de Celestino Silván, natural de esta villa y parroquia, y de Agustina Hernández, natural de Villamor de los Escuderos, braceros del campo, domiciliados en la calle de San Salvador. Nació dicho niño a las diez de la noche del día treinta del último setiembre, y le impuse el nombre Gerónimo. Son sus abuelos paternos Ángel Silván Martín y María Dobal Alejo; maternos Miguel Hernández Hernández, natural del expresado Villamor, y Margarita Martín, que lo es de Villaescusa. Fue su padrino Felipe Silván Hernández, casado, hermano consanguíneo del bautizado y natural como los abuelos paternos de esta misma villa, al que advertí el parentesco espiritual y consiguientes obligaciones.

Y para que así conste, firmo la presente partida, fecha ut supra.

Daniel Casaseca (rubricado)".

Zamora, a 17 de noviembre de 2011

ARCHIVO HISTÓRICO DIOCESANO ZAMORA

J. Rivera

TRANSLATION OF BAPTISMAL DOCUMENT FOR JERONIMO SILVÁN

In the parish church of Santa Maria del Castillo of the village of Fuentesaúco, bishopric of Zamora, on the fourth of October, 1877. I the signer and trustee of the same one I baptized solemnly a boy, legitimate son of Celestino Silván, natural of this village and parish, And of Agustina Hernández, natural of Villamor of the Escuderos, braceros of the field, resident of San Salvador Street. The said boy was born at ten o'clock at night on the thirtieth of the September, and I imposed the name Gerónimo on him.

The paternal grandparents are Ángel Silván Martin and María Dobal (Dovales) Alejo; maternal Miguel Hernández Hernández, natural of the aforesaid one Villamor, and Margarita Martin, of the village, Villaescusa.

His godfather is Felípe Silván Hernández, married, related by blood, brother of the baptized and natural as the paternal grandparents of this same village. I notified the godparents their spiritual and consequent obligations.

And so that thus be evident, I sign and date…. Endorsed by Daniel Casaseca

Santa Maria del Castillo, Diocese & Province of Zamora
Codigo 120.2, Book 12, Page 207
Archivo Historico Diocesano, Zamora

Marginal notes: Contracted canonical marriage with Doña Joaquina Bragado Vicente in the parish of Arcenillas, on the day August 30, 1919."

Joaquina had a child named Felisidada. I have not found any supporting information to show Gerónimo and Joaquina had children together. We do, however, have information related to Felisidada through Eusebio Gonzales, Jr. (Sab) as shared with me by his daughters, Linda and Patte.[5]

~

Crescéncia Silván Gonzales and Gerónimo exchanged many letters where she begged him to join her and his brothers in California. He did not sail to America. He did, however, sail to Cuba.

A ship's manifest from the S.S. *MANUEL CALVO* sailing from Santiago de Cuba and Habana[6] on 23 June 1931 lists him at age 54. Crescéncia kept all of his letters inside a large purse dangling from a closet hook.[7] Over the years the letters have been lost.

To shed light on Jerónimo's life, I painstakingly researched Cuba and its history at the time he and his brother, Agustin, were in Cuba to decipher the pull from Spain to Cuba. Just as their brothers before them, the lure of earning a substantial wage compared to the meager way of life in their homeland generated restlessness and meager hope.

What was the pull to Cuba for Jerónimo and Agustin, the sugar cane, coffee or tobacco fields, highway construction? Those industries called workers at that time.

What was the push that made Jerónimo, Joaquina and Agustin leave Cuba in 1930 and 1931?

---

[5] Felisidada information can be found in Part 6 – Other Silván Family

[6] Source: www.ancestry.com

[7] Source: Theresa Gonzales Sackett

About Cuba:

Cuba is the largest and western-most island of the Antillean archipelago, situated at the key approaches to the Atlantic Ocean, the Gulf of Mexico, and the Caribbean Sea – 90 miles south of the Florida Keys. Spain officially designated the island as "Fortress of the Indies" and "Key to the New World."

Cuba extends 750 miles in length, surrounded by more than 1600 coastal keys and islets, measuring more than 46,000 square miles. The coastline of the main island extends approximately 2500 miles in length. At its widest point, the island measures 124 miles; at its narrowest point, it barely reaches 22 miles.

The ship manifest shows that Jerónimo and Joaquina's Cuban residence was Santiago on the southeastern shoreline. Agustín's Cuban residence is shown as Havana.

In the 1860s, Cuba was the richest and most populated of Spain's two remaining American colonies, faced serious economic and political problems. In the later eighteenth century, Cuba was the world's foremost sugar producer. However, the production and export of sugar's growing competition from European and American sugar beet and new sugar-cane producing regions posed a threat to Cuba's future.

Soon after major political upheavals, elite Cubans desired Spanish immigration in order to 'whiten' Cuba's population. Spanish elites helped avert Cuban vengeance by encouraging reconciliation between Cubans and Spaniards that persisted from the first occupation through the early 1930s.

Cuba was devoted to growing sugar and the massive immigration from Spain after 1898 fueled the venture. The United States purchased about 80% of their sugar. The *Chaparra Sugar Company* in central Cuba moved to import labor to the sparsely populated *Camaguey* and *Oriente* provinces by welcoming Spanish workers and their families. Many migrants left the sugar plantations after one or two harvests to resettle in the urban centers, such as Havana or Santiago de Cuba.

The sugar cane farmers were eager to place Gerardo Machado in control since he was open to their demands. He remained in power from 1925 – 1933. One of his most notable accomplishments was building Cuba's central highway, called *La Carretera Central*, which ran practically the entire length of the island from Pinar del Rio in the west to Santiago de Cuba, a distance of over 700 miles. It touched the coast in only three places, Havana, Matanzas and Santiago de Cuba.

The price of sugar began to drop; the economy floundered and the United States responded to the crisis in an attempt to halt declining world prices by decreasing Cuban exports. Moratoriums were imposed on new planting. Efforts proved futile. The depression came to Cuba, shadowing the United States' fall in October of 1929. A year later, the U.S. increased the duty on Cuban sugar. The Cuban share of the market declined down to 49% in 1930.

Between 1930 and 1931, the Machado government inaugurated drastic salary cuts for all public employees except military with pay reductions up to 60%. Civil servants were laid off; highway construction employing 15,000 workers in 1928 were suspended. By mid 1931, 200 post offices, seven public hospitals, nurseries, schools and agricultural stations closed. Female employees were fired. Salaries were cut again and then fell into arrears.

Labor began to organize, union membership expanded and strikes increased leading to national labor militancy. Between 1929 and 1932, strikes halted production of sugar, cigar manufacturing, railroads, metallurgy, construction, and textiles. In March 1930, the outlawed CNOC organized a stunning general strike involving more than 200,000 workers, paralyzing Cuba; ending only after government violence and repression.

In April, workers and soldiers clashed again. On May 1, 1930, at a celebration in Regla, demonstrators were killed and injured. Several weeks later, railroad workers struck, paralyzing national rail transportation. Strike organizers were arrested and trains resumed operations under army direction. Encouraged by the events, the CNOC[8] established provincial groups, expanding into the countryside to organize agricultural workers and peasants.

Government and political clashes increased and the *Union Nacionalista* organized a political rally in Artemisia; before speakers addressed the assembled thousands, the army opened fire to disperse the panic-stricken crowd resulting in eight deaths and hundreds wounded, including children.

June, 1930 = Jerónimo and Joaquina left Cuba to return to Spain.

~

In 1931, Cuba joined six other sugar producing countries in signing the Chadbourne Plan, designed to raise floundering prices by restricting supplies for five years. The effect was devastating. Sugar production dropped 60%. Sugar producers found themselves with surplus sugar in search for new markets at a time of declining prices. Producers struggled to remain solvent by lowering wages and cutting production through layoffs. The length of the *zafra* was reduced a second time, this time to a 62-day harvest – that is only two months' work for tens of thousands of sugar workers.

Salaries and wages were reduced. Workers were laid off. Businesses and factories closed. Unemployment soared. Pay for agricultural workers declined by 75%. In the sugar zones, wages fell as low as twenty cents for a twelve-hour work day. On one large estate, workers received ten cents a day --- five in cash and

---

[8] CNOC = Confederación Nacional Obrera de Cuba

five in credits at the company store. As wages fell, the value of the peso decreased in purchasing power. The peso was worth 28 centavos less in 1928 than in 1913.

These conditions set the stage for political confrontation and social conflict on a scale unprecedented in the republic of Cuba. The road toward revolution was obvious.

June 1931, Agustin left Cuba and returned to Spain.

Cuba in the 1930s saw men wearing white hats, light colored pants and shirts and fedoras. Rumba was the native dance and royal palm trees were called the feather dusters of the gods. There were cars in Havana, but many more horses were used for transportation than automobiles. Many streets were created from cobblestone and giant earthenware jars caught rain water. They grew oranges on the western shore that were sweeter and juicier than Spanish oranges. The hillsides were similar to Spain; narrow sloping streets ran down between the white-washed buildings. Cubans idolized President Theodore Roosevelt and erected a statue in his honor. They were proud of the Bacardi Rum facility where they brewed first-rate rum and still do.

LIST OR MANIFEST OF ALIEN PASSENGERS FOR THE UNITED

ALL ALIENS arriving at a port of continental United States from a foreign port or a port of the insular possessions of the United States, and all aliens arriving at a port of said insular possessions from a foreign port, a port of continental United This white sheet is for the listing of

S. S. "MANUEL CALVO", Passengers sailing from SANTIAGO DE CUBA AND HABANA , JUNE , 19 31.

No. on List	Name in Full (Family name)	(Given name)	Age (Yrs.)	Sex	Calling or occupation	Able to read	Nationality (Country of which citizen or subject)	Race or people	Place of birth (Country)	(City or town, State, Province or District)	Final destination	Last permanent residence (Country)	(City or town, State, Province or District)
1	Iglesias Conde	Mercedes	34	F	home	Spanish yes	Spanish	Spanish	Spain	Orense	in transit to Spain	Cuba	Santiago
2	Rodriguez Gonzalez	America	9	F	-	yes	do	do	do	Cuba	Santiago	do	do
3	Rodriguez Gonzalez	Alfredo	6	M	-	yes	yes	do	do	do	do	do	Palto (Orte.)
4	Castro Fernandez	Nieves	34	F	home	no	do	no	do	Spain	Lugo	do	do
5	Balcarcel Castro	Aurora	12	F	-	yes	do	yes	do	do	do	do	do
6	Balcarcel Castro	Milolita	9	F	-	yes	do	yes	do	do	do	do	do
7	Balcarcel Castro	Virginia	7	F	-	no	do	no	do	do	do	do	do
8	Balcarcel Castro	Carmen	3	F	-	no	do	no	do	Cuba	Palto (Oriente)	do	do
9	Balcarcel Castro	Luis	1	M	-	no	do	no	do	do	do	do	do
10	Fernandez Gallego	Maria R.	53	F	home	no	yes	do	Spain	Leon	do	do	Chaparra
11	Blanco	Celestina	30	F	do	yes	yes	do	do	do	do	do	Santiago
12	Perez Aira	Maria	44	F	do	no	no	do	do	do	Lugo	do	do
13	Gonzalez Gonzalez	Dolores	34	F	do	no	no	do	do	do	Leon	do	do
14	Piris Girard	Vicente	38	M	merchant	yes	do	yes	do	do	Balearos	do	do
15	Mestre Moll	Magdalena	38	F	home	yes	do	yes	do	do	do	do	do
16	Piris Mestre	Magdalena	4	F	-	no	do	no	do	Cuba	Santiago	do	do
17	Piris Mestre	Maria	1	F	-	no	do	no	do	do	do	do	do
18	Aira Gonzalez	Manuel	40	M	merchant	do	yes	do	Spain	Lugo	do	do	do
19	Roca Roca	Jaime	36	M	carpenter	yes	do	yes	do	do	Gerona	do	do
20	Prieto Menias	Antonia	30	F	home	yes	do	yes	do	do	Leon	do	do
21	Roca Prieto	Jaime	8	M	-	no	do	no	do	Cuba	Santiago	do	do
22	Roca Prieto	Antonia	6	F	-	no	do	no	do	do	do	do	do
23	Roca Prieto	Manuel	3	M	-	no	do	no	do	do	do	do	do
24	Delgado Sanchez	Maximiano	30	M	merchant	yes	do	yes	do	Spain	Salamanca	do	do	do
25	Capel Nacedo	Santiago	58	M	laborer	no	do	no	do	do	Granada	do	do	do
26	Lopez Aguilar	Jesus	40	M	dependent	yes	do	yes	do	do	Lugo	do	do	do
27	Silvan Hernandez	Geronimo	54	M	laborer	no	do	no	do	do	Zamora	do	do	do
28	Bragado Vicente	Joaquina	55	F	home	no	do	no	do	do	do	do	do	do
29	Lopez Arias	Amador	28	M	merchant	yes	do	yes	do	do	Lugo	do	do	do
30	Gayoso Gonzalez	Elvira	26	F	home	yes	do	yes	do	do	do	do	do	do

Total passengers . . . . .
U. S. citizens . . . . . .
Aliens . . . . .

Line 27: Gerónimo Silván Hernández, age 54
Line 28: Joaquina Bragado Vicente, age 55

List 1.

The entries on this sheet must be typewritten or printed.

STATES IMMIGRATION OFFICER AT PORT OF ARRIVAL

States, or a port of another insular possession, in whatsoever class they travel, MUST be fully listed and the master or commanding officer of each vessel carrying such passengers must upon arrival deliver lists thereof to the immigration officer
THIRD-CLASS PASSENGERS ONLY

Arriving at Port of PHILADELPHIA AND NEW-YORK in transit to Spain , JUNIO 10 , 1931.

233

No. on List	The name and complete address of nearest relative or friend in country whence alien came, or if none there, then in country of which a citizen or subject.	Final destination		By where paid passage paid?		Whether ever before in the United States, and if so, when and where?				Whether going to join a relative or friend; their name and complete address, and if a relative, exact relationship	Purpose of coming to United States									Condition of health, mental and physical	Deformed or crippled Nature, length of time, and cause	Height	Color of—	Marks of identification
1	in transit to Spain	Spain	Orense	as self	- No	No	No	No	in transit to Spain	in transit	no no no	no	no no no	good none	5 -	fairblk brwn	zona
2	do	do	do	mother	- do	do	do	do	do	do	do do do	do	do do do do	do	3 7	do do	do
3	do	do	do	do	- do	do	do	do	do	do	do do do	do	do do do do	do	3 4	do do	do
4	do	do	Lugo	as self	- do	do	do	do	do	do	do do do	do	do do do do	do	5 1	do brwn	do
5	do	do	do	mother	- do	do	do	do	do	do	do do do	do	do do do do	do	4 8	do do	do
6	do	do	do	do	- do	do	do	do	do	do	do do do	do	do do do do	do	4 4	do do	do
7	do	do	do	do	- do	do	do	do	do	do	do do do	do	do do do do	do	3 9	do do	do
8	do	do	do	do	- do	do	do	do	do	do	do do do	do	do do do do	do	3 6	do do	do
9	do	do	do	do	- do	do	do	do	do	do	do do do	do	do do do do	do	2 5	do do	do
10	do	do	Leon	as self	- do	do	do	do	do	do	do do do	do	do do do do	do	5 1	do do	do
11	do	do	do	do	- do	do	do	do	do	do	do do do	do	do do do do	do	5 2	do do	do
12	do	do	Lugo	do	- do	do	do	do	do	do	do do do	do	do do do do	do	3 3	do do	do
13	do	do	Leon	do	- do	do	do	do	do	do	do do do	do	do do do do	do	5 1	do do	do
14	do	do	Balnares	do	- do	do	do	do	do	do	do do do	do	do do do do	do	5 6	do do	30
15	do	do	do	husband	- do	do	do	do	do	do	do do do	do	do do do do	do	5 2	do do	do
16	do	do	do	father	- do	do	do	do	do	do	do do do	do	do do do do	do	3 4	do do	do
17	do	do	do	do	- do	do	do	do	do	do	do do do	do	do do do do	do	2 8	do blnd	do
18	do	do	Lugo	as self	- do	do	do	do	do	do	do do do	do	do do do do	do	6 1	do blck	do
19	do	do	Barcelona	as self	- do	do	do	do	do	do	do do do	do	do do do do	do	5 8	do do	do
20	do	do	do	husband	- do	do	do	do	do	do	do do do	do	do do do do	do	5 -	do do	do
21	do	do	do	father	- do	do	do	do	do	do	do do do	do	do do do do	do	4 1	do do	do
22	do	do	do	do	- do	do	do	do	do	do	do do do	do	do do do do	do	3 6	do do	do
23	do	do	do	do	- do	do	do	do	do	do	do do do	do	do do do do	do	3 3	do do	do
24	do	do	Salamanca	as self	- do	do	do	do	do	do	do do do	do	do do do do	do	5 7	do do	do
25	do	do	Almeria	do	- do	do	do	do	do	do	do do do	do	do do do do	do	5 6	do do	do
26	do	do	Lugo	do	- do	do	do	do	do	do	do do do	do	do do do do	do	5 7	do do	do
27	do	do	Zamora	do	- do	do	do	do	do	do	do do do	do	do do do do	do	5 9	do do	do
28	do	do	do	husband	- do	do	do	do	do	do	do do do	do	do do do do	do	5 4	do do	do
29	do	do	Lugo	as self	- do	do	do	do	do	do	do do do	do	do do do do	do	5 8	do do	do
30	do	do	do	husband	- do	do	do	do	do	do	do do do	do	do do do do	do	5 4	do do	do

year:

Age: 54

Gender: Male

Port of Departure: Santiago of Cuba and Havana

Ethnicity/Race- /Nationality: Spanish

Ship Name: Manuel Calvo

Search Ship Database: Search the Manuel Calvo in the 'Passenger Ships and Images' database

Port of Arrival: New York, New York To Philadelphia, Pennsylvania

NATIVITY: Spain

Line: 27

Microfilm Serial: T715

Microfilm Roll: T715_4982

Birth Location: Spain

Birth Location Other: zamora

Page Number: 233

ancestry

Microfilm roll: T715_4982; Line: 27; .

Source Information: Ancestry.com. New York Passenger Lists, 1820-1957 [database on-line]. Provo, UT, USA: Ancestry.com Operations, Inc., 2006. Original data:

- Passenger Lists of Vessels Arriving at New York, New York, 1820-1897; (National Archives Microfilm Publication M237, 675 rolls); Records of the U.S. Customs Service, Record Group 36; National Archives, Washington, D.C.

- Passenger and Crew Lists of Vessels Arriving at New York, New York, 1897-1957; (National Archives Microfilm Publication T715, 8892 rolls); Records of the Immigration and Naturalization Service; National Archives, Washington, D.C.

LORENZO SILVÁN HERNÁNDEZ
5 September 1880 - Unknown

Lorenzo was the ninth child born to Celestino Silván Dovales and Agustina Hernández Martin. Besides the baptismal record, there is a ship manifest that tells a story of this brother. He was three years younger than his brother, Gerónimo, and four years older than his sister, Crescéncia. He was 5' 4" with brown eyes, brown hair and a dark complexion. He may have been the shortest Silván brother.

As a passenger on the SS MUNARGO leaving Antilla, Cuba[9]. He lists his friend as Santo Ramuiz from Santiago. Lorenzo Silván was a single male, could read and write, and was 40 years old at the time he was on this ship. After scrutinizing the ship manifest, one can see the date of his last permanent address was Santiago de Cuba since February of 1911, the same time the Orteric sailed his brothers to Hawaii without him.

Lorenzo later sailed on the SS MUNARGO in February of 1923 into New York. Many ships leaving Cuba sailed to New York before sailing to its final destination. It is unknown whether he returned to Spain after that date as his two brothers (Agustin and Gerónimo) did when they sailed from Cuba in 1930 and 1931. He did not join his siblings in California[10].

---

[9] Antilla is a municipality and town in Holguin Province of Cuba, located on the northeastern shore of Cuba on a peninsula between the Gulf of Nipe and Banes Bay.

[10] Based on the ship manifest, it appears Lorenzo Silván had a mentor in America named Valentin Aguirre who helped many Spaniards and Basques by acting as their "friend" at the arrival port for ease in traveling from Spain to America. James Fernandez, professor from New York and administrator of the "Spaniards in the United States" Facebook page,

Assumptions:

Lorenzo Silván is shown on the ship manifest living in Cuba from February of 1911 until he sailed from Cuba in February 2, 1923. Since two of his brothers (Victorino and Juan Francisco) and his sister (Crescéncia) sailed from Gibraltar in February 1911 after proving good health and showing documentation of good character, I believe Lorenzo made the trip south with his siblings but did not pass the health exam.

Hawaii required men of working age to pass a health exam to be assured people could hold their end of the work required. Both South America and Cuba accepted laborers such as Lorenzo if they did not pass the health exam for the Hawaii offering because their rules were less strict.

New York, Passenger Lists, 1820-1957 about Lorenzo Silvan

Name:	**Lorenzo Silvan**
Arrival Date:	6 Feb 1923
Birth Date:	abt 1883
Birth Location:	Spain
Birth Location Other:	prov of samaria
Age:	40
Gender:	Male
Ethnicity/ Nationality:	Spanish
Port of Departure:	Antilla,cub
Port of Arrival:	New York, New York
Ship Name:	Munargo
Search Ship Database:	Search the Munargo in the 'Passenger Ships and Images' database

View Passenger List

OBISPADO de ZAMORA

ARCHIVO HISTÓRICO DIOCESANO

CERTIFICACIÓN LITERAL DE PARTIDA DE BAUTISMO

Parroquia Santa
María del Castillo.
Fuentesaúco

Diócesis Zamora

Provincia Zamora

Código 120.2

Libro 12

Folio 107v

Núm.

Notas marginales

No tiene

Don José Ángel Rivera de las Heras, Encargado del Archivo Parroquial de Santa María del Castillo de Fuentesaúco en depósito en el Archivo Diocesano, Diócesis de Zamora, Provincia de Zamora,

CERTIFICA: Que el acta al margen reseñada, correspondiente al Libro de bautizados donde se asienta la partida de Lorenzo Silván Hernández, y literalmente dice así:

" En la iglesia parroquial de Santa María del Castillo de la villa de Fuentesaúco, diócesis de Zamora, y en el día ocho de setiembre de mil ochocientos ochenta, yo el infrascrito cura párroco de la misma, bauticé solemnemente un niño hijo legítimo de mis feligreses Celestino Silván, natural de esta villa, y Agustina Hernández, de la de Villamor de los Escuderos. Nació expresado niño a las diez y media de la noche del día cinco del mismo setiembre, y le impuse el nombre de Lorenzo. Son sus abuelos paternos Ángel Silván y María Dobales, naturales de esta villa; maternos Miguel Hernández, natural de dicho Villamor, y Margarita Martín, de Villaescusa. Fue su madrina Teresa Lema Baquero, casada, de esta naturaleza y vecindad, a quien advertí el parentesco espiritual y consiguientes obligaciones.

Y para que esto así conste, firmo y rubrico la presente partida, fecha ut supra.

Daniel Carrascal (rubricado)".

Zamora, a 9 de marzo de 2012

Obispado de Zamora
V.º B.º:
El Vicario General,

TRANSLATION OF BAPTISMAL DOCUMENT FOR LORENZO SILVÁN HERNÁNDEZ

Don Jose Ángel Rivera de las Heras, responsible for the parochial file of Santa Maria del Castillo inside the Archive Diocese File of Zamora, Province of Zamora.

CERTIFY: That the actual margin and correspondence of the baptismal book where Lorenzo Silván Hernández is listed is literal to say:

"In the parroquial church of St. Mary of the Castle of this village of Fuentesaúco, diocese of Zamora, and the 8th day of September, 1880, I, signer and priest of the same, baptised solemnly, a boy, the legitimate son of parishioners Celestino Silván, native of this village and Agustina Hernández of Villamor de los Escuderos. The aforesaid boy was born at half past ten at night the 5th day of September and I imposed him the name Lorenzo. His paternal grandparents are Ángel Silván and Maria Dobales, natives of this village; Maternal grandparents are Miguel Hernández native of said Villamor and Margarita Martin, of Villaescusa. It was his godmother Teresa Lema Baquero, married, of this natural neighborhood, to whom I notified the spiritual relationship and consequent obligations.

And so that this thus be evident, I sign and endorse the present part and date, Daniel Carrascal (endorsed)

Santa Maria del Castillo, Diocese & Province of Zamora
Codigo 120.2, Book 12, Page 107v
There are no notes in the margin
Archivo Historico Diocesano, Zamora

11

AGUSTÍN SILVÁN HERNÁNDEZ
Born about 1887 - Unknown

Agustín Silván Hernández was the last Silván child born in Fuentesaúco, Province of Zamora, Spain to Celestino Pedro Silván Dovales and Agustina Hernández Martin in the fall of 1887. His paternal grandparents were Ángel Silván Martin and Maria Dovales Alejo. His maternal grandparents were Miguel Hernández Hernández of Villamor de los Escuderos and Margarita Martin of Villaescusa.

He was 5' 7" tall. We can only assume he remained in Spain except for a short time in Cuba based on the ship manifest; he left Cuba on the SS CRISTOBAL COLON from Santiago, Cuba.

Based on Agustin's and Gerónimo's residence villages shown on the manifests, I pinpointed they may have worked on the Chaparral Sugar Plantation although at that time, the island also employed massive amounts of people to build roads and work in the coffee plantations.

The ship sailed out of Havana harbor in June of 1931. His homeland is listed as Zamora, line 16 of the manifest shows Agustin Silván, age 43, single male, white hair and black eyes. He sailed from Havana to New York in transit to Spain.

ancestry

New York Passenger Lists, 1820-1957

Name:	**Agustin Silvan**
Arrival Date:	23 Jun 1930
Birth Year:	abt 1887
Birth Location:	Spain
Birth Location Other:	zamora
Age:	43
Gender:	Male
Ethnicity/Race/Nationality:	Spanish
Port of Departure:	Havana, Cuba
Port of Arrival:	New York, New York
Ship Name:	Cristobal Colon
Search Ship Database:	

Source Citation: Year: 1930; Microfilm Detail: T715; Microfilm Roll: T715_4697; Line: 16; Page Number: 132.

Source Information:

Ancestry.com. New York Passenger Lists, 1820-1957 [database on-line]. Provo, UT, USA: Ancestry.com Operations, Inc., 2010.

Original data:

• Passenger Lists of Vessels Arriving at New York, New York, 1820-1897 (National Archives Microfilm Publication M237, 675 rolls); Records of the U.S. Customs Service, Record Group 36; National Archives, Washington, D.C.
• Passenger and Crew Lists of Vessels Arriving at New York, New York, 1897-1957 (National Archives Microfilm Publication T715, 8892 rolls); Records of the Immigration and Naturalization Service; National Archives, Washington, D.C.

LIST OR MANIFEST OF ALIEN PASSENGERS FOR THE UNITED

S. S. "CRISTOBAL COLON"   Passengers sailing from ____ HAVANA ____ , 190_

No.	Family name	Given name	Age	Sex	Married/Single	Calling or occupation	Read	Write	Nationality	Race or people	Country	City or town	Immigration Visa Number	Issued at	Date	Country	City or town
1	Biarna	Francisco	30	M	S	Laborer	Yes	Spanish	Yes	Spain	Spanish	Spain	Lugo				Cuba	Havana
2	Araujo	Manuel	27	M	M	DO	DO	DO	DO	DO	DO	Coruña				DO	DO
3	Vales	Jose	28	M	S	DO	DO	DO	DO	DO	DO	do				DO	DO
4	Ibies	Cayetano	40	M	M	DO	DO	DO	DO	DO	DO	Pontevedra					
5	Villarino	Narciso	38	M	M	DO	DO	DO	DO	DO	DO	Lugo				DO	DO
6	Dorado	Carmen	36	F	M	DO	DO	DO	DO	DO	DO	do				DO	DO
7	Villarino	Carmen	8	F	S	-	DO	DO	DO	DO	DO	DO	do				DO	DO
8	Villarino	Antonio	1	M	S	-	DO	DO	DO	DO	DO	Cuba	Havana				DO	DO
9	Fernandez	Maria	23	F	S	Home	DO	DO	DO	DO	DO	Spain	Zamora				DO	DO
10	Rivera	Fulgencio	37	M	M	Laborer	DO	DO	DO	DO	DO	DO	Coruña				DO	DO
11	Rodriguez	Rosa	30	M	S	do	DO	DO	DO	DO	DO	DO	do				DO	DO
12	Sanchez	Nicolás	41	M	S	do	DO	DO	DO	DO	DO	DO	do				DO	DO
13	Garcia	Manuel	38	M	M	do	DO	DO	DO	DO	DO	DO	do				DO	DO
14	Gallo	Francisco	19	M	S	do	DO	DO	DO	DO	DO	DO	Orense				DO	DO
15	Tomil	Juan	28	M	S	do	DO	DO	DO	DO	DO	DO	Coruña				DO	DO
16	Silvan	Agustin	43	M	S	do	DO	DO	DO	DO	DO	DO	Zamora				DO	DO
17	Diaz	Concepcion	26	F	S	Home	DO	DO	DO	DO	DO	DO	Orense				DO	DO
18	Garcia	Manuel	24	M	S	Laborer	DO	DO	DO	DO	DO	DO	Coruña				DO	DO
19	Viala	Francisco	28	M	S	do	DO	DO	DO	DO	DO	DO	do				DO	DO
20	Lopez	Jose	30	M	S	do	DO	DO	DO	DO	DO	DO	Lugo				DO	DO
21	Fernandez	Rosa	25	F	S	Home	DO	DO	DO	DO	DO	DO	do				DO	DO
22	Bermudez	Gregorio	47	M	M	Laborer	DO	DO	DO	DO	DO	DO	Coruña				DO	DO
23	Negreira	Andrés	37	M	M	do	DO	DO	DO	DO	DO	DO	do				DO	DO
24	Rey	Pedro	42	M	M	do	DO	DO	DO	DO	DO	DO	do				DO	DO
25	Blanco	Valentin	29	M	S	do	DO	DO	DO	DO	DO	DO	Lugo				DO	DO
26	Iglesia	Patricio de la	48	M	M	do	DO	DO	DO	DO	DO	DO	Salamanca				DO	DO
27	Diaz	Florencia	46	F	M	Home	DO	DO	DO	DO	DO	DO	do				DO	DO
28	Iglesia	Francisco de la	20	M	S	do	DO	DO	DO	DO	DO	DO	do				DO	DO
29	Iglesia	Francisco de la	8	M	S	Student	DO	DO	DO	DO	DO	Cuba	Habana				DO	DO
30	Iglesia	Gregorio de la	1	M	S	-	DO	DO	DO	DO	DO	do	do				DO	DO

List 13

STATES IMMIGRATION OFFICER AT PORT OF ARRIVAL

STEERAGE PASSENGERS ONLY

131

Arriving at Port of ___ N E W Y O R K ___, June 23 th ___, 19 30.

PART 3

Immigrant Silváns from Spain to Hawaii and into America

Victorino Luciano Silván Hernández

Juan Francisco Silván Hernández

Crescéncia Silván Hernández (Gonzales)

Family Group Sheet for Victorino (Vitorino) Luciano SILVAN Hernandez

Husband:		Victorino (Vitorino) Luciano SILVAN Hernandez
	Birth:	21 Jul 1868 in Fuentesauco, Province of Zamora, Spain
	Death:	15 Dec 1925 in San Leandro, Alameda, California
	Burial:	Oakland, Alameda County, California, USA
	Father:	Celestino Pedro SILVAN Dovales
	Mother:	Agustina Hernandez Martin

Wife:		Romana MARTINEZ Lorenzo
	Birth:	09 Aug 1874 in Fuestesauco, Zamora, Spain
	Death:	29 Mar 1955 in San Leandro, Alameda, California USA
	Burial:	Oakland, Alameda County, California, USA
	Father:	Pedro Martin
	Mother:	Sabina Lorenzo

	Children:	
1 F	Name:	Theodora "Dora" Martin Silvan
	Birth:	06 Sep 1899 in Fuentesauco, Zamora, Spain
	Death:	24 Jul 1991 in Pleasanton, Alameda County, California USA.
	Marriage:	Apr 1919 in Hanalei, Kauai, Hawaii Territory
	Spouse:	John Bento Souza
2 F	Name:	Felisa (Alice) Martin Silvan
	Birth:	06 Nov 1904 in Fuentesauco, Zamora, Spain
	Death:	10 Dec 1991 in Alameda County, California, USA
	Burial:	Hayward, Alameda County, California, USA
	Marriage:	05 May 1924 in Alameda, California, USA
	Spouse:	Seraphim Andrews (Joe) Medeiros
3 M	Name:	Jacinto Martin Silvan
	Birth:	19 Jul 1906 in Fuentesauco, Province of Zamora, Spain
	Death:	Apr 1911 in At sea, Orteric from Gibralter to Honolulu
4 M	Name:	Celestino Martin Silvan
	Birth:	20 Jul 1906 in Fuentesauco, Zamora, Castilla-Leon, Spain
	Death:	01 Jul 1983 in San Leandro, Alameda, California, United States of America
	Burial:	Oakland, Alameda County, California, USA

Notes

Theodora "Dora" Martin Silvan
Teodora / Theodora aka DORA

VICTORINO LUCIANO SILVÁN HERNÁNDEZ
and
ROMANA MARTINEZ LORENZO

VICTORINO LUCIANO SILVÁN HERNÁNDEZ
21 July 1868 – 15 December 1925

Victorino Luciano Silván Hernández had a dark bushy mustache that could have rivaled Salvador Dali's. I believe he must have been a strong, independent and thoughtful man to uproot his family and leave his mother behind. He was the oldest in the group of Silváns to immigrate from Fuentesaúco, Province of Zamora, Spain where he was born to Celestino Silván Dovales and Agustina Hernández Martin.

His paternal grandparents were Ángel Silván Martin and Maria Dovales Alejo. His maternal grandparents were Miguel Hernández Hernández of Villamor de los Escuderos and Margarita Martin of Villaescusa. His Godfather was Luciano Prieto. The name is not in the family tree, so this may have been a very close friend.

There is not much information to be found for this older brother except for a short mention in the book, *Mama and Dad and their Fifteen Kids* by Rose Ruiz Gobert. At the time Rose was born, she mentions her Aunt Ramona helping at her birth but she left the next morning because her "husband was sick in bed and he needed her at home". This would have been Uncle Victorino.

CERTIFICACIÓN LITERAL DE PARTIDA DE BAUTISMO

Parroquia Santa María del Castillo. Fuentesaúco.

Diócesis Zamora

Provincia Zamora

Código 120.2

Libro 10

Folio 309r

Núm.

Notas marginales

No tiene

Obispado de Zamora
V.º B.º.
El Vicario General,

José F ...

Don José Ángel Rivera de las Heras, Encargado del Archivo Parroquial de Santa María del Castillo de Fuentesaúco en depósito en el Archivo Diocesano, Diócesis de Zamora, Provincia de Zamora,

CERTIFICA: Que el acta al margen reseñada, correspondiente al Libro de bautizados se asienta la partida de Víctor Luciano Silván Hernández, y literalmente dice así:

" En la iglesia parroquial de Santa María del Castillo de esta villa de Fuentesaúco, diócesis y provincia de Zamora, y día veinticinco de julio de mil ochocientos sesenta y ocho, yo el infrascrito párroco de ella, bauticé solemnemente un niño que había nacido el veintiuno del mismo, hijo legítimo de Celestino Silván, natural de esta, y Agustina Hernández, de Villamor, a quien puse por nombre Víctor Luciano. Abuelos paternos Ángel y María Dobales, difuntos; maternos Miguel, del dicho Villamor, y Margarita Martín, difunta, de Villaescusa. Fue su padrino Luciano Prieto a quien advertí el parentesco espiritual y obligaciones.

Y lo firmo.
Juan Antonio Álvarez *(rubricado)*".

Zamora, a 17 de noviembre de 2011

The Silván families continued to multiply along with a mounting discontent as the siblings began to mumble. They feared for their future and they weighed their options after seeing a poster asking for workers in Hawaiian sugar fields looking far from home.[12]

By the end of 1910, four of the siblings decided to trust the plantation agents from Hawaii and with legal documents in hand, they prepared to leave Fuentesaúco and Spain.

Money was scarce. They pooled everything they had and rode the train over the mountains to Seville, sailed down the Guadalquivir River to Sanlúcar and then walked and camped the remaining way to La Linea at Gibraltar where a ship waited and their adventure began.

The immigrant ship, ORTERIC, sailed from Gibraltar on February 24, 1911 carrying the Silván families; all except their brother, Lorenzo, who did not pass the health exam.

During the 48-day voyage, death struck down his five-year old son, Jacinto Silván Martin, from measles. His burial at sea was numbing as his small body was interred in a watery grave. Rosary beads, prayers, and tears could not take away the pain.

Within a couple of weeks, their cousin, 2-year old Simon Martin, died and the heaviness of their loss was insurmountable.[13]

At 43, Victorino was the oldest Silván brother on the sugar plantations of Kauai and Oahu. The planting, furrowing, cutting, carrying, and long days took its toll. But he persevered to guarantee his family received what the infamous poster promised. His children were educated, fed and clothed.

---

[12] See *The Girl Immigrant* for complete story and copy of the poster proclaiming the wonders of Hawaii, jobs etc.

[13] *The Girl Immigrant* describes this time in the Silván family's life on board the SS Orteric

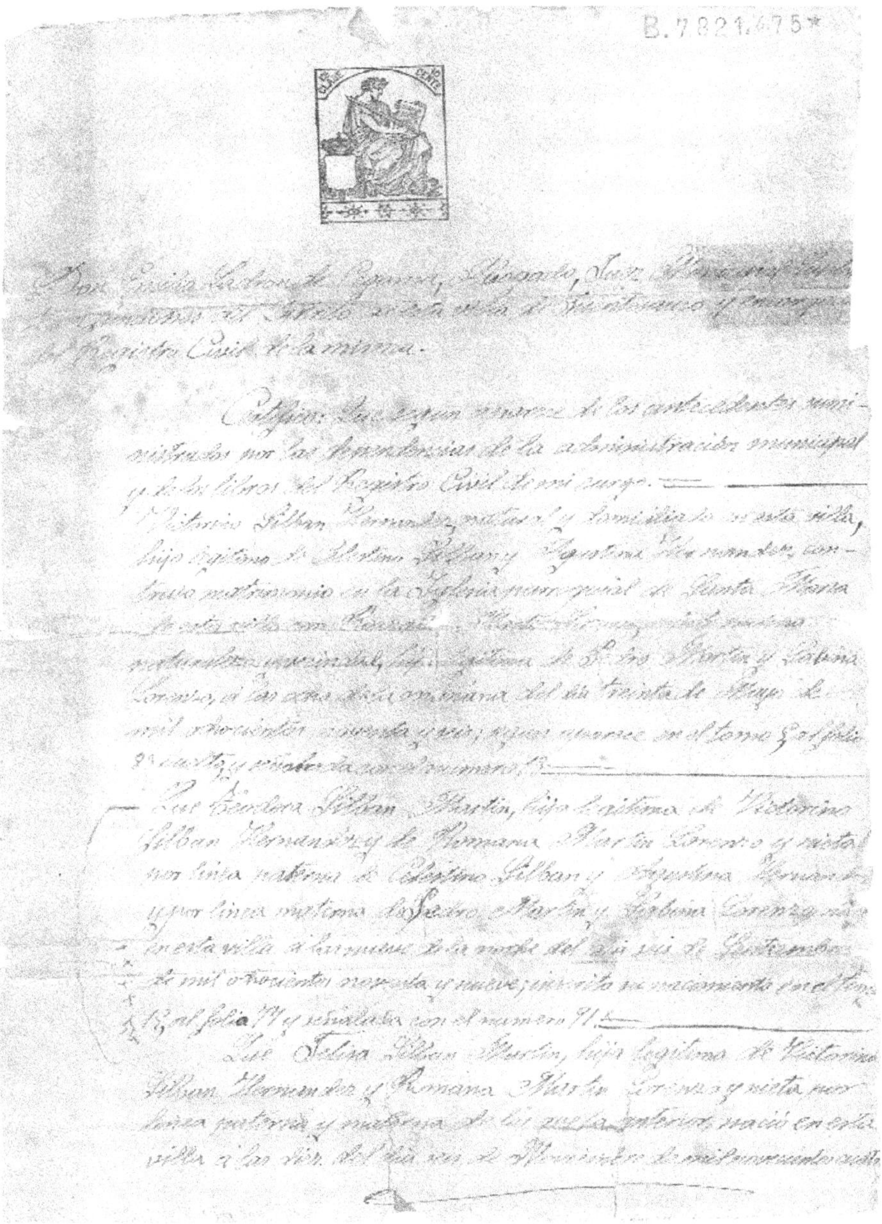

B.7821475*

Don Emilio Silvan de Ugarre, Abogado, Juez [illegible] del Partido de esta villa de [illegible] y encargado del Registro Civil de la misma.

Certifico: Que segun aparece de los antecedentes suministrados por las dependencias de la administración municipal y de los libros del Registro Civil de mi cargo.

Victorino Silban Hernandez, natural y domiciliado en esta villa, hijo legítimo de Celestino Silban y Agustina Hernandez, contrajo matrimonio en la Iglesia parroquial de Santa María de esta villa con Romana Martin Lorenzo, de igual naturaleza y vecindad, hija legítima de Pedro Martin y Sabina Lorenzo, a las ocho de la mañana del día treinta de Mayo de mil ochocientos noventa y seis; segun aparece en el tomo 2 al folio 9º vuelto y señalada con el número 13.

Que Teodora Silban Martin, hija legítima de Victorino Silban Hernandez y de Romana Martin Lorenzo y nieta por línea paterna de Celestino Silban y Agustina Hernandez y por línea materna de Pedro Martin y Sabina Lorenzo, nació en esta villa a las nueve de la noche del día seis de Septiembre de mil ochocientos noventa y nueve; inscrito su nacimiento en el tomo 13, al folio 77 y señalado con el número 91.

Que Felisa Silban Martin, hija legítima de Victorino Silban Hernandez y Romana Martin Lorenzo y nieta por línea paterna y materna de los [illegible] anteriores, nació en esta villa a las diez del día seis de Noviembre de mil novecientos [illegible]

Watching Celestino learn to swim and grow on the island soothed Victorino's heart but he worried his son might never recover from Jacinto's death. He watched him pound the hard shells of coconuts and drink their milk. He watched him eat his first banana and shared a laugh when they realized bananas must be peeled before eating its fruit. He watched his son earn his first coins selling fish he caught himself. Despite feeling old, Victorino did not regret leaving Spain, but he missed his oldest son, his mother, his brothers and his country. He, like other Spaniards, kept those feelings tightly locked inside of their hearts and did not speak of it often.

The Silván families chose plantations close to one another that could offer jobs to all of them but Crescéncia and Felix Gonzales stayed on Oahu at the Ewa Plantation for a time before eventually joining the others on Kauai.

Celestino, Teodora, Victorino, Romana and Felisa
abt 1917-1918
(Corner inset photos are Celestino as an adult at various ages)

Victorino and Romana watched over their daughters. Family and friends often ate together, danced, talked and looked forward to restful time away from the Kilauea Sugar Plantation fields on the north shore of Kauai. While living in the small village of Hanalei, they became good friends with the Souza family.

They saw Teodora's eyes wander toward the youngest Souza boy, John, who was a quiet Portuguese boy, two years older than their daughter. John Souza Bento limped from a machete injury while working in the sugar fields. By the spring of 1919, Teodora married John Souza at St. Sylvester's Church in Kilauea.[14]

Victorino watched his brother, John, and sister, Christina, sail a year earlier for San Francisco, California in January 1918. But, he did not want to leave his daughter behind in Kauai, not yet.

However, within three years (April 1921), they sailed to San Francisco[15] with Felisa and Celestino. Teodora and John with their new baby, Josephine, (b. April 1920) followed them soon afterward.

They settled in the Oakland area and eventually bought a white Victorian house at 214 Dabner Street; a porch in the front with a bank of stairs leading into the yard and gardens. Ramona planted lots of flowers and made their house a home.

Within four years, Victorino's health diminished. He was grandfather to Teodora's three children, Josephine, Victor and Alfred and Felisa's first child, Melvin. By December, Victorino Luciano Silván Hernández died of a lung abscess just before Christmas in 1925, not living to see his next five grandchildren. He was fifty seven years old.

---

[14] This is the church listed on six baptismal records for the Souza Bento family, so the church as the venue for their wedding is based on that documentation. No marriage records could be found at the Roman Catholic Church in the State of Hawaii's Chancery Office in Honolulu, the archdiocese in Kauai, or the vital statistic records.

[15] Documents show them on the 1920 census in Hanelei, Kauai, but I cannot find the ship manifest showing them sailing from Hawaii to California. It is only through family stories that we know they settled in San Leandro, Alameda, California.

He is buried in St. Mary's Cemetery, 4529 Howe St, Oakland, CA 94611.   Ramona would later be buried beneath the same gravestone[16] thirty years later when she died of a cerebral vascular stroke.

Gravestone of Victorino Silván – 1925

---

[16] And a third grave etched on the same gravestone would hold Alice's younger brother, Celestino eighteen years later in October, 1973.

Translation of Document[17] B. 7.821.475

Don Emilio Ladron de Cegama, Attorney and Deputy Municipal Justice for the Fuentesaúco District and administrator of the Municipal Civil Registry of said district certifies to the following:

Certificate: That according to the entries recorded in the archives of the Civil Registry.

Victorino Silban a native and resident of this village, natural son of **Celestino Silban** and **Agustina Hernández**, married **Romana Martin Lorenzo** a native and resident of the same village, natural daughter of **Pedro Martin** and **Sabina Lorenzo**. The marriage ceremony took place at the parochial church of *Santa Maria* in the same village on 30 of May in 1896 at 8:00 a.m. as recorded in volume 9, page 83, column 13 of the Registry.

That **Teodora Silban Martin** natural daughter of **Victorino Silban Hernández** and **Romana Martin Lorenzo**, paternal granddaughter of **Celestino Silban** and **Agustina Hernández**, maternal granddaughter of **Pedro Martin** and **Sabina Lorenzo**, was born in this village at 9:00 p.m. on 6 September 1899 as recorded in volume 19, page 77, column 99.

That **Felisa Silban Martin**, natural daughter of **Victorino Silban Hernández** and **Romana Martin Lorenzo**, granddaughter of the aforementioned couples, was born in this village at 10 a.m. on 6 November, 1904 as recorded on volume 16, page 298, column 117.

That **Celestino Silban Martin** natural son of **Victorino Silban Hernández** and **Romana Martin Lorenzo,** granddaughter of the aforementioned couples, was born in this village on 20 July 1906 as recorded on volume 12, page 30, column 76.

That **Jacinto Silban Martin** natural son of **Victorino Silban Hernández** and **Romana Martin Lorenzo**, granddaughter of the aforementioned couples, was born in this village at 11:00 p.m. on 19 July 1906 as recorded on volume 17, page 312, column 81.

I grant this statement at the request of **Victorino Silban** for immigration purposes. The Municipal Justice of Fuentesaúco has affixed his Seal of Office on this 27th day of January, 1911.

Signed: Julio Corrales, Secretary

Document courtesy of Linda Medeiros Ely

Lines 6-11 list Victorino Silban Hernández and family
Column 11 shows relative they left behind: Agustina Hernández, mother, Fuentesaúco

This census was dated January 1920 in Hanalei, Kauai, Hawaii –
just west of Kilauea
ADDRESS LISTED AS: Kilauea Road, Camp G

Victorino Luciano "Vitorino" Silvan [Edit Name]

| Memorial | Photos | Flowers | | Share | Edit |

Learn about removing the ads from this memorial...

[Transfer Management] [Edit] [Delete

Birth: Jul. 21, 1868
           Zamora
           Castilla y Leon, Spain
Death: Dec. 15, 1925
           Oakland
           Alameda County
           California, USA [Edit Dates]

Victorino Luciano Silvan Hernandez was born
in Fuentesauco, Province of Zamora, Spain,
the son of Celestino Silvan Dovales and
Agustin Hernandez Martin. He married Romana
(Ramona) Lorenzo Martin in 1896. They
emigrated, along with their 4 children and
Silvan siblings and families to the sugar fields
of Hawaii on the SS ORTERIC from Gibraltar in
1911. Their 5 year old son, Jacinto, died of
measles and was buried at sea.

Several years after working in Hawaii, they all
moved to California where they raised their
children. He is buried in the shared grave plot
with his wife, Romana and his remaining son,
Celestino.
[Edit Bio]
Family links: [Edit]
 Spouse:
  Romana Lorenzo *Martin* Silvan (1874 - 1955)

 Children:
  Theodora Martin *Silvan* Souza (1899 - 1991)*
  Felisa *Silvan* Medeiros (1904 - 1991)*
  Celestino Martin Silvan (1906 - 1983)*

*Calculated relationship

[Add Marker Transcription]
[Add Note]

Burial: [Edit]
Saint Marys Cemetery
Oakland
Alameda County
California, USA [Add Plot]

Edit Virtual Cemetery info [?]

Created by: Patricia Steele
Record added: Feb 02, 2012
Find A Grave Memorial# 84368255

Added by: Patricia Steele

Added by: Patricia Steele

Cemetery Photo

WIFE OF VICTORINO SILVÁN HERNÁNDEZ:
ROMANA MARTINEZ LORENZO
9 August 1874 – 29 May 1955

It is believed that Romana was cousin to Agustina Hernández Martin through her father, Pedro Martin. We know their children were cousins and the Martin name appears to be the only link. She and Victorino were married fifteen years before they made the decision to leave Spain and accompany his younger brothers and sister to Hawaii. Her parents were Pedro Martin and Sabina Lorenzo as shown on the legal documents required to emigrate from Spain.

She left her home village with four children and arrived in the Hawaiian Islands with three, losing one of her sons on the ship due to measles or small pox. A burial at sea is something I cannot imagine and wonder if this woman ever got over such a horrific tragedy.

Her granddaughter, Dorothy Souza Petersen, told me during our interview that her grandmother loved music and dancing. When she and her siblings were young, her grandmother Ramona would demand they sit on the couch like little ducks in a row while she danced for them.

"We were a captive audience," Dorothy laughed.

Top photo: Alien Certificate from Hawaii – March 19, 1921

Bottom photo: Ramona (with apron) watches her daughter, Teodora (Dora) hold her granddaughter, Vicki Souza, child of Victor John Souza in the fall or winter of 1949.

Romana Lorenzo "Ramona" *Martin* Silvan [Edit Name]

| Memorial | Photos | Flowers | | Share | Edit |

Learn about upgrading this memorial...

[Transfer Management] [Edit] [Delete]

Birth: Aug. 9, 1874
          Zamora
          Castilla y Leon, Spain
Death: Mar. 29, 1955
          Oakland
          Alameda County
          California, USA [Edit Dates]

Romana MARTIN Lorenzo was born in
Fuentesauco, Province of Zamora, Spain to
Pedro Martin and Sabina Lorenzo. She married
Victorino Luciano SILVAN Hernandez May 30,
1896 at Santa Maria Church del Castillo in
Fuentesauco.

They had 4 children (Teodora, Felisa, Jacinto
and Celestino). In 1911, they traveled with
her husband's brother and sister and their
families to Gibraltar and sailed to Hawaiian
sugar fields on the SS ORTERIC, where their
twin son, Jacinto, contracted Measles and
died (buried at sea).

Added by: Patricia Steele

They lived in Hawaii until they sailed to
California about 1921 and lived in Oakland
area. She shares a grave plot with her
husband and remaining son, Celestino Martin
Silvan.
[Edit Bio]
Family links: [Edit]
 Spouse:
  Victorino Luciano Silvan (1868 - 1925)*

 Children:
  Theodora Martin *Silvan* Souza (1899 - 1991)*
  Felisa *Silvan* Medeiros (1904 - 1991)*
  Celestino Martin Silvan (1906 - 1983)*

*Calculated relationship

Added by: Patricia Steele

[Add Marker Transcription]
[Add Note]

Burial: [Edit]
Saint Marys Cemetery
Oakland
Alameda County
California, USA [Add Plot]

Edit Virtual Cemetery info [?]

Created by: Patricia Steele
Record added: Feb 02, 2012

Cemetery Photo

JUAN FRANCISCO SILVÁN HERNÁNDEZ
and
EUSTOQUIA RITA TRASCASAS MARZO

Family Group Sheet for Juan Francisco SILVAN Hernandez

Husband:	Juan Francisco SILVAN Hernandez
Birth:	16 Aug 1875 in Fuentesauco, Province of Zamora, Spain
Death:	05 May 1945 in Benicia, Solano, California, USA
Marriage:	23 Apr 1900 in Fuentesauco, Zamora, Spain
Father:	Celestino Pedro SILVAN Dovales
Mother:	Agustina Hernandez Martin

Wife:	Eustoquia Rita Trascasas Marzo
Birth:	29 Sep 1880 in Toro, Province of Zamora, Spain
Death:	13 Jun 1953 in Woodland, Yolo, California, United States
Burial:	Jun 1953 in Benicia, Solano County, California, USA
Father:	Manuel Trascasas Alonso
Mother:	Manuela MARZO Garcia

Children:

1 F	Name:	Manuela Trascasas SILVAN
	Birth:	25 Jun 1901 in Fuentesauco, Province, of Zamora, Spain
	Death:	21 Apr 2001 in Woodland, Yolo, California, United States of America
	Burial:	Winters, Yolo County, California, USA
	Marriage:	16 Oct 1919 in Alameda, Alameda, California, USA
	Spouse:	Bernardo Romero Ruiz

2 M	Name:	Agustino Marzo Silvan
	Birth:	29 Mar 1908 in Fuentesauco, Province of Zamora, Spain
	Death:	03 Sep 1994 in Homer, Kenai Peninsula, Alaska, United States of America
	Spouse:	Maria Ernestasia Fernandez

3 M	Name:	Jose Marzo Silvan
	Birth:	08 Jun 1910 in Fuentesauco, Province of Zamora, Castilla-Leon, Spain
	Death:	17 Aug 1979 in Sacramento, Sacramento, California, USA
	Burial:	Sacramento, Sacramento County, California, USA
	Marriage:	11 Nov 1939 in Reno, Washoe, Nevada, USA
	Spouse:	Encarnacion "Carrie" Alva

4 F	Name:	Maria Trascasas Silvan
	Birth:	07 Mar 1914 in Kapaa, Kauai, Hawaii, USA
	Death:	10 Jul 1997 in Vacaville, Solano, California, United States
	Marriage:	24 Dec 1931 in Sacramento, Sacramento, California, United States
	Spouse:	Francisco Pareja Cuellar

5 F	Name:	Juanita Trascasas Silvan
	Birth:	07 Mar 1918 in San Lorenzo, Alameda, California, USA
	Death:	13 Jan 1981 in Loveland, Larimer, Colorado, United States
	Burial:	Jan 1981 in Fort Collins, Larimer County, Colorado, USA
	Marriage:	26 Oct 1932
	Spouse:	Eugene Vidept Watkins

6 M	Name:	Celestino Fernandez Silvan
	Birth:	30 Jun 1919 in Pittsburg, Contra Costa, California, United States
	Death:	13 Jul 1973 in Carmichael, Sacramento, California, United States of America
	Burial:	Sacramento, Sacramento County, California, USA
	Marriage:	1943 in Benicia, Solano, California, USA
	Spouse:	Frances Surname Unknown

7 F	Name:	Ramona Trascasas Silvan
	Birth:	09 Mar 1922
	Death:	22 Aug 1922 in Yolo, California, USA
	Burial:	Winters, Yolo County, California, USA

Notes

Juan Francisco SILVAN Hernandez
Juan Francisco Silvan Hernandez was 5'3" tall with brown hair and blue eyes

JUAN FRANCISCO SILVÁN HERNÁNDEZ
16 August 1875 - 5 May 1945

Proven document states:
Juan Francisco Silván Hernández (tomo 5, fol. 162-163v). Casado en la Iglesia de Santa María de Fuentesaúco el 23 de abril de 1900 (tomo 5, fol. 145v), con Rita Marzo Trascasas Marzo, natural de Toro, en 1881, hija de Manuel Trascasas y Manuela Marzo, naturales de Toro.

Music was in his blood; his drum, he called el bombo was his magic carpet to other places. Remembered as the man with the drum, he sang songs and encouraged others to dance.

Born in Fuentesaúco, Zamora, Spain to Celestino Silván Dovales and Agustina Hernández Martin in the summer of 1875, he learned at an early age to negotiate or get lost along the way. Raised in Fuentesaúco, he and his horse pulled bulls out of the bullring as matadors finished with them. Despite the busy work, he would always find time for music, singing and his drum. He was dark skinned, had brown hair, bright blue eyes and stood 5′ 6″ tall. He smoked a cigar or a pipe and kept his dark, luxuriant mustache twisted and twirled.

He was hard working, loyal, responsible and friendly. By 1900, he had a musical band called *John's Song and Drums*, tempting listeners to tap their feet.

Eustoquia Rita Trascasas Marzo, from the nearby hilltop village of Toro, was accompanied by her mother and two uncles to hear the music in Fuentesaúco.

Soon afterward, the music was from bells ringing on April 23, 1900 as they were married in Fuentesaúco at Santa Maria del

Castillo Church. Their first child, Manuela Silván Trascasas was born fourteen months later, June 25, 1901[18]. This was my grandmother (abuelita). It was seven years before Agustín was born in 1908.

Spain experienced flooding that destroyed most of the country's crops. Young men were conscripted into the military; there was unrest, threats, challenges, small wages. People cried.

Amid the turmoil that surrounded the villagers, a poster was circulated promising fortunes through hard work in a faraway place called Hawaii by sugar plantation owners. The year their son, José, was born, short conversations morphed into in-depth discussions and their dream was born.

At the end of 1910, Victorino, Juan, Lorenzo, and Crescéncia's husband, Felix, met with the civil registrar to prepare legal documents of good standing; each child was listed to meet immigration requirements. A ship would sail from Spain to Hawaii; they must get to La Linea and Gibraltar's pier.

The biggest hurdle Juan faced was selling their dream to his mother, Agustina Hernandez Martin, and facing the grim fact that he'd never see her again. His family's lives would change from a dusty village to the unknown across an ocean.

He would leave family members behind. When the mass exodus blew through their village, he left the graves of his ancestors for the promises of strangers. He took his family and his drum. He left his mother and brothers.

Juan was heartbroken but stoic for his wife, Rita. She was leaving her mother and family behind in Toro also. His children would be leaving their grandmothers. He would be leaving his mother. His guilty heart squeezed from the joy of new adventures to a little knot of apprehension.

---

[18] I can only assume Rita may have birthed one or more children who died young because it was seven years before their son; Agustín Silván Marzo was born in 1908,

SPANISH DOCUMENT REVEALS: *Juan Francisco Silván Hernández (tomo 5, fol. 162-163v). Casado en la Iglesia de Santa María de Fuentesaúco el 23 de abril de 1900 (tomo 5, fol. 145v), con Rita Marzo Trascasas Marzo, natural de Toro, en 1881, hija de Manuel Trascasas y Manuela Marzo, naturales de Toro.*

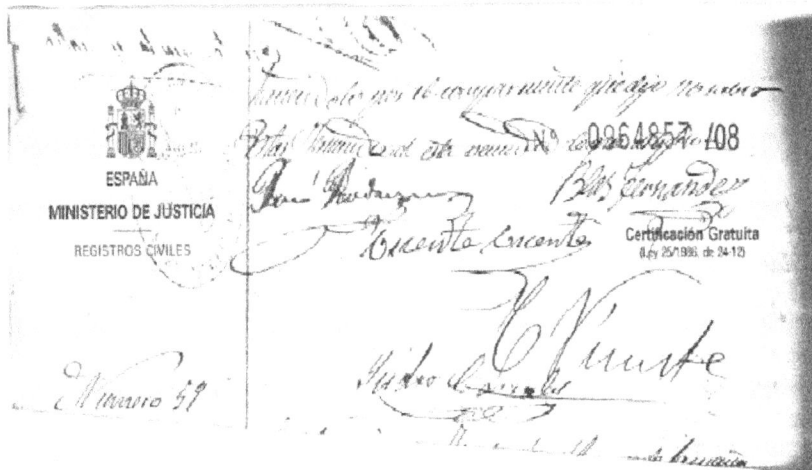

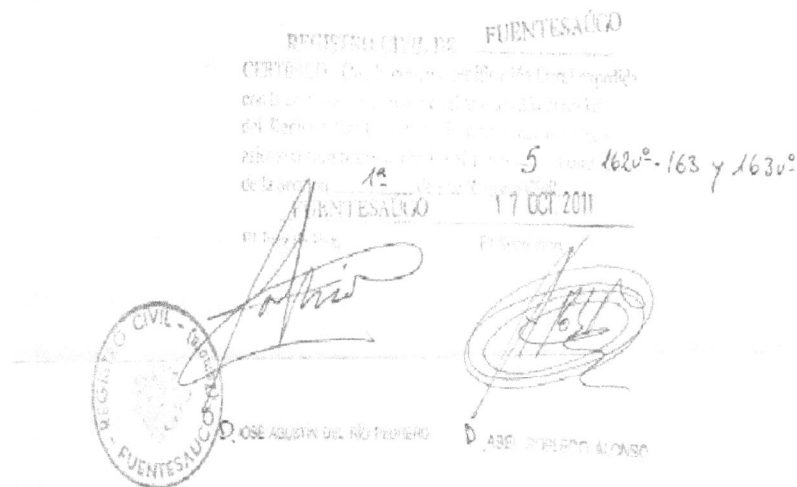

Birth Certificate
Juan Francisco Silván Hernández / Side note: Matrimony Information

Ship's Manifest ~ S.S. Orteric sailing from Gibraltar Feb 24, 1911.
Lines 1-5 list Juan Silban Hernández and family

Finally in Honolulu, Hawaii, they honored their commitment to the Hawaiian plantation owners by working in various sugarcane fields; their first Hawaiian-born child, María Silván, was born in 1914, at Kapa'a, a community designated as *Kealia*. From there, they moved north to the Kilauea Plantation. They'd exchanged their individuality with bango numbers when they worked in the cane fields[19] and John felt he was getting nowhere when his earnings went to the company store.

John Silvan and his family sailed to San Francisco on the HERMAN GOVERNOR with his sister, Crescéncia and her husband, Felix Gonzales less than seven years after arriving in Hawaii.

Friends greeted them and shared their home in San Lorenzo in Alameda County until they found a home of their own. John

---

[19] *Bango*: An ID tag made of brass or aluminum with a number stamped on one side worn on a chain around their neck; different shapes determined a worker's race. Every plantation used the *bango* system and laborers were required to wear them during working hours. Plantation accounts were kept by *bango* number; deductions for infractions, store purchases, laundry services, etc. were all kept in account books under the *bango* number and on pay day, workers presented their *bango* at the payroll desk; no pay without it.

and Rita, with Manuela, Gus, José and María, soon rented a small house with two other families. They had separate living spaces with a community kitchen and housed Crescéncia, Felix, Alejandro, Juan, María Gregoria, Christina Barceliza, Agustína and Victorina Gonzales, Dioniseo Leigones Herrero, Dominiquez Perez and their four children. There were 19 in the household.

Two months later, on March 7, 1918, Rita gave birth to a daughter named Juanita Silván Trascasas. Their last son, Celestino Fernandez Silván, was born in June 1919.

John's family lived a time in the Santa Clara Valley (San Jose area) and worked in Suisun, California in the pear harvests before moving to Winters, California. The Silvans picked fruit and packed fruits. Juan also worked in the orchards and cannery.

He built an outside conical oven, lined with bricks called *el horno* to bake their bread. Rita Silván grew herbs in her garden and ground fresh parsley and garlic by mortar and pestle[20].

Juan also grew grapes, produced red wine to fill several barrels each fall and stored them in the cool cellar. He kept a wine jug at his feet beneath the dinner table. The Silvans were mostly self-sufficient; they bartered with neighbors in exchange for the crops they did not grow themselves.

Juan trained his boys to work in the fields from an early age. They learned to hold the implements steady to keep the rows in order, how deep to plant the variety of seeds; they grew peas, string beans, corn and garbanzo beans. Pears, peaches, apricots, apples, figs, prunes and almond trees grew on the ranch in Winters.

At harvest time, Juan, Gus, José and later John's younger sons and daughters worked in the fields cutting and packing fruit into boxes to sell, eat and trade.

---

[20] Source: Story by Millie Ruiz Cortopassi; memories of helping Grandma Rita crush herbs

John Silván never lost his love for music; the family sang and danced while he played his drum and the Silván and Gonzales families visited often; their children played together and their lives became enmeshed on American soil. The adults played cards amid grumbling and laughter. Often, the partners in their card games were John and Christina against Rita and Felix. And the winners were most often Rita and Felix despite the bantering that erupted between the two.[21]

A curious mystery involves Felix Gonzales and his Spanish military[22] history. **The family story: The Spanish government sent a letter offering him a *Marquis* position to thank him for his military service. Rita read and destroyed the letter so he would not receive the honor offered to him out of pettiness. The story saddened me so I researched it and found:

(1) Only the royalty in Spain received Marquis Status. So, what honor did Spain's government offer Felix? (2) Rita could not read.[23]

---

[21] Source: Victorina Gonzales Weber

[22] Fernando Hidalgo Lerdo de Tejada, a genealogist in Seville, researched military history. He said as a poor Spaniard, he was sure Felix was recruited in the obligatory military service (so, he passed to "segunda reserva")

[23] Military story passed down through the family until it filtered to Eusebio (Sab) Gonzales to Patte Kronlund and Linda Rhoades. We are all stumped.

April 12, 1930, Federal Census, California Solano County, Silveyville Township.

		Name	Relation				Sex	Color	Age	Marital	Age at marriage			Birthplace	Father birthplace	Mother birthplace	
125	125	Silven	John F.	Head	O		M	W	54	M	24	No	No	Spain	Spain	Spain
		—	Pete	Wife-H			F	W	48	M	18	No	No	Spain	Spain	Spain
		—	Jose?	Son			M	W	20	S		No	Yes	Spain	Spain	Spain
		—	Mary	Daughter			F	W	16	S		No	Yes	Madrid Spain	Spain	Spain
		—	Vicente	Daughter			F	W	13	S		No	Yes	California	Spain	Spain
		—	Philittos	Son			M	W	11	S		Yes	Yes	California	Spain	Spain
3	126	Ruby	Ben	Head	O		M	W	30	M	20	No	No	Spain	Spain	Spain
		—	Mildred	Wife-H			F	W	29	M	19	No	No	Spain	Spain	Spain
		—	Frank	Son			M	W	9	S			Yes	California	Spain	Spain
		—	John	Son			M	W	7	S			Yes	California	Spain	Spain
		—	Rose	Daughter			F	W	6	S			Yes	California	Spain	Spain
		—	Mike	Son			M	W	5	S			No	California	Spain	Spain
		—	Mary	Daughter			F	W	2	S			No	California	Spain	Spain
3	127	Sabin	August	Head	R		M	W	22	M		No	Yes	Spain	Spain	Spain
		—	Marie	Wife-H			F	W	16	M		No	No	Spain	Spain	Spain
		—	John	Son			M	W	1 4/12			No		California	Spain	Spain

The residence is listed as"*Hill roads in the Olive District off Pleasant Valley Road.*"

Photo: Manuela, Gus, Joe, Mary and Juanita. Is Celestino behind the camera?

When John Silván had a stroke in 1939, his ranching days were over. John's sister, Crescéncia Gonzales and her husband, Felix, invited John and Rita to live with them at Putah Creek near the Olive School.

The Silváns sold their ranch October 20, 1943 to Rafael and Ruth Lopez when he became bedridden. The property is defined as "Lots 1, 2, 26, 27 and 28 Block 1 of Emery's Addition in Winters[24]. The sale price was $1,500. The down payment was $500 and payments were $25 per month without interest until the remaining $1,000 was paid off.

They were moved to Benicia to live with their daughter, Juanita and her husband, Manuel Castelar, where they lived until his death May 5, 1945.

---

[24] Emery's addition was the area just west of Emery Street in Winters which is off of what is now called West Main Street. There are houses there now but there probably were still orchards around the houses in 1943. Emery was a developer from the Berkeley Bay Area who came to Winters and built some houses in that area around 1913.

www.findagrave.com ~ MEMORIAL #84168251

Newspaper Obituary list in the HERALD-NEW ERA, BENICIA, CALIFORNIA

John Silván's death certificate lists father's name as Agustín; it should be listed as Celestino. His middle initial is listed as "A" but his middle name was Francisco

Thursday, May 10, 1945

Final Rites Held For John A. Silvan

John A. Silvan, 75, died last Saturday night at the home of his daughter, Mrs. Juanita Castelar of 310 East M street, Benicia. A native of Spain, Silvan had resided in Benicia for the past five years.

He is survived by his wife, Rita; two other daughters, Mrs. Mary Cuellar of Vacaville, and Mrs. Mildred Ruiz of Winters; three sons, August of Napa, and Joseph and Celestino of Benicia, and a sister, Christina Gonzolas of Winters.

Funeral services under the direction of Chisholm and Passalacqua Funeral Home were held Tuesday at St. Dominic's church. A rosary was said at the home on Monday night.

Pvt. Robert S. Miller Killed In Action

Private Robert S. Miller of the Marine Corps reserve, whose wife resides in Benicia, has been killed in action, the Navy Department reported Tuesday.

Stamp Collectors Here You Are

A revised edition of the official booklet containing descriptions and illustrations of U. S. postage stamps from the date of their introduction, 1847, until April 1, 1945, is now available. Postmaster Alma Pometta announced this week. It may be obtained for 30 cents in post note, postal money order or check from the Superintendent of Documents, Government Printing Office...

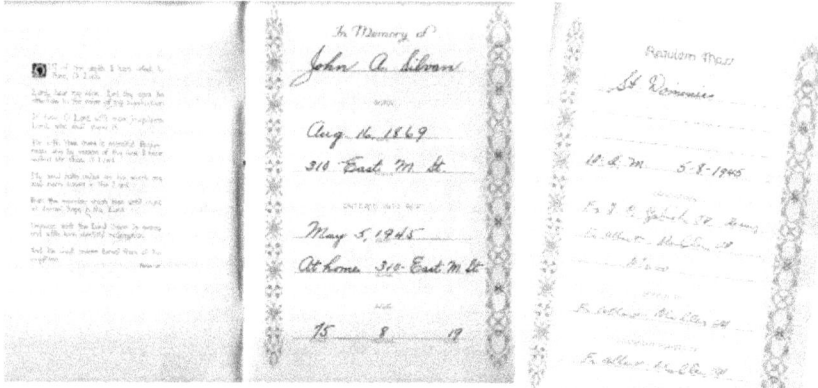

Juan Francisco "John" *SILVAN* Hernandez

| Memorial | Photos | Flowers | | Share | Edit |

Learn about sponsoring this memorial...

[Transfer Management] [Edit] [Delete]

Birth: Aug. 16, 1875
Zamora
Castilla y Leon, Spain
Death: May 15, 1945
Benicia
Solano County
California, USA [Edit Dates]

Juan Francisco SILVAN Hernandez was the son of Celestino SILVAN Dovales and Agustina Hernandez Martin, born in Fuentesauco, Province of Zamora, Spain. He was the 6th child of nine children.

He married Eustoquia Rita TRASCASAS Marzo on May 11, 1900 at Santa Maria del Castillo Church in the same village. Their first child, Manuela was born June 25, 1901, followed by 2 sons, Agustin Marzo Silvan in 1908 and Jose Marzo Silvan in 1910.

Juan and his family emigrated from Spain in 1911 on the SS ORTERIC from Gibraltar with his brother (Victorino and family) and his sister (Crescencia Silvan Hernandez Gonzales and family) to Hawaii. The families later sailed to San Francisco in 1918 and 1921.

Juan was an orchardist most of his life, loved playing his drum (el bombo) and was known as a loving father and husband. He died at his daughter's (Juanita)home in Benicia where she cared for her parents, John and Rita, for five years.

He died of heart disease at age 75 years, 8 months and 19 days. A rosary was said at the home on May 7, 1945 and he was buried May 8, 1945 by Chisholm and Passalacqua. The death certificate states the name of his father incorrectly as "Augustin". It should read "Celestino".
[Edit Bio]
Family links: [Edit]
Spouse:
Eustoquia Rita Trascasas Marzo Silvan (1880-1953)

Added by: Patricia Steele

This Agreement, Made and entered into this 20th. day of October , A. D. 19 45.

Between Juan Silvan Hernandez and Estonia Trescass Silvan Hernandez,

the parti es of the first part, and Rafael A Lopez and Ruth Lopez, his wife, in joint tenancy,

the parties of the second part,

Witnesseth, That the said parti es of the first part, in consideration of the covenants and agreements on the part of the said part i es of the second part hereinafter contained, agree to sell and convey unto the said parties of the second part, and said second part i es agree to buy all th the certain lot or parcel of land, situate in the Town of Winters County of Yolo State of California and bounded and particularly described as follows, to-wit:

That certain real property situated in the Town of Winters, County of Yolo, State of California, described as follows, to-wit:

Lots 1, 2, 26, 27, and 28, Block 1 of Emry's Addition to the Town of Winters, according to the map or plat of said addition on file and of record in the office of the County Recorder of said County of Yolo.

for the sum of Fifteen hundred and no /100 Dollars,

Five hundred dollars down, receipt of which is hereby acknowledged, and twenty dollars per month with no interest, until the balance of the One thousand dollars is paid.

In Witness Whereof, the said parties to there presence have hereunto set their hands and seals, the day and year first above written.

+ John Silvan
+ Estonia trescas
Rafael A Lopez
Ruth A Lopez

William J Jerome

Harry A Leavitt Jr.

Agreement
For Sale of Real Estate

Juan Silven Hernandez and Estonia Trescass Silvan Hernandez.
—to—
Rafael A. and Ruth Lopez, in joint tenancy.

DATED October 20th, 1945

Recorded at the Request of

WIFE OF JUAN FRANCISCO SILVÁN HERNANDEZ:
EUSTOQUIA RITA TRASCASAS MARZO,
28 September, 1880 - June 13, 1953

She was fiesty as a young woman and ornery as an adult. Barely five feet tall, Eustoquia Rita Trascasas Marzo had tenacious courage and made snappy judgements. Born in the hill town of Toro high above the road between Fuentesaúco and Madrid, her teenage years were spent dodging a stepfather and mourning her father's and sister's deaths.

Rita's father was nearly sixty years old and had been widowed twice already when he married her mother, Manuela Marzo, who was young and wanted a family. Rita had half siblings in Toro, a village with various Trascasas bloodlines. Her dark brown hair and chocolate, brown eyes danced with delight when her sister, Jacinta Modesta arrived when she was three and a half years old. The girls were inseparable.

Growing up, Rita thought her life would always be rosy, filled with a loving family that included many uncles, aunts and various cousins on the Trascasas and Marzo sides. The village of Toro encapsulated her life as she skipped through the ancient stone arches within the plaza mayor, *Iglesia Parroquial de Santo Tomas Cantuariense* and through their extended family homes near her.

She was almost eleven when her world crashed.
Her young sister died. Then, her father.
Not long afterward, her life again changed drastically when her mother remarried a man to support them; she felt she'd lost her

mother too. The next years were tough; her uncles watched over them while her mother trembled to keep Rita safe.

Rita's young life was charged with electricity , never docile; she wanted a life of adventure and music. And then she met Juan Silván Hernández, his music, and her life changed once again.

Rita was a seamstress, sewing matador's costumes that were called Suits of Lights. Long skirts, fringed shawls, castenets, fans, roses in her hair…that was the culture of a young Spanish woman in 1900.

With Juan, she also became a wife, mother and a grandmother. She'd followed her husband across the world to Hawaii and then to California where they bought property known as the Silván Ranch in the Olive District off Pleasant Valley Road in Winters, California.

Rita was remembered for her thrifty decisions, saucy comebacks, spirited conversations --- in Spanish --- her Matanza chores, cooking, crocheting, baking and wine making that became a part of their lives. And she loved her wine.

She always wore dark clothing, as if clinging to the old world; black dresses, black cardigan sweaters, black hightop button shoes although bunions plagued her and distorted her feet and the shoes. Black cotton stockings covered her legs, which were anchored with an elastic band at the top called "legas". Or she pulled her stockings upward, grabbed the top and twisted a small knot at the side before tucking it tightly to secure them.

She wore aprons with huge pockets that enabled her to store seeds for the chickens, hold candy for the children or store buttons, pennies or crochet thread. And the scarf tied about her head was a mainstay, well remembered by her children and grandchildren.

Her typical day included waking at dawn, cooking breakfast for her husband and workers at the ranch, feeding chickens, washing clothing on a washboard and hanging the clothes on the clothesline. Then, she washed dishes, cleaned the kitchen and began lunch preparations.

On a day when chores allowed her some free time, she wrapped her headscarf around her head, pulled on a sweater and walked down the gravel road toward town. She might spend a couple dollars in the 5 & 10-cent store where she loved looking, looking, looking. But her typical purchases were yarn, thread, buttons and colored embroidery thread. She and her thrifty soul always made it home in time to put dinner on the table. She was sly; she'd put a big pot of garbanzo beans on the stove early morning and by dinnertime – viola! Dinner was served.

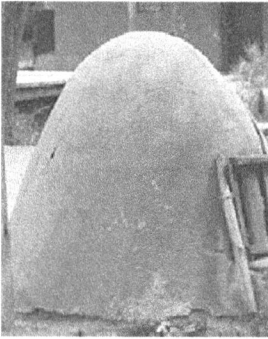

She baked bread once a week in the outside brick oven John built near the kitchen door on the ranch. (This photo is a typical horno, not the original used in the Silván family).

Rita lined her bread box with a sheet before placing bread loaves inside to keep out the mice. The aroma of baking bread lured many drop-in visits.

Other days she would sit beneath the grape arbor or persimmon tree with crochet needles and thread and create doilies, table cloths and linens to adorn the tables to keep or give away. She'd knit long socks without looking at them --- if visitors arrived, she would click…click away and talk as if her fingers were an automated tool in her lap. She didn't waste time. She always had a spoon, a broom or needlework in her hands and she constantly warned her children and grandchildren to do the same. Idle hands are….

Rita Silván was an excellent seamstress. She often mended, attached buttons and virtually remade clothing to make it last; she also sewed a three-piece suit for her husband, John, by hand with tiny tight stitches without a pattern.

She never learned English. Unless the children learned to speak Spanish, they were lost in the conversational dust. She did learn enough English to get her point across though; "no" and "coffee". She was too ornery to learn English; she had children to speak for her, right?

After birthing seven children that we know of, her body started breaking down. Several stomach surgeries left her belly crumpled, scarred and weak. I'm told she had a heavy banding around her belly because the wall of her stomach was thin, leaving a hole the size of a small coffee can. When she stood up, she often needed to lie down for someone to wrap a binder around her belly to keep her intestines inside[25].

Her eyeglasses were thick and she was nearly deaf by the late 1940s. My personal childhood memories of my great grandmother, Eustoquia Rita Trascasas Marzo Silván, were those thick glasses, her black clothing, her grumpiness; I had to yell to be heard.

[26] After John Silván's death in 1945, Rita remained in Benicia with her daughter, Juanita. When Juanita divorced Manuel Castelar and moved to Colorado, Rita moved to San Jose with Mary Louise and Celestino Silvan for several months. When they also moved to Colorado to be closer to Mary Louise's family, Rita moved again.

Rita bounced between her daughter, Mary (and her husband Frank Cuellar in Winters), Gus and his wife, Ruby, and later to her daughter, Manuela's, at 745 First Street in Woodland, California. She also lived awhile with her granddaughter, Rose, in Saratoga, California. She moved from one child's house to the next during her waning years, where she became a bit senile and nearly blind.

By 1953, returning to Manuela's, Rita was under constant doctor's care by Roy Newmann, M.D., from February 25, 1953 until she died at the Yolo General Hospital on June 13, 1953 of a carcinoma of the left lung with abscess, which her death certificate

---

[25] This information came from Mary Louise Silván, her daughter in law.

[26] Source: Millie Ruiz Cortopassi

stated she'd suffered with about 14 months. She is buried beside her husband, John Silván Hernandez, at St. Dominic's Catholic Cemetery in Benicia, Solano County, California.

Rita died the summer before my 7th birthday. I can remember her in a tall-backed chair in the bay-windowed room of abuelita Manuela's house on First Street in Woodland, California. The sun shot beams of light across her black-clad lap and little dust motes danced in the light. Her hands were knotted tightly in her lap and one of her black stockings had slipped down and I was afraid to point it out to her. Yes, she was ornery and frightened me at times but the memory of that long-ago day is better than the memory later... In the church or the funeral parlor (I cannot remember which), when my father picked me up and told me to kiss abuela goodbye. I held tightly to his neck and I still feel my head shaking wildly, *please no*. To this day I do not know if I kissed her cold face or not. I just remember being traumatized and the fear of doing so.

Dn. Antonio Gonzalez Garcia, Cura Parroco de Sto Tomás Cantuariense de la Ciudad de Toro, en el Obispado de Zamora,

Certifico: que en el libro noveno de bautizados de esta demarcación al folio ciento cuarenta, se halla la siguiente partida —

Eustoquia Rita
hija de Manuel
Trascasas y Manuela
Marzo Garcia

"En treinta de Diciembre de mil ochocientos ochenta, yo Dn. Vicente Prantes Cordero del Orden Premostratense, Cura Ecónomo de la Iglesia parroquial de Sto Tomás Cantuariense de esta ciudad de Toro, bauticé solemnemente a una niña que nació el dia veintiocho de dichos mes y año á las dos y media de la tarde, á la que puse por nombre Eustoquia Rita, es hija legítima de Manuel Trascasas y de Manuela Marzo Garcia, bautizada en la parroquia de Sn Sebastian y mis feligreses; abuelos paternos Santiago y Maria Alonso, y los maternos Gregorio y Teresa Garcia, todos naturales de esta ciudad. Fué su padrino Jacinto Marzo tio carnal de la bautizada, á quien advertí el parentesco espiritual y demas obligaciones. Y por ser verdad lo mismo Pba ut supra" — Vicente Prantes Cordero. — Hay una rúbrica —

Concuerda con el original á que me remito; y para que conste, á petición de la interesada y al objeto de que acreditar pueda ante el parroco de su domicilio su aptitud para contraer matrimonio canonico, la extiendo en este pliego de papel de oficio firmandola y sellandola con el de esta parroquia, en Toro á diez y seis de Febrero de mil novecientos.

Antonio Gonzalez
Garcia

Baptismal document, 30 September 1880
Eustoquia Rita, hija de Manuel Trascasas, Manuela Marzo Garcia

Family Tree of EUSTOQUIA RITA TRASCASAS MARZO

<u>Santiago Degracious Trascasas Conejo married Maria Alonso de la Vega.</u>
They had ten children between 1821 and 1845:
Manuel Trascasas Alonso, Pablo A. Trascasas Alonso, Candida E. Trascasas Alonso, Jeronima R. Trascasas Alonso, Micaela Trascasas Alonso, Juliana J. Trascasas Alonso, Pascuala Trascasas Alonso and Tomas T. Trascasas Alonso.

<u>Gregorio Marzo married Teresa Garcia</u>
Children (that I could find) born between (circa) 1875 to 1890:
José Marzo Garcia,
Manuela Marzo Garcia
Jacinto Marzo Garcia.

*Eustoquia Rita Trascasas Marzo's parents:
Manuela Marzo García (1855), Manuel Trascasas Alonso, (1840-1850)
*Paternal grandparents: Santiago Trascasas Conejo, María Alonso de la Vega
*Maternal grandparents: Gregorio Marzo, Sr. + Teresa García
*Godfather: (Uncle) Jacinto Marzo
*Sister: Jacinta Modesta Trascasas Marzo, died- age 8, buried Toro, Spain

Collage identification:
Left: Manuela Marzo García, mother of Eustoquia Rita Trascasas Marzo.
Middle: Manuela Marzo's brother: Jacinto Marzo Garcia;
Family photo with son, Gregorio.
Children: Right: Andres and María / Bottom right: María and Gregorio.
Far right, young boy in uniform: Andres.
(Jacinto was Manuela Marzo Garcia's godfather)
(Toro, Zamora, Spain)

Birth document- Manuela Marzo García
(Mother of Eustoquia Rita Trascasas Marzo)

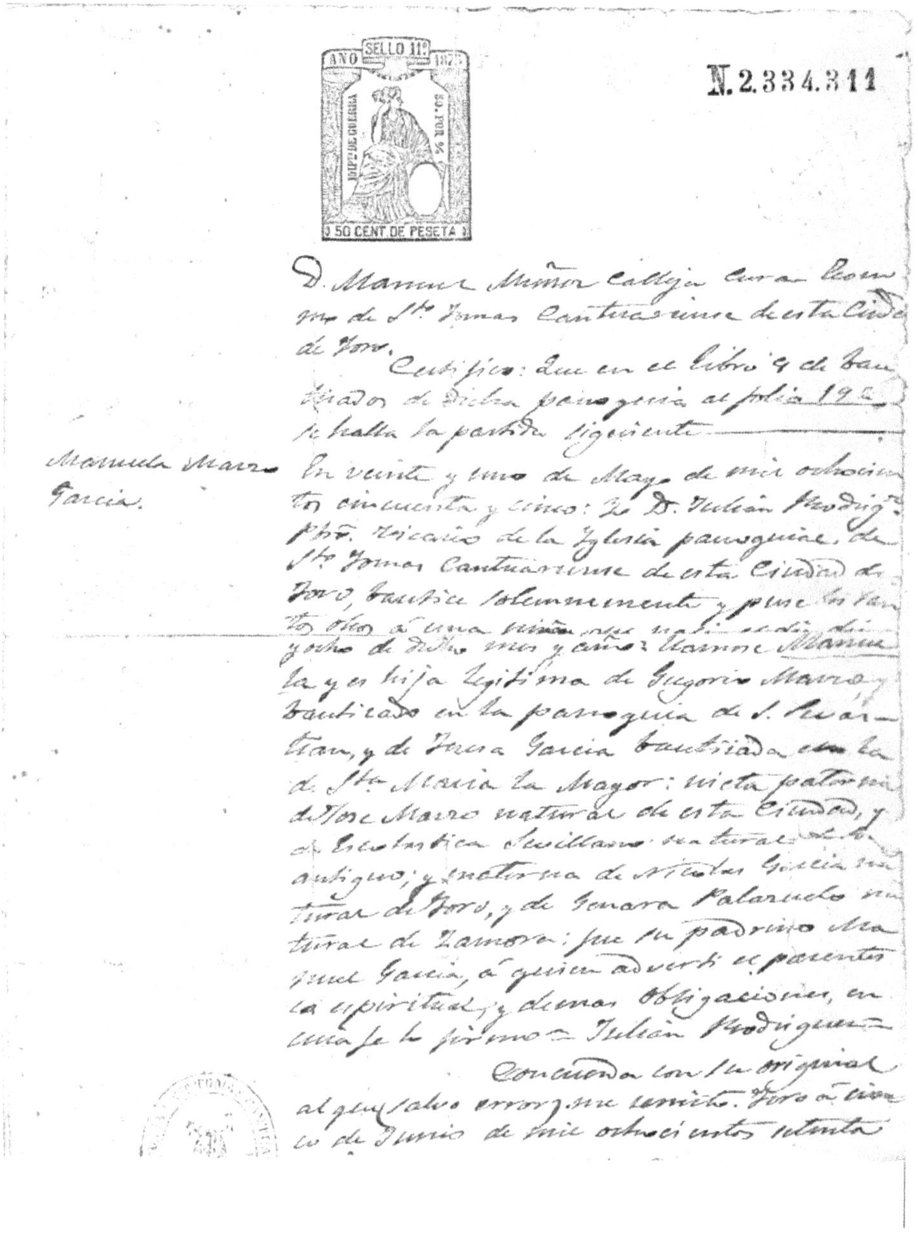
AÑO 1875 SELLO 11º
DIPN DE GUERRA 50 POR %
50 CENT. DE PESETA

N. 2.334.311

D. Manuel Muñoz Callejo Cura Ecónomo de Sto Tomas Cantuariense de esta Ciudad de Toro.

Certifico: Que en el libro 9 de bautizados de dicha parroquia al folio 19 se halla la partida siguiente

Manuela Marzo García.

En veinte y uno de Mayo de mil ochocientos cincuenta y cinco: Yo D. Julian Rodriguez Pbro. Vicario de la Iglesia parroquial de Sto Tomas Cantuariense de esta Ciudad de Toro, bauticé solemnemente y puse los santos oleos á una niña que nació en dia diez y ocho de dicho mes y año: llamose Manuela y es hija legítima de Gregorio Marzo y bautizado en la parroquia de S. Sebastian, y de Teresa Garcia bautizada en la de Sta Maria la Mayor: nieta paterna de Jose Marzo natural de esta Ciudad, y de Escolastica Sevillano natural de lo antiguo; y materna de Nicolas Garcia natural de Toro, y de Genara Palazuelo natural de Zamora: fue su padrino Manuel Garcia, á quien adverti el parentesco espiritual, y demas obligaciones, en cuya fe lo firmo = Julian Rodriguez

Concuerda con su original al que salvo error me remito. Toro á cinco de Junio de mil ochocientos setenta

Marriage Document of Manuel Trascasas Alonso and Manuela Marzo Garcia

NOTE:
Rita Silván's death certificate shows date of birth, September 19, 1875.
This should read September 28, 1880 as confirmed in her birth certificate.
Informant was her daughter, Mary Silván Cuellar where she lived in Vacaville,
California at the time of her death.

CERTIFICATE OF DEATH

STATE FILE NO. 53-050865
STATE OF CALIFORNIA—DEPARTMENT OF PUBLIC HEALTH

DECEDENT PERSONAL DATA

1a. NAME OF DECEASED—FIRST NAME: RITA MIDDLE NAME: none LAST NAME: SILVAN
2a. DATE OF DEATH: June 13, 1953 2b. HOUR: 12:30A

3. SEX: female 4. COLOR OR RACE: white widowed
6. DATE OF BIRTH: Sept 19, 1875 7. AGE: 77 YEARS

8a. USUAL OCCUPATION: at home 8b. KIND OF BUSINESS OR INDUSTRY: — 9. BIRTHPLACE: Spain
10. CITIZEN OF WHAT COUNTRY: Spain

11. NAME AND BIRTHPLACE OF FATHER: unk.
12. MAIDEN NAME AND BIRTHPLACE OF MOTHER: Mildred Trascasas, Spain
13. NAME OF PRESENT SPOUSE: John Silvan, deceased

14. WAS DECEASED EVER IN U.S. ARMED FORCES? no
15. SOCIAL SECURITY NUMBER: none
16. INFORMANT: Mrs. Frank Cuellar

PLACE OF DEATH

17a. COUNTY: Yolo 17b. CITY OR TOWN: Near Woodland 17c. LENGTH OF STAY IN THIS CITY OR TOWN: 3½ mo
17d. FULL NAME OF HOSPITAL OR INSTITUTION: Yolo General Hospital 17e. ADDRESS: West Woodland

LAST USUAL RESIDENCE

18a. STATE: California 18b. COUNTY: Yolo 18c. CITY OR TOWN: Woodland 18d. STREET OR RURAL ADDRESS: 745 First

PHYSICIAN'S OR CORONER'S CERTIFICATION

19a. CORONER ... June 13, 1953
19b. PHYSICIAN ... Roy A. Neumann M.D.
19c. DEGREE OR TITLE: M.D. 19d. ADDRESS: Yolo General Hosp. Woodland
19e. DATE SIGNED: 6/13/53

FUNERAL DIRECTOR AND REGISTRAR

20a. BURIAL 20b. DATE: 6-15-53 20c. CEMETERY OR CREMATORY: St. Dominics,
21. SIGNATURE OF EMBALMER: 1949
22. FUNERAL DIRECTOR: J.C. McHARY 23. DATE RECEIVED: JUN 15
24. SIGNATURE OF LOCAL REGISTRAR

MEDICAL AND HEALTH DATA

CAUSE OF DEATH

25. DISEASE OR CONDITION DIRECTLY LEADING TO DEATH: Carcinoma of left lung (abscess — pathological report to follow) 14 months

26. OTHER SIGNIFICANT CONDITIONS CONTRIBUTING TO DEATH: None

OPERATIONS

27a. DATE OF OPERATION 27b. MAJOR FINDINGS OF OPERATION 28. AUTOPSY: X

DEATH DUE TO EXTERNAL VIOLENCE

29a. ACCIDENT 29b. PLACE OF INJURY 29c. LOCATION
29d. TIME OF INJURY 29e. INJURY OCCURRED 29f. HOW DID INJURY OCCUR

John and Rita Silván are buried in a spousal grave at
St. Dominic's Catholic Cemetery, Benicia, California.
John F (Francisco) and Rita M (Marzo) SILVÁN

Woodland (Calif.) Daily Democrat, Monday, June 15, 1953   3

Benicia Services Set For Mrs. Rita Silvan

Graveside services will be held in St. Dominic's cemetery Benicia this afternoon for Mrs. Ruth Silvan, who died Saturday in Yolo General hospital.

Mrs. Silvan is survived by six children, Joe M. Silvan, Del Paso Heights; August Silvan, San Jose; Celestino Silvan and Mrs. Juanita Hyhts, both of Colorado; Mrs. Mary Cuellar, Vacaville, and Mrs. Mildred Ruiz, with whom Mrs. Silvan made her home in Woodland.

Services will be held at 2:30 p.m. at the cemetery, with the Mc-Nary funeral home of Woodland in charge of arrangements, Interment will take place beside the grave of her husband, John Silvan, who died May 5, 1945.

www.findagrave.com ~ Memorial#84168739

Eustoquia Rita Trascasas Marzo Silvan [Edit Name]

| Memorial | Photos | Flowers | | Share | Edit |

Learn about upgrading this memorial...

[Transfer Management] [Edit] [Delete

Birth: Sep. 28, 1880
          Zamora
          Castilla y Leon, Spain
Death: May 13, 1953
          Benicia
          Solano County
          California, USA [Edit Dates]

Eustoquia Rita Marzo Trascasas was born in
Toro, Spain to Manuela MARZO Garcia and
Manuel TRASCASAS Alonso .

She married Juan Francisco SILVAN Hernandez
on May 11, 1900 at Santa Maria del Castillo
Church in Fuentesauco, Zamora, Spain, 17
miles from Toro. Their first child, Manuela was
born June 25, 1901, followed by 2 sons,
Agustin Marzo Silvan in 1908 and Jose Marzo
Silvan in 1910.

Juan and his family emigrated from Spain in
1911 on the SS ORTERIC from Gibraltar with
his brother (Victorino and family) and his sister
(Crescencia Silvan Hernandez Gonzales and
family) to Hawaii. The families later sailed to
San Francisco in 1918 and 1921.

Rita was a homemaker most of her life, a
baker, a cook and remembered as very thrifty.
They lived on their ranch in the Olive district
near Winters, California until her husband had
a stroke. When she could no longer care for
him, they moved in with his sister, Christina
Gonzales in Putah Creek before moving to
Benicia, where Rita and Juan's daughter,
Juanita, cared for John until he died of heart
disease at age 75 years.

Rita, in frail health, lived with her various
children before dying at Yolo General Hospital
in Woodland, California of carcinoma of the
left lung with abscess. She'd been ill 14
months before her death. She was buried with
her husband, John/Juan Silvan in Benicia,
California on June 15, 1953 at St. Dominic's.
Pallbearers were her grandsons, Tony Ruiz,
Frank Ruiz, John Ruiz, Joe Ruiz, Frank Cuellar
and Michael Ruiz.

Added by: Patricia Steele

Added by: Patricia Steele

This photo[27] of Crescéncia Silván Hernandez Gonzales and Eustoquia Rita Trascasas Marzo, sisters-in-law both dressed in black generated a lot of family curiosity.

Were they both pregnant?

Were they both in mourning?

Were they in California or still in Hawaii?

---

[27] Thanks to Dutch Huckaby for finding this photo and thanks to his brother, Felix, for touching it up. The original was cracked, broken and tarnished. Felix brought it back to life and old and broken or new and shiny, the ladies faces still tell a story that only they are aware of.

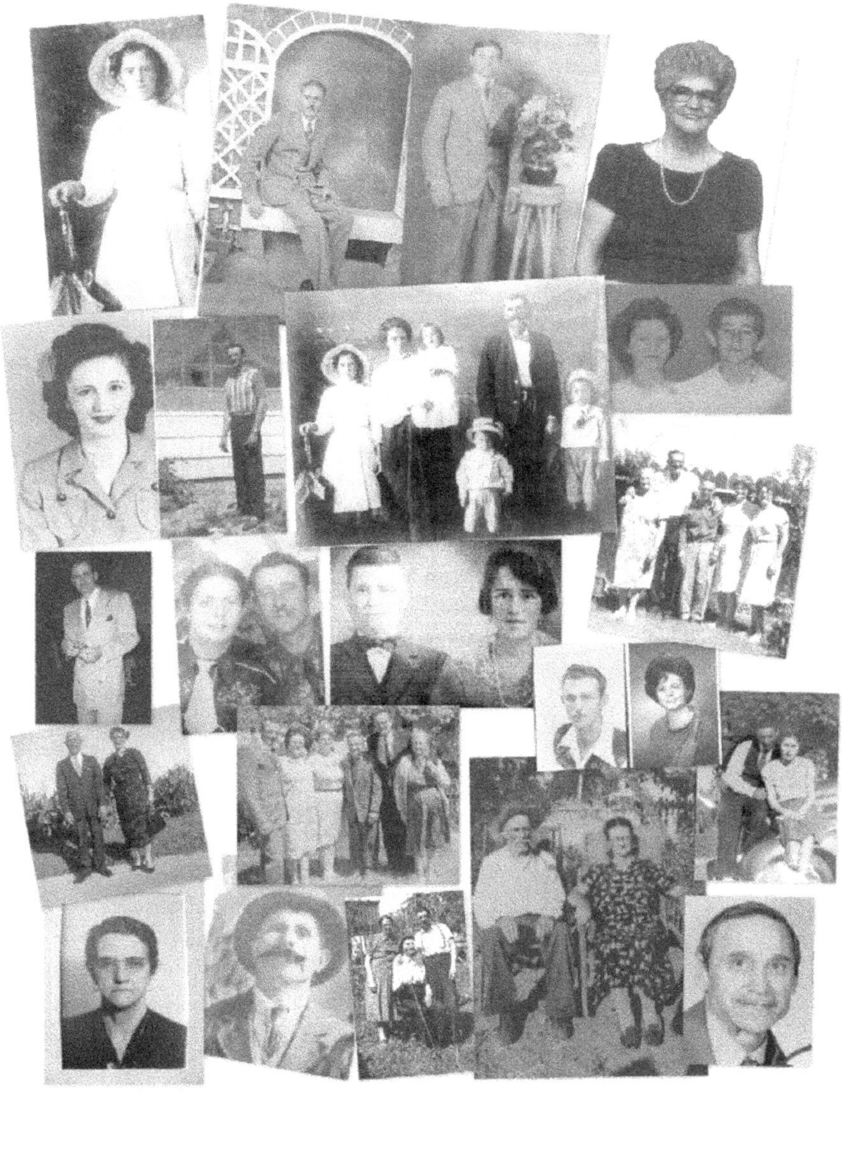

(30) Grandchildren

Manuela married Bernardo "Ben" Ruiz when she was eighteen and delivered her first child, a son named Frank (after Ben's father) ten months later on August 18, 1920. Another son followed, named Juan (after Manuela's father) sixteen months after Frank was born. Then Rose was born in 1923, (named after Ben's mother) and then little Benny nine months later, who died[28] just after his third birthday; the first of three grandchildren Juan and Rita would lose and grieve over with Manuela. Michael was just seven months old when Benny was buried and then Mary (named after Ben's stepmother) was born in November 1928. Two years later, Manuela was born and they called her Millie, then the next October in 1931 Jose (named for Manuela's brother) was born. Manuela had a seventeen-month hiatus before Dolores was born in March of 1933. Rita Christina was born in December of 1934; Antoinette in April of 1936, Josephine Agustína (named after Manuela's grandmother) was born in June of 1937. The year Antonio was born in 1938, little Dolores (Lola) came down with Spinal Meningitis and died at the San Francisco Children's Hospital. Many of the siblings grieved a very long time and her grandparents were scarred with her loss. Two more children were born after Lola died; Encarnacion (Carnie) in October of 1941 and then a stillborn daughter in 1943 they named Bernarda.

Agustín married twice. There is some question about whether his first wife's child, John Silván, listed on the 1930 Census

---

[28] Mary Ruiz Sanderson – She contracted Diphtheria but had been inoculated. Benny had not been inoculated because Ben, his father, was working in the fields and needed to finish the job. They postponed his shots. So, when he contracted the dreaded disease, he died.

was indeed his child. I found no birth record showing parents but the census listed the family as Gus Silván, María Silván and John Silván (child). It is believed this child was later known as John Fernandez, taking his mother's maiden name growing up in Winters, California.

Jose married Encarnacion "Carnie" Alva and had one son, Joe, Jr. in December of 1945.

Maria (Mary) married Frank Cuellar; Frank, Jr. was born 1933, Fred born 1934 (died in 1999), Rose Marie born 1936 and Helen born 1937.

Juanita (Jenny/Nita) married several times and had three children, Theresa Marie Watkins in 1934 from her first husband; Roberta Rose Hyatt in 1948 and John Carl Hyatt in 1949 by her third husband, Robert Hyatt. Robert Hyatt adopted Theresa. She married twice more after her divorce from Bob Hyatt.

Celestino married and divorced Frances (no children). He later married Mary Louise Hutcheson. They had six children, Celestino Robert born in 1950, Christina Louise born in 1954, LuCinda Ann born in 1958, Mary Kathleen (Kathy) born in 1962 and Troy Purl in 1963, who died in 1995 and is buried at Brownsville Cemetery, Brownsville, Yuba County, California. Mary is buried near her son, Troy Purl in Brownsville Cemetery.

CRESCENCIA SILVÁN HERNÁNDEZ
And
FELIX GONZALES HERNÁNDEZ

Photo courtesy of:
Anna Alex Gonzales Manley, daughter of Alejandro "Red" Gonzales

Family Group Sheet for Crescencia SILVAN Hernandez

Husband:	Felix Hernandez GONZALES	
Birth:	14 Aug 1881 in Fuentesauco, Zamora, Spain	
Death:	27 Dec 1963 in Winters, Yolo, California, USA	
Burial:	Winters, Yolo County, California, USA	
Marriage:	06 May 1906 in Fuentesauco, Province of Zamora, Spain	
Father:	Ascencion GONZALES	
Mother:	Gregora Hernandez	

Wife:	Crescencia SILVAN Hernandez	
Birth:	15 Jun 1884 in Fuentesauco, Zamora, Castilla-Leon, Spain	
Death:	24 Oct 1946 in Winters, Yolo Co., California, USA	
Burial:	Winters, Yolo County, California, USA	
Father:	Celestino Pedro SILVAN Dovales	
Mother:	Agustina Hernandez Martin	

Children:

1 M	Name:	Alejandro "Red" Silvan Gonzales	
	Birth:	09 Jul 1908 in Fuentesauco, Province of Zamora, Castilla-Leon, Spain	
	Death:	07 Sep 1975 in Woodland, Yolo Co, California USA	
	Marriage:	Abt 1926 in California	
	Spouse:	Adeline "Lena" Fernandez	

2 M	Name:	John (Juanitco) Silvan Gonzales	
	Birth:	27 Jan 1910 in Fuentesauco, Province of Zamora, Spain	
	Death:	11 Apr 1961 in San Francisco, California, USA	
	Marriage:	Abt 1937 in Reno, Washoe, Nevada, USA	
	Spouse:	Hazel Spurlock Robinson	

3 F	Name:	Maria Gregora Gonzales	
	Birth:	11 Apr 1912 in Ewa Plantation, Oahu, Hawaii, USA	
	Death:	08 Jun 2004 in Citrus Heights, Sacramento, California, USA	
	Marriage:	21 May 1934 in Reno, Washoe, Nevada, USA	
	Spouse:	Orville Benjamin Miller	

4 F	Name:	Christina 'Sally' Barceliza Gonzales	
	Birth:	31 Mar 1915 in Ewa Plantation, Oahu, Hawaii	
	Death:	27 Feb 2003 in Sacramento, Sacramento, California, United States	
	Marriage:	04 Feb 1939 in Reno, Washoe, Nevada, USA	
	Spouse:	Allen Elmer Huckaby	

5 F	Name:	Augustina (Tina) F. Gonzales	
	Birth:	27 Sep 1916 in Kilauea, Kauai Hawaii USA	
	Death:	10 Feb 2005 in Winters, Yolo, California	
	Burial:	Winters, Yolo County, California, USA	
	Marriage:	24 Oct 1937 in California, USA	
	Spouse:	Charles Robert Coombs	

6 F	Name:	Victorina Gonzales	
	Birth:	03 Oct 1917 in Kilauea, Kauai Hawaii, USA	
	Marriage:	1942 in Reno, Washoe, Nevada, USA	
	Spouse:	Alvin Carl Weber	

7 M	Name:	Alfredo Geronimo "Jerry" or "Dutch" Gonzales	
	Birth:	09 Aug 1919 in Putah, Yolo, California, USA	
	Death:	01 Nov 1999 in Sacramento, Sacramento, California, United States of America	
	Burial:	Santa Nella Village, Merced County, California, USA	
	Marriage:	Abt. 1954 in California, USA	
	Spouse:	Cecelia LaLuc	
8 F	Name:	Theresa (Olivia) Gonzales	
	Birth:	31 Jan 1921 in Yolo, California	
	Marriage:	25 Jun 1946 in Reno, Washoe, Nevada, USA	
	Spouse:	Buel Arthur Sackett	
9 M	Name:	Eusebio Felix "Sab" Gonzales	
	Birth:	18 May 1923 in Oakland, Alameda, California, USA	
	Death:	11 Jun 2004 in Elk Grove, Sacramento, California, USA	
	Marriage:	Jul 1948 in Winters, Yolo, California USA	
	Spouse:	Phyllis H Yankee	

CRESCÉNCIA SILVÁN HERNÁNDEZ GONZALES
June 15, 1884 - October 24, 1946

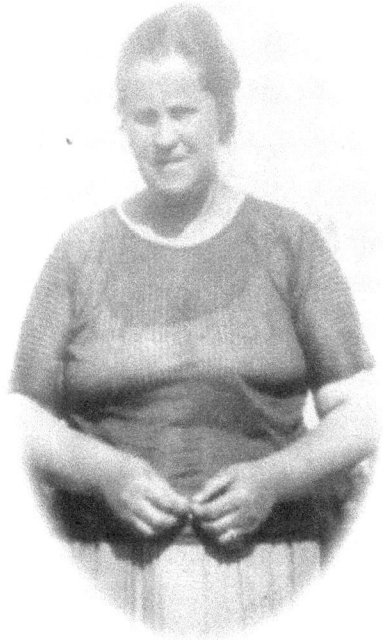

By 1911, she[29] was the only living daughter of eleven children born to Celestino Silván Dovales and Agustina Hernández Martin. Born in Fuentesaúco, she spent her childhood and early adult life in this small village northwest of Madrid.

Santa Maria del Castillo Church[30] in Fuentesaúco was the family church for the Silváns where baptisms and marriages took place.

And this was the church where she married her husband, Felix Gonzales Hernandez on May 6, 1906. Her grandchildren, Linda, Patte and Phil have a piece of this ancestral church --- stones their father, Sab, brought back to California from Fuentesaúco. They are emotional reminders of a time long past and a link to the Silván family 100 years earlier.

---

[29] Various documents show her name spelled as Crescencia and Crestencia. Her birth document shows Crescéncia.

[30] When Crescéncia's youngest son, Sab and his wife, Phyllis visited Fuentesaúco, it was being renovated. He was very moved when he was allowed to bring pieces of the old part of the church back to California with him. His daughters each carried a piece of the Fuentesaúco family church with them when they walked down the aisle with their father to marry their husbands and have since placed the stones in special glass cases for posterity.

Proven Birth Document:

Crescencia Silván Hernández, natural de Fuentesaúco, 15 junio 1884, tomo 10, pág. 114, hija de Celestino y Agustina. Casada en Fuentesaúco con Félix González Hernández, el 5 de mayo de 1906 (tomo 5, fol. 257).

During the time Crescéncia lived in Fuentesaúco, it was a small, country village, mostly an agricultural community and remains so today. Her grandparents were born in villages smaller than Fuentesaúco nearby, Villamor de los Escuderos and Villaescusa.

Crescéncia was a cherished little sister with blue eyes and red hair, standing just 5' 1 ¾" tall. She learned from an early age the art of being a homemaker and could sew fine sampler stitches and small fancy tucks in dresses and blouses. She was referred to as a *Modista*[31]and was hired by an affluent family as a live-in.

Just before Crescéncia's 22nd birthday, she married Feliz (Felix) Gonzales Hernandez at the Santa Maria Church in Fuentesaúco on May 6, 1906. He was 25.

Based on family stories and calculations, it is believed her first child died either stillborn or as an infant before her first son, Alejandro was born in 1908.

Less than five years after their marriage, she and Felix joined her brother's families in exhaustive discussions about leaving Spain for a better life. Hawaiian agents displayed posters to advertise the wonders of Hawaii and the money that could be earned, far and above their current situation, while working in the sugar plantations of the islands.

Although leaving her mother, Agustina, was beyond her comprehension, she agreed with her husband and three brothers

---

[31] *Modista* is a dressmaker or fashion designer.

that maybe it was their only option. Food was scarce and the recent flooding made their prospects for a good harvest even worse. She enjoyed her life in Fuentesaúco with the bull fights, the peanuts, musical family events and her heart tripped at the sacrifices leaving her home would entail.

The boys were little, only one and two years old. Could they handle the type of trip the men described? Could she? She felt a measure of excitement about the adventure of a train ride and a ship, the ocean beyond and the poster's promises but leaving her mother and siblings behind? She begged Gerónimo to come along but his decision was made to stay with the others. She pouted. As the youngest sister, it usually worked, but not that time.

As Felix purchased the tickets and met with the alcalde (judicial magistrate of the village) in Fuentesaúco to request the documents required to be accepted on the ship at Gibraltar to take them to Hawaii, she began the arduous task of packing. She gave away many of her things to family friends, her mother, her brothers and tried to focus on the awesome challenges ahead. The trunk looked big at the beginning of the process. It soon looked the size of a thimble as she sat amid the scattering of her possessions and bits of clothing. But he said one trunk. So, she must have bitten her lip and persevered because the one trunk was all they took with them.

They had to get their papers in order and legitimize their preparation to leave Fuentesaúco, which was their pueblo or hometown as we know it. They had to prove they were healthy, free of encumbrances such as debt and that their children were their own natural children.

The Cedula Personal or head tax was a form of taxation which replaced the tributary system in 1884. This served as a paper which was used as proof that one was a colony of Spain and a legitimate member of a pueblo, an ID card.

Everything was in order. They gathered their belongings, hauled the trunk aboard the wagons that her brothers (Gerónimo and Agustin) drove to the train station in Salamanca and the trip began.[32]

The trek south, the train ride, camping, cooking, sleeping, parading the children and keeping a stiff upper lip through it all must have been overwhelming but they made it to *La Linea* in the timeline proscribed by the poster and saw the Rock of Gibraltar. Exhausted, dirty and not just a little hungry, they arrived en masse to flow through a river of people all with the same dreams and hopes she carried within. The gigantic rock of an island across from *La Linea* called Gibraltar stood above the rocking ship, waiting for its immigrant passengers to fill the void.

On February 24, 1911, the SS ORTERIC sailed from Gibraltar down around Cape Horn stopping only once, at *Puente Arenas* to fuel up and let off some passengers. History states many jumped into the water to get off the ship to put their feet on land and never looked back.

The ocean got rougher just past *Puente Arenas* and children began getting sick. Crescéncia watched and cried as her little nephew, Jacinto contracted the measles, died and was slipped overboard into his watery grave. Then her friend's daughter sickened and died named Maria Corrales; and then her cousin's child, Simon Martin. The children's deaths were so frightening; she kept her two little boys, Alejandro and Juanitco, close, rarely allowing them from her sight.

It was with some great relief when they arrived in the port of Honolulu in the Territory of Hawaii on April 14, 1911 so she could leave the filthy confines of the ship and inhale the lovely scented winds of the tropical island.

During their life in Hawaii, Felix Gonzales tended to the horses and mules for the plantation workers at Ewa Plantation on

---

[32] The trip from Fuentesauco overland by train to Seville and boat to Sanlúcar before boarding the SS ORTERIC at Gibraltar is a comprehensive non-fiction narrative in the book titled, THE GIRL IMMIGRANT.

Oahu and the Kilauea Plantation on Kauai. He also worked on a dairy and eventually had a dairy of his own. They lived in the Hawaiian Islands nearly seven years and during that time, their family grew from two to six. Born in Hawaii were Maria Gregoria, stillborn twins[33], Christina Barceliza, Agustína and Victorina.

After seven years, Felix Gonzales applied for permission to leave Hawaii and was released from the Selective Draft on December 11, 1917 in the Territory of Hawaii by paying a $4 tax requested by the United States to regulate the immigration of aliens, a law that became effective July 1, 1907.

On January 12, 1918, their family boarded a military boat, SS HERMAN GOVERNOR, along with her brother, Juan Francisco and his wife Eustoquia Rita Trascasas Silván and their children, Manuela, Agustin, Jose and Maria.

Crescéncia and Felix, with their growing family, lived in Oakland, California in a two-story wooden framed house with an outer stairway adorned over an arbor by a climbing grapevine. This was just after WWI ended and jobs were scarce, but Felix found work in a Chevrolet plant, a sugar factory and a meat packing plant to support his family.

While in Oakland, three more children were born; Acension (Alfred) called Dutch, Theresa (Teet) and Eusebio Felix later known as Sab. Their family was complete[34].

---

[33] Many of the family members told me Crescencia lost twins at birth but nobody knew if it was in Hawaii or California. After carefully studying the dates of birth, I found a gap of nearly three years between Maria and Barceliza. After discussing my assumption with her daughter, Victoria, she agreed this was probably correct.

[34] After Alfred, a baby girl was born before the next child, Theresa. Family folklore say this baby died when María (Marie) accidentally dropped her. Too young to nanny so many siblings as she readied the younger children for school, she couldn't manage the baby. I am told carried the guilt all her life. Crescencia did not speak of this family crisis Marie voiced her regrets to several family members.

During the summers, he would follow the fruit crops like many of the Spanish immigrants for extra money and he'd camp his family on the banks of Putah Creek[35]. During those summers Felix and Crescéncia were lured to Putah Creek in Winters, California, which would later become Diversion Dam. The family camped on a meadow below Pleasant Valley Road. They created their own entertainment and the Gonzales children hold fond memories; the boys walking on stilts and rolled rubber tires, the girls walking with tin cans pressed to their feet. [36]

Putah Creek had clean wet sand along its banks. Crescéncia often placed soapy dishtowels on small rocks and larger boulders embedded in the sand to bleach them in the hot sun. The water flowed and glistened and the family enjoyed the peaceful area.

Across the road and up on a hill, they later purchased 107 acres of land covered with pine, green oak, and beautiful white bark buckeye trees by Lake Berryessa. Felix and Crescéncia were thrilled to buy this land for their family partially with money they'd saved plus a loan from the Federal Land Bank of Fairfield. The land had an orchard, a small vineyard and barn. They drilled a well and bought horses to plow the land, plows, a seed planter and large and small cultivators. They built a larger redwood barn to house their implements, the horse and milk cow.

The barn also housed the family at one end while they built a new home on the first knoll that overlooked Putah Creek. There was a large screened porch along the entire front and south side of

---

[35] Putah Creek is described as follows: Putah Creek is not what you would expect in the inner coastal ranges of California. It is a clear, rushing stream that flows at about the same rate all year long because of the releases from Monticello Dam. Just downstream from Lake Solano County Park is a diversion dam, which creates Lake Solano. Putah Creek and environs have been classified as a Nationally Important Bird Area because of Yellow-billed Magpie, a species endemic to California. The Highway 29 to Lake Berryessa stretch of Putah Creek in California is 16 miles long

[36] Family history from Theresa Gonzales Sackett

the house. Downstairs was a storage area; a garage the summer kitchen and cooling cellar.

Her youngest son, Sab, said Crescéncia loved children and always had a very generous heart. She invited disadvantaged youths from the Oakland area to help turn their lives around. Others said it was a mixed blessing since the ranch always needed workers; they had helpers and the youths received a chance to learn a better life. There was always work on a ranch and these young people worked with Felix and his older children to plant apricots, plums and almonds.

The children were growing and married, raising children of their own but many continued to help on the ranch.

Felix created his own trucking company in Winters to haul fruit and other commodities throughout the area, especially to the Bay area where international markets were located.[37]

Their lives were filled with hard work, disappointments and family gatherings. The traditional *Matanza* included butchering two hogs in early winter when they made chorizo, blood sausage and bacon. The fat was rendered and the excess meat was seared and placed into 10 and 15 gallon crocks and covered with fresh lard. Then, the crocks were moved to the cool cellar to avoid the heat that could turn it rancid.

Crescéncia was an efficient manager and oversaw many parts of the daily routines. There was the domed outside oven where bread was baked once a week called *el horno*. Then, those barrels of red wine each fall that were placed in the cooling cellar before the grapes burned on the vines. She watched over the children as they crushed the grapes in large wooden tanks with their bare feet before being placed in a presser. If the wine became too warm and started to sour, she was happy to have the wine vinegar it created.

---

[37] Story source: Eusebio Gonzales (Sab)

Her children attended nearby Olive School, walking down a paved road to join the other families on Olive School Lane. It was a one-room school house that was split into two rooms where the students marched into class to the beat of a clapper against the inside of the bell. The children often hoped it would crack. Many students were Spanish (including the Silván and Ruiz cousins) or Japanese and other ethnic nationalities.

Crescéncia repeatedly asked her brother, Geronimo, to leave Spain to join her in California. He never did. She saved his letters in a purse on a hook inside her closet. The letters are long gone but Victorina Gonzales Weber's memory made me smile. Victorina was bilingual and read the letters to her mother until Crestencia found a translator. The letters were saved all her life, never giving up hope. Nobody knows what happened to the letters.

She was plagued with diabetes in her later years, often wearing soft slippers on her throbbing and burning feet. I believe this was probably due to neuropathy, a severe burning and throbbing in the feet which is a symptom of diabetes.

Old bricks can still be found on the property; the locals still refer to the patch of land as the Gonzales Ranch. The land still has its original slopes. A new home is now built on the flat portion of the property. The new landowner allows family members to take bricks and Alicia Gonzales says she cherishes them; a reminder not only of her grandmother, but of her trip to the old place with her father, Ascension (Alfred) Gonzales before he died.

CERTIFIED COPY OF BIRTH DOCUMENT

MINISTERIO DE JUSTICIA
Registros Civiles

737380

Serie BS   N° 396904

CERTIFICACION EN EXTRACTO DE INSCRIPCION DE NACIMIENTO

Sección 1.ª

Tomo ___10___

Pág. ___114___

Folio (1) _____

Registro Civil de ___FUENTESAUCO___

Provincia de ___ZAMORA___

D. Mª ___CRESCENCIA SILVAN HERNANDEZ___
(Nombre y dos apellidos del nacido)

hija de ___Celestino___ y de ___Agustina___
(Nombre)   (Nombre)

nació en ___Fuentesauco___ (Zamora)

el día ___quince___ de ___Junio___
(En letra)

de ___mil ochocientos ochenta y cuatro.___
(En letra)

Esta certificación en extracto sólo da fe del hecho del nacimiento, de su fecha y lugar y del sexo del inscrito (Reglamento del Registro Civil de 14 de noviembre de 1958, art. 29).

—(Para notas y otras indicaciones) (2)

(Sello del Registro Civil)

CERTIFICA: Según consta de la página registral reseñada al margen, el Encargado D. Agustin del Rio Romero (Secretario)

Fuentesauco ___, a 17 de Diciembre de 1981.—

(En los Juzgados de Paz, firmarán el Juez y el Secretario)

Importe de la certificación:

Tarifa Tributaria, n.º 32 (en pólizas)....   ptas.
Tasas (Decreto de 18-6-59, art. 4.º y artículo 37, tarifa 1.ª)...............   »
Busca (art. 40, tarifa 1.ª) (3)...........   »
Urgencia (art. 41, tarifa 1.ª) (4).......   »
Impreso (5)..........................   »
                        TOTAL...............

(1) Se consignará el folio y no la página, si se certifica de libros ajustados al modelo anterior a la Ley vigente del Registro Civil; en otro caso, se consignará sólo la página.
(2) Se inutilizará con una raya de tinta el espacio sobrante.
(3) CINCO PESETAS por cada período de busca de tres años, quedando exento el primer período de tres años.
(4) CINCO PESETAS cuando se despache dentro de las veinticuatro horas.
(5) Modelo oficial de acuerdo con la Orden de 24 de diciembre de 1958.

COPY OF ORIGINAL BIRTH DOCUMENT

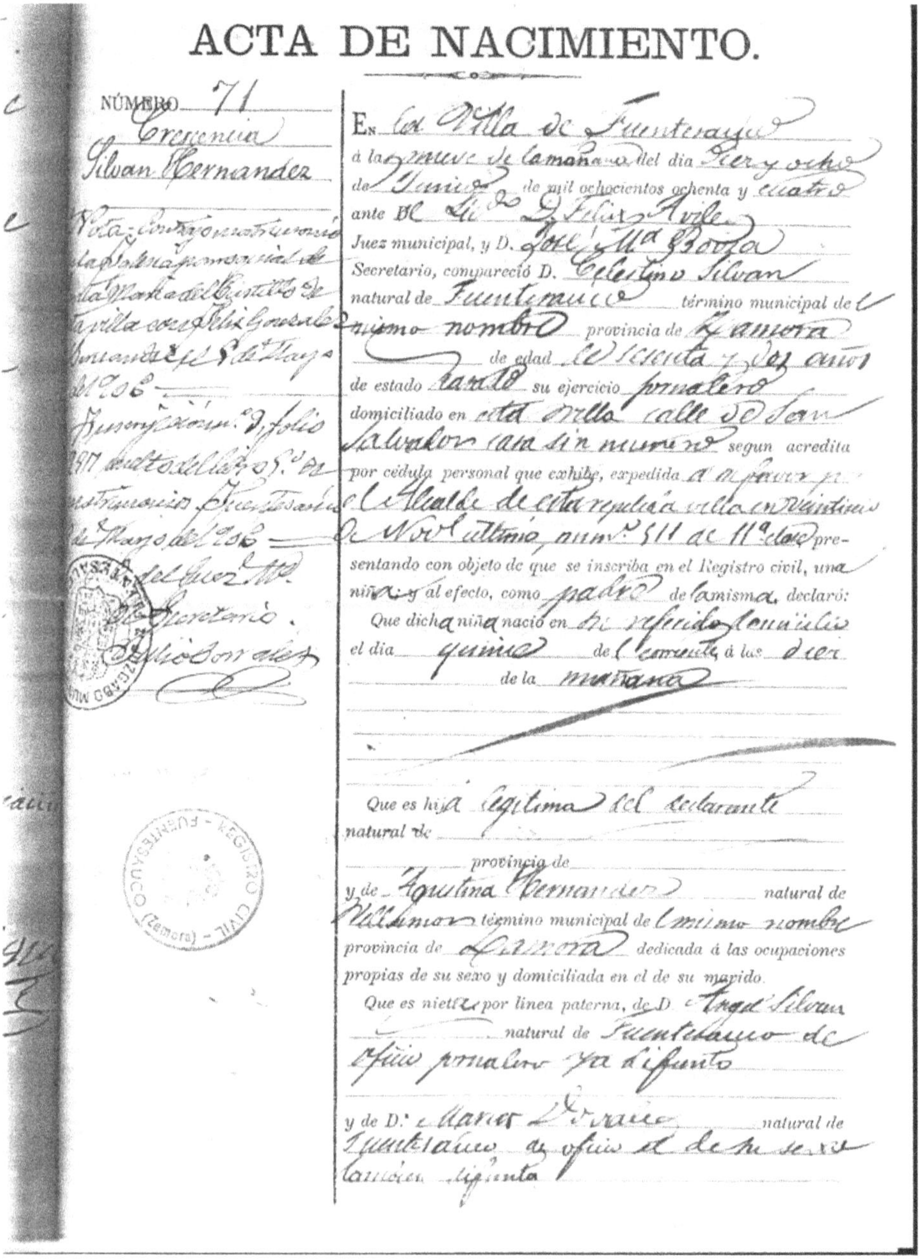

ACTA DE NACIMIENTO.

NÚMERO 71

Crecencia Silvan Hernandez

Nota - [illegible] Santa María del Castillo de esta villa con Felix Gonzalez Fernandez el 8 de Mayo de 1906 [illegible] folio 187 [illegible] de Mayo de 1906 [illegible] El Secretario [illegible]

En la Villa de Fuentesaúco á las nueve de la mañana del dia diez y ocho de Junio de mil ochocientos ochenta y cuatro ante el Ldo D. Felix Avila Juez municipal, y D. José Mª Borja Secretario, compareció D. Celestino Silvan natural de Fuentesaúco término municipal de el mismo nombre provincia de Zamora de edad de treinta y dos años de estado casado su ejercicio jornalero domiciliado en esta villa calle de San Salvador casa sin número segun acredita por cédula personal que exhibe, expedida a su favor por el Alcalde de esta repetida villa en veintiuno de Nov. último, núm. 511 de 11ª clase presentando con objeto de que se inscriba en el Registro civil, una niña y al efecto, como padre de la misma declaró:

Que dicha niña nació en su referido domicilio el dia quince del corriente á las diez de la mañana

Que es hija legítima del declarante natural de provincia de y de Agustina Hernandez natural de Villamor término municipal de el mismo nombre provincia de Zamora dedicada á las ocupaciones propias de su sexo y domiciliada en el de su marido.

Que es nieta por linea paterna, de D. Angel Silvan natural de Fuentesaúco de oficio jornalero ya difunto y de Dª Maria [illegible] natural de Fuentesaúco de oficio el de su sexo también difunta

FUENTESAUCO - REGISTRO CIVIL (Zamora)

y por línea materna de D. *Miguel Hernandez*
natural de *Villamor de los [...]* de
[...] formalase ya difunto

y de D. *Margarita Martin* natural de
Villa[...] de [...]
bien difunta

Y que á la expresada niña se le había de poner el
nombre de *Crescencia*

Todo lo cual presenciaron como testigos D. *Agustin*
Rodriguez y Benigno [...] ma-
yores de edad, naturales
y domiciliados en esta villa, *[...]*
labrador y Peaton de Villanueva y
[...]

Leída integramente esta acta, é invitadas las personas que
deben suscribirla á que la leyeran por sí mismas, si así lo creían
conveniente, se estampó en ella el sello del Juzgado municipal,
y la firmaron el Sr. Juez *no haciéndolo el de-*
clarante por manifestar no saber á
su ruego lo haz Emilio Gonzalez

y de todo ello, como Secretario, certifico.

Emilio Gonzales

Agustin Rodriguez

Translation of Document[38] B. 7.821.478

Don Emilio Ladron de Cegama, Attorney and Deputy Municipal Justice for the Fuentesaúco District and administrator of the Municipal Civil Registry of said district certifies to the following:

Certificate: That according to the entries recorded in the archives of the Civil Registry.

Felis Gonzales Hernández a natural citizen of this village, legitimate son of **Ascension Gonzales** and **Gregoria Hernández**[39], entered into matrimony in the Church of San Maria in this villa with **Crescéncia Silban Hernández** of the same nationality and place, the legitimate daughter of **Celestino Silban** and **Agustina Hernández** at eight o'clock on the fifth of May, 1906 as recorded in volume 9 of the Registry.

That **Alejandro Gonzales Silván,** legitimate son of **Felix Gonzales Hernández** and **Crescéncia Silban Hernández**, naturalized and domiciled in this villa, grandson of the paternal line of Ascension and Gregoria and maternal line of **Celestino** and **Agustina** born in this village at 12:00 o'clock on 9 July 1908 as recorded in volume 79, page 310, in book 17 of births.

That **Juan Gonzales Silván**, legitimate son of **Felix Gonzales** and **Crescéncia Silván Hernández** and paternal and maternal same as entered above, born in this village at 10 o'clock on the 31st of January, 1910, as recorded on volume 17, page 496, column 16.

I grant this statement at the request of **Felix Gonzales** for immigration purposes. The Municipal Justice of Fuentesaúco has affixed his Seal of Office on this 27th day of January, 1911.

The Secretary, PLM
Signed by: Julio Corrales

---

[38] Document received from Patte Gonzales Kronlund and Linda Gonzales Rhoades, translated by their father, Eusebio Felix Gonzales, youngest son of Crescencia and Eusebio Gonzales.

[39] I was told after his parents died and he was made a ward of the Catholic Church, he wasn't adopted but was taken in by a family for awhile before he joined the military and then returned to Fuentesauco.

Name: *Hernandy Silvan* *Cristencia* Age: 26
Sex: F Citizen of SPAIN
Steamer ORTERIC Line
Date APR 1 8 1911 Port of Hon.'ulu, Hawaii
Group No. 04 List No. 25

Honolulu, Hawaii, Passenger Lists, 1900-1953

Name	Cristencia Silvan Hernandez
Age	26
Gender	Female
Birth Year	abt 1885
Port of Departure	Gibraltar
Departure Date	24 Feb 1911
Ship	Orteric
Port of Arrival	Honolulu, Hawaii
Arrival Date	13 Apr 1911
Ethnicity/Race/Nationality	Spanish
Last Residence	Spain

Name	Abejandro Gonzalez Silvan Hernandez
Age	3
Gender	Male
Birth Year	abt 1908
Port of Departure	Gibraltar
Departure Date	24 Feb 1911
Ship	Orteric
Port of Arrival	Honolulu, Hawaii
Arrival Date	13 Apr 1911
Ethnicity/Race/Nationality	Spanish
Last Residence	Spain

Record Index

Name:	Cristencia Silvan Hernandez
Age:	26
Gender:	Female
Birth Year:	abt 1885
Port of Departure:	Gibraltar
Departure Date:	24 Feb 1911
Ship:	Orteric
Port of Arrival:	Honolulu, Hawaii
Arrival Date:	13 Apr 1911
Ethnicity/Race/Nationality:	Spanish
Last Residence:	Spain

Source Information

Record URL: http://search.ancestry.com/cgi-bin/sse.dll?h=9547498&db=HonoluluPL&indiv=1

Source Citation: Repository Name:*National Archives and Records Administration (NARA); NARA Series:A3422; Roll 29.*

Source Information: Ancestry.com. *Honolulu, Hawaii, Passenger Lists, 1900-1953* [database on-line]. Provo, UT, USA: Ancestry.com Operations, Inc., 2009. Original data: Passenger Lists of Vessels Arriving at Honolulu, Hawaii, 1900-1953; (National Archives Microfilm Publication A3422, 269 rolls); Records of the Immigration and Naturalization Service, Record Group 85; National Archives, Washington, D.C.

Copy of Ship's Manifest ~ S.S. Orteric sailing from Gibraltar Feb 24, 1911. Lines 24-30 list Felizo Gonzalez[40] Hernández and family

---

[40] Gonzales was often misspelled to read Gonzalez or the name was changed between then and arriving in America

SILVÁN LEAVES   Patricia Ruiz Steele

In California:
Goat transport in
Oakland….

Crescéncia Silván Hernández
Gonzales – Photo taken about
1938

139 | P a g e

They sailed into the San Francisco harbor on the 18th of January, 1918. Lines 3 - 6

Form 500-B
U. S. DEPARTMENT OF LABOR
IMMIGRATION SERVICE

Record on this blank United States citizens and citizens of insular possessions of the United States arriving at a port of continental United States from a foreign port or a port of the insular possessions of the United States, and such citizens arriving at a port of said insular possessions from a foreign port, a port of continental United States, or a port of another insular possession.

54

LIST OF UNITED STATES CITIZENS
(FOR THE IMMIGRATION AUTHORITIES)

S. S. GOVERNOR sailing from HONOLULU January 15, 19 18. Arriving at Port of San Francisco January 19 18

No.	Family Name	Given Name	Age Yrs. Mos.	Sex	IF NATIVE OF U.S. INSULAR POSSESSION OR IF NATIVE OF UNITED STATES, GIVE DATE AND PLACE OF BIRTH (CITY OR TOWN AND STATE).	IF NATURALIZED, GIVE NAME AND LOCATION OF COURT WHICH ISSUED NATURALIZATION PAPERS AND DATE OF PAPERS	ADDRESS IN UNITED STATES
1	de Deo	Juan	1	M S	Ewa, Hawaii	November 9, 1916.		California.
2	Cassão	Maria J. Dias	2 6	F S	Ewa, Hawaii	June 26, 1915.		"
3	Goncalves	Maria C	6 9	F S	Nolon, Hawaii	May 18, 1918.		"
4	Goncalves	Barcelina	2 9	M S	Honsululi, Haw	April 1915.		"
5	Goncalves	Augustina	1 4	F S	Koalia, Hawaii	September 1916.		"
6	Goncalves	Victoria	4	F S	Koalia, Hawaii	October 1917.		"
7	Moreno	Atancio	6 6	F S	Ewa, Hawaii	May 21, 1912.		San Francisco.
8	Moreno	Juliana	3 9	M S	Ewa, Hawaii	February 16, 1914.		"
9	Moreno	Edvaria	1 8	M S	Ewa, Hawaii	May 21, 1916.		"
10	Villela	Declinia	2 8	M S	Kapia, Hawaii	April 1917.		"
11	Rios	Gregorio	6	M S	Jabala, Hawaii	November 1912.		"
12	Del Rio	Antonio	1 8	M S	Pahola, Hawaii	December 1916.		"
13	Aponte	Edvard	33	M M	Ponce, P. R.	December 1884.		"
14	Aponte	Rosie	18	F M	Ponce, P. R.	May 1899.		"
15	Aponte	Elena	4	F S	Manila	August 1913.		"
16	Rosales	Jose	2 6	F S	Wailuku, Hawaii.	May 21, 1914.		"
17	Silvan	Maria	3 9	F S	Koalia, Hawaii	March 29, 1914.		"
18	Silvan	Antonio R	3 -	M S	Hilo, Hawaii	March 1914.		"
19	de Mello	John	23	M M	Honolulu, Hawaii.	September 3, 1917.		"
20	de Mello	Saterina	22	F M	Spain			"
21	Garcia	Rafael	4	M S	Ewa, Hawaii	March 1914.		"
22	Garcia	Cecelio	1 10	M S	Ewa, Hawaii	February 1916.		"
23	de Mello	John	6		Honolulu, Hawaii	June 1917.		"
24	Contreras	Marcesle	3 5	F S	Wailuku, Hawaii.	August 2?, 1914.		"
25	Sousa	Lydia	4	F S	Funene, Hawaii	September 9, 1913.		"
26	Fernandes	Manuel	2 6	M S	Wailuku, Hawaii	June 30, 1915.		"
27	Fernandes	Phillipe	4 6	M S	Wailuku, Hawaii	July 24, 1913		"
28	Fernandes	Vicenteus	- 10	M S	Lahaina, Hawaii	March 25, 1917.		"
29	Pena	Geronima	1 6	M S	Honolulu, Hawaii	1916.		"
30	Sobrism	Medalina	6	F S	Honolulu, Hawaii	1916.		"

Admitted Jany 15/18

IMPORTANT NOTICE.—1. Great care should be taken not to place on this list the name of any passenger who was not born in the United States or who has not taken out final naturalization papers.
2. Where one or more members of a family are aliens, the names of all such members should be recorded upon the alien manifest. Suitable notation may be made upon such manifest opposite the names of those members who claim citizenship.
3. Failure to observe the terms of this notice may result in delay to passengers at the port of arrival.
4. List on this form only U. S. citizens or citizens of an insular possession of the United States.

California, Solano County, Silveyville Township, April 12-15, 1930, Enumeration
District No. 48-13o, Supervisor's District No. 5 – 15th Census of the United States.
They lived on Pleasant Valley Road in Winters, California

The 1930 U. S. Federal Census

Eusebio (Sab) , Victorina (Vic), Allen Huckaby, Theresa – About 1938
Christina and Felix Gonzales, November 30, 1943
Bottom photo: Felix Gonzales with Red's children

Crescéncia Silván Hernández Gonzales died in an Auburn Hospital following an illness of seven weeks. Prior to going to the Auburn Hospital, where she spent three days before she died, she spent two weeks in Sutter Hospital, Sacramento, California.

Pallbearers at the graveside rites were Alexander (Alejandro/Red) Gonzales, Buel Sackett, John L. Morgan, Frank Boise, Johnny Djubek and Allen Huckaby.

Graveside Rites Held Here Saturday For Mrs. Christina Gonzales

Graveside funeral services were held here Saturday for Mrs. Christina Gonzales, well known local resident, who died in an Auburn hospital October 24 following an illness of seven weeks. Rev. Father Madden officiated.

Mrs. Gonzales had been a patient at the Auburn hospital three days. Prior to hospitalization there she had spent two weeks in Sutter hospital, Sacramento. She was a native of Spain and had been a resident of Winters for 50 years.

Beside her husband, Felix Gonzales, the following children survive: Alexander and Felix, Jr. of Winters, John of Santa Rosa, Alfred of San Francisco, Mrs. Marie Miller of Sebastopol, Mrs. Augustina Coombs and Mrs. Theresa Sackett of Winters, Mrs. Victoria Weber of Lodi and Mrs. Barceliza Huckaby of Auburn.

Rosary was recited Friday night in the Lukens, Vettestad and Bryan Chapel in Auburn.

Pallbearers at the graveside rites were Alexander Gonzales, Buell Sackett, John L. Morgan, Frank Boisa, Johnny Djubek and Allen Huckaby.

CARD OF THANKS

We wish to express our heartfelt thanks to all those who so kindly assisted and for the words of sympathy and beautiful floral offerings received on the death of our beloved wife and mother.

Mr. Felix Gonzales and Family

www.findagrave.com ~ Memorial #326563214

Christina *Silvan* Gonzales [Edit Name]

| Memorial | Photos | Flowers | | Share | Edi |

Learn about removing the ads from this memorial...

[Transfer Management] [Edit] [Dele

Birth: Jun. 15, 1884
          Zamora
          Castilla y Leon, Spain
Death: Oct. 24, 1946
          Winters
          Yolo County
          California, USA [Edit Dates]

Christina Gonzales was born in Fuentesauco,
Province of Zamora, Spain as Crescencia
Silvan Hernandez, the daughter of Celestino
Silvan Alejo and Agustina Hernandez Martin.
She married Eusebio Feliz Gonzales May 6,
1906 in Santa Maria del Castillo Church in her
village.

Less than five years after their marriage, she
and Eusebio joined her three older brother's
families and sailed on the SS Orteric from
Gibraltar to Hawaii to work in the sugarcane
fields. At that time, in 1911, Alejandro and
Juan were their only children. (Her brother,
Lorenzo, did not board)

During their life in Hawaii, Eusebio Gonzales
tended to the horses and mules for the
plantation workers at Ewa Plantation on Oahu
and later worked on the Kilauea Plantation on
Kauai. They lived in the Hawaiian Islands
nearly seven years and during that time, their
family grew from two to six.

They sailed to America with family members
and two more children were born. She died in
Placer County and is buried in the Winters
Cemetery beside her husband, Eusebio
Gonzales.

[Edit Bio]
[Link family members]
[Add Marker Transcription]
Note: died in Placer Co 64 Yr 3 Mo 22 Days old
spouse of F.G. Gonzales
[Edit]

Burial: [Edit]
Winters Cemetery
Winters
Yolo County
California, USA

Added by: Patricia Steele

Added by: Patricia Steele

Cemetery Photo
Don't show cemetery photos

(Gravestone lists Crescéncia's year of birth at 1882. It should read 1884)

HUSBAND OF CRESCÉNCIA SILVÁN HERNÁNDEZ:

FELIX GONZALES HERNANDEZ

14 August 1881 - 27 December 1963

Felix loved horses. The son of Ascension Gonzales and Gregoria Hernández, he and his sister, Isabella, were orphaned at a very young age.

The family story related to me by his daughter, Theresa Gonzales Sackett, notes the children became wards of the Catholic Church with the hopeful prospect of adoption. Isabella was adopted by a family who had only daughters. They did not want boys, so Felix remained a ward of the church where he endured forced labor; he was beaten and the foundlings were not offered an education. He was often sent to bed without meals if he did not adhere to their strict regimen. By the time he turned fourteen, I am told that he ran away to Valladolid, Spain to join the military with the King's Cavalry.

He was 5' 7 ½" tall with blue eyes and brown hair. He had a mole on the left side of his face and a small scar near the hairline on the left side of his head.

To add to the history before this chapter, when Felix applied for permission to leave the Territory of Hawaii to sail to the United States, he brought his family to settle in the Oakland, California area and started working at the Chevrolet plant. It was during this time the last three Gonzales children were born, Theresa, Alfredo and Eusebio.

Felix eventually accumulated enough money to buy 107 acres in Solano County just outside Winters along Putah Creek consisting of a small orchard, vineyard and barn. The barn was their home while he built the house. He planted apricots, plums and almonds and everyone worked on the ranch.

Felix was rarely idle. During this time, he also had a trucking business in Winters where he hauled fruit and other commodities through the area, especially to the bay area where the best marketing was located.

As his ranch prospered, he was able to add mules and horses to help with the farm work. Along with his children who were growing up to learn the hard work on the ranch, he also had help from some of the under-privileged boys Crescéncia tried to help from the Oakland area. Hard work and long hours was a regimen the Gonzales children learned, both boys and girls. They drove the truck through the orchards long before they were legal age, they smoked behind the barn and generally look back on their lives with laughter and the memory of smoke in the air.

Great excitement arose with the eventual purchase of a tractor. The Gonzales clan took turns jumping on it for photographs.

An incorrect birth record was received by the Gonzales family from the ayuntamiento (city hall) in Fuentesaúco for a man named Eusebio Gonzales Hidalgo. Due to this mix up, over the years the Gonzales family has believed Felix Gonzales was named Felix Eusebio Gonzales Hidalgo although other documents listed his name as Felix Gonzales Hernandez, Feliso G. Hernandez and Felis Gonzales. Another unfortunate result of the incorrect birth document is my book, *The Girl Immigrant*, lists him as Eusebio in error. His gravestone is also etched with the name, "Eusebio".

The importance of documents and the spelling of names cry for proof but what can a family believe when the village in Spain sends a birth document for the wrong man? Felix's father was named Ascension. I am told one of his sons was named Ascension "Dutch" but he gave himself a middle name, "Jerry." Felix named his daughter, María Gregoria, after his mother, Gregoria Hernandez.

Family stories say Felix Gonzales was in the "Spanish Cavalry under Generalissimo Francisco Franco" and a few years later he received a letter, honoring him as a Marquis by the King of Spain. What honor was offered? How could he become a Marquis in Spain's royalty? Was it a commendation?

Researching Felix Gonzales' military history, I found answers from a genealogist in Seville. He doubted Felix was in the "King's Army" because those soldier's rich fathers purchased their son's commissions. Felix was an orphan.

My research regarding marquis status:

Francisco Franco was ten years old when Felix Gonzales was military age. Franco became the Fascist leader during the Spanish Civil War in 1936 and remained as the dictator until 1973. It is true the king can bestow the rank of Marquis on noblemen. The king could never bestow the rank on a commoner for any reason.

I studied any and all medals and commendations made for military service in that time period. When King Alfonso VIII took control in 1902 from his mother/regent Queen María Christina, a medal was established but it is unclear if it was used to honor military service members. I found the Royal Cavalry Armory, General Military Archives and Archivos General de Indies plus the Spanish Military Archives in Segovia but they had no records of this type of commendation.

In Seville's military

museum, I found various medals offered to Spanish military but no notations regarding the cavalry. We know Felix was in the cavalry due to his care, knowledge and experience with horses.

At this point, the only way to solve this mystery is to study the photograph of Felix Gonzales in full military uniform. His children know it exists but as of this publication, it hasn't surfaced. If my genealogist can see the uniform's insignia he can help.

This *Cedula Personal* ticket shows Felix lived on Doctor Armeuteros Street, Fuentesaúco.

This Matson document shows he paid the alien tax to enter the United States from Hawaii.

Hello Patricia,

I've received your family's certificates but... I think there is a problem with your information because Eusebio González Hidalgo and Félix González Hernández are not the same person, as you can see in the attached with all the information the certificates have given to us. In fact, Eusebio González Hidalgo married another person in 1907 and died in Fuentesauco in 1977... and Félix González Hernández married Crescencia in 1906...

II.- Celestino Silván. Natural de Fuentesaúco, en 1822. Jornalero. Casado con Agustina Hernández, natural de Villamor, hija de Miguel Hernández, natural de Villamor, jornalero, fallecido antes de 1884, y Margarita Martín, natural de Villaescusa (Zamora), fallecida antes de 1884. Fueron padres de:

⊛ Juan Francisco Silván Hernández (tomo 5, fol. 162-163v). Casado en la Iglesia de Santa María de Fuentesaúco el 23 de abril de 1900 (tomo 5, fol. 145v), con Rita Marzo Trascasas Marzo, natural de Toro, en 1881, hija de Manuel Trascasas y Manuela Marzo, naturales de Toro.

⊛ Crescencia Silván Hernández, natural de Fuentesaúco, 15 junio 1884, tomo 10, pág. 114, hija de Celestino y Agustina. Casada en Fuentesaúco con Félix González Hernández, el 5 de mayo de 1906 (tomo 5, fol. 257).

Eusebio González Hidalgo. Natural de Fuentesaúco, Zamora, 14 agosto 1881, tomo 8, página 171, hijo de Luciano González Vicente, natural de Fuentesaúco, jornalero, hijo de Bernardo González, labrador, fallecido antes de 1881, e Isabel Vicente, naturales de Fuentesaúco, y María Hidalgo, natural de Fuentesaúco, hija de Ángel Hidalgo, jornalero, y Marcelina Antón, naturales de Fuentesaúco. Casado con Gabina Alba Zamorano en Fuentesaúco el 27 de abril de 1907. Falleció en Fuentesaúco el 9 de marzo de 1977 (tomo 2, folio 130).

Source: Fernando Hidalgo Lerdo de Tejda, Genealogist, Seville, Spain

Felix Gonzales Hernandez ~ 1961

THE SELECTIVE DRAFT
TERRITORY OF HAWAII

HONOLULU, HAWAII

December 11, 1957.

TO WHOM IT MAY CONCERN:

This is to certify that

FELIX GONZALES HERNANDEZ

REGISTRATION NO.____ OVER AGE

has this day signified his desire to leave the Territory

for ___ SAN FRANCISCO

and has registered his future address at Headquarters.

There is no objection on the part of the draft

to his travel to ___ SAN FRANCISCO

www.findagrave.com ~ Memorial #33364237

Felix Hernandez Gonzales [Edit Name]

| Memorial | Photos | Flowers | | Share | Edit |

Learn about removing the ads from this memorial...

[Transfer Management] [Edit] [Delete]

Added by: Patricia Steele

Birth: Aug. 14, 1881
         Zamora
         Castilla y Leon, Spain
Death: Dec. 28, 1963
         Winters
         Yolo County
         California, USA [Edit Dates]

Felix GONZALES Hernandez was born in
Fuentesauco, Province of Zamora, Spain. It is
believed he was orphaned young. He married
Crescencia (Christina) Silvan Hernandez on
May 6, 1906 in Santa Maria del Castillo Church
in her village.

Less than five years after their marriage, they
joined his brother's in law and their families
and sailed on the Orteric from Gibraltar to
Hawaii to work in the sugarcane fields. At that
time, in 1911, Alejandro and Juan were their
only children.

During their life in Hawaii, Felix Gonzales
tended to the horses and mules for the
plantation workers at Ewa Plantation on Oahu
and later at the Kilauea Plantation on Kauai.
They lived in the Hawaiian Islands nearly
seven years and during that time, their family
grew from two to six.

Added by: Patricia Steele

They sailed to America in 1918 with family
members and two more children were born. He
is buried in the Winters Cemetery beside his
wife, Crescencia Silvan Hernandez Gonzales

In September 2013, new documentation
proved Felix's name was not EUSEBIO. An
incorrect birth document was received from
Spain. His name was Felix Gonzales Hernandez
in Spain, but in America the second surname
was dropped.
[Edit Bio]
Family links: [Edit]
 Spouse:
   Christina *Silvan* Gonzales (1884 - 1946)

[Add Marker Transcription]
Note: 84 yrs old

Cemetery Photo
Don't show cemetery photos
on this memorial [?]
Added by: Vicki

GONZALES FAMILY. It was 1918 when the Gonzales family sailed from Hawaii to Oakland and bought 107 acres of virgin land along Putah Creek. From left to right are (seated) mother Christina holding Eusebia and father Eusebio holding Theresa; (standing) Victoria, Tina, John, Alexander, Marie, Sally, and Alfred. Both parents were born in northern Spain, married there, and came to Hawaii, where they monitored the influx of immigrants into this country under a seven-year contract. (Courtesy of Theresa Gonzales Sackett.)

(32) Grandchildren

(12) When he was 17, Alejandro (Red) married Adeline "Lena" Fernández and they had six (6) children. His first son, John, was born in 1926 but died two years later in 1928. He is buried at Winters Cemetery. Christina was born in 1927 and died in Carmichael, California in 2006. Geronimo (Herman) Alejandro was born in 1929. Felestino (Mac) and Felix (Willie) were born by 1931 quickly followed by Clara Dean in 1932[41]. The marriage became dysfunctional; Lena and baby Clara Dean moved in with her parents in the Oakland area, leaving the four children to be raised by their grandparents. Edna Jo Flint raised Red's four children plus five children she and Red had; Edna Jo, John Alex, Lois, Ralph and Buell William. Later in Red's life, he and Edna became estranged. She cared for Red's father, Felix, in Vacaville until his death. Red moved south and later married Anna Sandvigen. Red's last daughter, Anna, was born in 1965.

(3) John married Hazel Spurlock Robinson about 1937 and they had two children, Barbara (Bobbie) Joan in 1939 and John Alfred in 1943. John was also the father of a third child named Kristen, born in May of 1947 whose mother was Betty Jean Galbraith.

(4) María Gregoria (Marie) married Orville Miller sometime after 1930 and they had four children; Orville, Jr., John, James and Christina.

---

[41] Source: Victorina Gonzales Weber. At this writing, I have not found Clara Dean but my research continues.

(3) Christina "Sally" Barceliza married Allen Huckaby in Reno in February, 1939. They had three children, Christina Rosella in 1940, Allen "Dutch" Noel in 1942 and Felix Victor in 1946.

(1) Augustina "Tina" married Charles Robert Coombs in 1937. They had one daughter, Judith Fay in 1939.

(2) Victorina (Vic) married Alvin Weber in 1942. He had a son from a previous marriage (Walter). Vic and Alvin had two children, James Herman who was born in 1945 but died in 1971, and Sally Victoria who was born in 1948.

(2) Alfred "Dutch" married twice. In the early 1950s, he married Cecelia La Luc and they had one daughter in 1954, Theresa Joanne. They divorced in 1966 and he later married Sarah Anne (Sally) Brown. They had one daughter, Alicia J., born in 1967.

(2) Theresa married Buel Arthur Sackett in 1946 (a few months before her mother died). They had two sons, Buel Arthur, Jr. in 1955 and Chester "Chet" Hiram II in 1959.

(3) Eusebio Felix "Sab" married Phyllis Yankee in 1949. They had three children, Linda Alicia in 1951, Patricia "Patte" in 1956 and Phillip Gale in 1957.

PART 4
FIRST GENERATION of
Silván Descendants in America

Victorino Luciano Silván Hernández (Ramona Lorenzo Martin)

Teodora, Felisa, Jacinto and Celestino

~

Juan Francisco Silván Hernández (Eustoquia Rita Marzo Trascasas)

Manuela, Agustín, José, María, Juanita and Celestino

~

Crescéncia Silván Hernández (Gonzales) (Felix Gonzales Hernandez)

Alejandro, Juan, María Gregoria, Christina Barceliza, Agustína, Victorina, Theresa, Ascensión and Eusebio

~

Supporting Documents and Sources

The Silván Family in America

A NOTE FOR THE FAMILY OF VICTORINO SILVÁN HERNANDEZ:

During my interview with Robert Souza, son of Theodora Silván Martin, I was stunned to learn he had an uncle, an older Silván son, who lost his leg in the Spanish/American war. He stayed behind in Spain. Obviously with only one leg, he would not have been accepted by the Hawaiian Plantation owners. Bob Souza did not know his mother's brother's name but had heard the story about her older brother and his medical issues directly from Theodora Silvan.

The disheartening fact that Victorino and Ramona Silván lost a son on the ship from Spain to Hawaii must have been a double loss since they'd not only left their parents and siblings behind but their older child.

Robert Souza did not know anything about him and assumed he died. There are stories, however, from several descendants about cousins in Spain who were nuns. They were Dora's and Felisa's nieces and came to America to visit in the early 1950s. They may have been the children of their older brother left in Spain. Some say other family members settled near Monterey, California.

DESCENDANTS OF:
Victorino Luciano Silván Hernández
(Ramona Martínez Lorenzo)

Teodora, Felisa, Jacinto and Celestino
This family photograph was taken in Hawaii about 1916.

Left to right: Celestino, Teodora/Theodora, Victorino Luciano Silván Hernandez, Romana (Ramona) Martin Lorenzo and Felisa.

Family members surmise the photos in the bottom corners of this photograph are different stages Celestino's life, who was the surviving son of Victorino and Ramona Silván.

TEODORA (Dora) SILVÁN MARTINEZ (Martin)

6 September 1899 - 24 July 1991
Fuentesaúco, Zamora, Spain
Married: John Souza Bento

Teodora Silván was an enigma; she often carried an aura of heavy sadness that her children did not understand.

Although, close to her siblings, they became estranged after their mother's death in 1955.

She was nearly twelve when she sailed on the immigrant ship, SS ORTERIC, from Spain from Gibraltar February 24, 1911 with her family, tio Juan Francisco Silván Hernández and tia Rita, their children Manuela, Agustin and Jose and tia Crescéncia Silván, tio Feliz Gonzales and their boys, Alejandro and Juan. Her tio Lorenzo was not allowed to board due to a rejected health exam.

As the oldest of nine Silvan children making their mass exodus from Fuentesaúco, she was often a surrogate mother to her siblings and cousins. We can only surmise that this burden generated resentment; years later, she appeared angry, sometimes bitter toward her children and with life itself. Or maybe it was the emotional pain when her little brother, Jacinto, contracted the measles and died during the immigrant voyage from Spain? When her mother grieved, was it up to Teodora to corral the little ones? Did she wonder if she could live through the heartbreak? When would she be able to grieve? Watching her mother grip her rosary beads and her father stare mutely at the horizon as little Jacinto was

dropped overboard in the inevitable burial at sea may have stunted her emotions before she'd become a woman on her own. Seeing her cousin, two-year old Simon Martin, join Jacinto in a watery grave shortly thereafter may have pulled her teetering emotions further inward.

Teodora spent ten years in Hawaii, helping her family in the sugar plantations. She told her niece, Cheryl, about riding a small gauge train to the fields to work, earning 25 cents per week.

At nearly twelve upon their arrival, her eligibility for the promised education for immigrant children was from May until July. Prospects were limited. Again, she was given the duty of overseer to her siblings. In the midst of their care, she learned to cook, harvest and can vegetables from their garden, bake bread and pies. She sewed a tight seam, crocheted picots around tablecloths and collars with the other women.

Teodora did not enjoy music as much as her sister and mother, but enjoyed the beat from the drum her tio Juan had carefully carried from Spain and dancing. She liked listening to others play instruments and smiled at Felisa and her cousin, Manuela, when they tapped to the beat.

She wasn't a child anymore but she wasn't an adult either. However, since the Spanish and Portuguese ethnic communities were sandwiched closely together, she often wound up with the adults.

As a teenager, she acknowledged that being with the adults had its pleasures. During the many fiestas, family and friends often ate together, danced together, talked together and generally looked forward to the restful time away from the fields of the Kilauea Sugar Plantation on the north coast of Kauai. While living in the small village of Hanalei of Waianae County in the Territory of Hawaii, the families became good friends with the Souza family.

Theodora and her mother, Ramona, had a tense relationship. She was not allowed to learn reading or writing because she had to care for Felisa and Celestino. Ramona favored the two younger children. Was this another reason for her sadness?

There were many Souzas but one stood out, John Souza Bento. He was two years older and a bit quiet but very interesting.

By the spring of 1919, Teodora became betrothed and a wedding was planned at St. Sylvester's Church in Kilauea.[42]

When Teodora's parents sailed to San Francisco in the spring of 1921[43] with Felisa and Celestino, she was adrift without them. Her new baby girl, Josephine, was born February 4, 1920 but she was lonely. John noticed. Conversations veered toward California.

---

[42] This is the church listed on six baptismal records for the Souza Bento family, so the church as the venue for their wedding is based on that documentation. No marriage records could be found at the Roman Catholic Church in the State of Hawaii's Chancery Office in Honolulu, the archdiocese in Kauai, or in vital statistic records. Based on baptismal records listing godparents, it is my assumption they married between the 3rd week of March and the end of April, 1919.

[43] Documents show them on the 1920 census in Hanelei, Kauai, but I cannot find the ship manifest showing them sailing from Hawaii to California. Romana's Alien Certificate is dated April 21, 1921. It is only through family stories that we know they settled in San Leandro, Alameda, California.

Yes, she'd miss wearing muumuus and the island air and tropical flowers and the even temperatures. But at 22 years old, she missed her family.

So, just after Josephine's first birthday, they packed their belongings and prepared to say aloha to their friends, the islands and the remaining Souza family. John purchased tickets and they boarded the SS MAUI in Honolulu on February 22, 1921. Sailing for eight days, they arrived into the port at San Francisco on March 1st.

By then, she was two inches taller than her sister, Felisa. She had large brown eyes, a round face and light, wavy brown hair. She was also five months pregnant (with Victor John) and anxious to have her second baby in California.

S. S. Maui ~ February 23, 1921
Line 18, 19 and 20: John L., Theodora, Josephine Bento
Theodora is listed as naturalized; John is a U.S. citizen

She shortened her name to Dora. Felisa now called herself Alice and she wanted to be more American. John would still be John and Celestino would still be Celestino, or Cel, but she and Felisa would fit in!

Her first son, Victor John Souza, was born four months after arriving in America on June 25, 1921 in Oakland where they lived near her parents and siblings. And then the Souza children kept coming until they totaled eight by the spring of 1935; Alfred, George, Dorothy, Lillian, Robert and Jerome[44].

As a young Spanish girl growing up between Spain and Hawaii, Dora learned the intricacies of needlework and cooking beyond those she'd learned in Hawaii.

Many of the people I have interviewed shared their thoughts about Dora and all have several threads of memory in common. She was well remembered for baking pies, cooking from scratch. Jars of canned vegetables lined the shelves of her pantry. In a nutshell, she was most remembered wearing an apron.

After careful sifting through the many memories that fill my notes, it appears that Dora was slightly bitter about her life. Her husband was remembered as distant, quiet and sometimes unfriendly. I asked her daughter, Dorothy, if her parent's marriage was arranged by their parents? No, she was sure it was not an arranged marriage. She was told their dating was watched very carefully by her mother, Ramona Silván, as he courted his way toward marriage.

Family relationships between Spanish on the plantations in Kauai and Portuguese nearby smoothed the way. They worked together, sometimes ate together, celebrated together, shared their Matanza,[45] held their babies and generally felt like family.

1920 Census: John, Theodora and baby Josephine on next page.

---

[44] I have confirmed that Felisa and Teodora both named their sons Jerome. Their descendants were very surprised.

[45] Matanza: traditional butchering of pigs. Everyone took part- butchering, carrying, grinding and preparing blood sausages, curing, placing bits in lard for many uses.

Her father, Victorino Silván, died of a lung abscess just before Christmas in 1925, not living to see his last five grandchildren. He is buried in St. Mary's Cemetery. After his death, Dora and Alice, along with Celestino, watched over their widowed mother, Ramona.

Nearly five years later, the April 7, 1930 Census in Oakland, Alameda County, California shown on the next page lists John earning $3,500 per year and the family lived at 1428 - 99th Avenue in Oakland. It lists John, Dora, Josephine, Victor, Alfred, George, Dorothy with Lillian who was one month old.

As their children grew to adulthood, each child seemed destined for different ways of life. Josephine became the favorite mother figure to the younger ones; Victor was tossed out of the house when he used his earnings to purchase a graduation-from-high school suit instead of giving the money to his father, so he joined the navy at eighteen without going to his graduation ceremony. He had already lived much of his teen years with his grandmother, Ramona. Her nurturing had softened his feelings as an adult. With his abuela, Ramona, he felt loved.

The younger children did not know their older brother as well as they would have liked; their years at home were hard ones. They worked in the fields at a young age, turning their money over to their father, a standard procedure rarely questioned.

When Dora's mother became too ill for her brother, Celestino, to care for her, Ramona was moved from her house at

214 Dabner Street to live with John and Dora at 877 Joaquin Avenue in San Leandro, Alameda County, California until she died on March 29, 1955. John Souza was the informant for her death certificate and handled the funeral arrangements with the H. W. Seramur Company for her burial at St. Mary's Cemetery April 1st.

Celestino inherited the house; since he'd already purchased the house next door, he sold his parents house and distributed the furniture and belongings among his sisters. There were a few items that brought contentious discussions and later caused a rift between Dora and Alice.

Dora grieved again when her son's (Robert) daughter, Denise, died on July 5, 1969 of leukemia when she was only seven years old. She had raised the child from 2 weeks to 4 years of age until her son, Bob and Jane married. Her mother, Cheryl Ayers abandoned the baby girl.

Dora's children scattered. Lillian flew to Paris to join her military husband, Bill Ross. Dora's oldest daughter, Josephine, was a member of the Orchid Society and a quilter of some renown. Alfred and George both joined the military just like their brother, Victor; Alfred army, George navy. Her daughter, Dorothy, loved horses. And her youngest son, Jerome, was a friend to all of them.

Dora became a widow at 74 just a few months after Alice's husband, Joe perished. Both sisters were widows the same year.[46]

---

[46] There is a short chapter on the Souza Bento family. See John Souza's biography

At the time of Dora's death, her residence was her daughter's (Dorothy) address in Hayward, Alameda, California. Dora died at the Pleasanton Convalescent Hospital in Pleasanton, California on July 24, 1991 at 91 years of age. The cause of death is listed on her Death Certificate as respiratory arrest from sepsis caused by bilateral lobar[47] pneumonia, dehydration and heart failure.

Dora's granddaughter, Cheryl Souza Edwards, kindly shared her grandmother's recipe below. She said when family members were ill; this dish always seemed to perk them up. Her daughter, Emily, assured her it worked for her influenza.

Long Rice or Bean Threads (with chicken)

Brown in pot:
1 ½ tablespoons olive oil
2 cloves garlic, chopped fine
½ medium onion, chopped fine
3 green onions, chopped fine
4 breasts, 4 thighs, 4 legs skin removed, or 1 whole chicken

After chicken is browned, then add:
20 oz. chopped tomatoes
20 oz. good water
¼ cup soy sauce
1 tablespoons parsley fresh
1 tablespoons sweet basil
1 teaspoon paprika

Simmer until chicken is done. Remove chicken and continue simmering sauce. Soak bean threads in cold water 20 minutes to soften. Return bean threads and add to sauce. Turn fire up and cook about 5 min. Do not overcook because it gets gooey.

Cheryl's note: I wrote this as it was dictated to my mother from grandma (Theodora) as she was illiterate, Cheryl.

---

[47] **lobar pneumonia** - pneumonia affecting one or more lobes of the lung; commonly due to streptococcal infection

HUSBAND OF TEODORA SILVÁN MARTIN
JOHN SOUZA BENTO
9 July 1897 - 17 October 1973

John Souza was born July 10, 1897 in Hanamaulu, Kauai in the Territory of Hawaii to parents who emigrated from Portugal to Hawaii in the late 1800s. His mother was María Bento Perreira, born in 1860 and his father was John Souza, Sr. born in 1855. His father died in Kilauea, Kauai, Hawaii. His mother migrated to California to join her sons based on a ship manifest of her arrival. They had three sons, Manuel (1883), Joe (1885) and John twelve years later. (1897) Could there have been births between Joe and John who did not survive? María was 37 when John was born.

It is assumed that the original Souza family worked in the sugar plantations of Hawaii after emigrating from Portugal with other family members and settled around Kauai based on several census lists from 1920 near Kilauea and a family story near Kapaá, a little farther south on the same island.

In the early years, the Souza boys worked in the sugar fields with their father. When John was a young man, he injured his leg badly with a machete during the cane cutting season. The leg was slow to heal and his leg never completely returned to normal. His conspicuous limp did not go unnoticed by the plantation owner, who asked him to work with the horses on the plantation, removing him from the fields. John was glad for the change, even though he had to walk about ½ mile to the main house every day. Being near horses was a much quieter and peaceful life compared to the cane fields with the dust, heat, sweat and stink. Every morning, he limped into the barns and greeted his charges. Feeding, watering, brushing, checking their feet and generally just maintaining the horse's overall needs was a job he considered worthy and admirable. After saddling the beautiful animals for his bosses to tour the sugar cane fields, [48]he shoveled, swept and generally mucked out stalls, making everything tidy until they returned from the fields. Then John wiped them down, brushed them again and returned them to clean stalls. He was one of several horse handlers and took his job very seriously. As they ate their oats and drank from the troughs, he headed back home again with his head held high. His leg healed and his limp lessened.

The Lihue Plantation was near Kapaá on the island of Kauai. The Kauai Historical Museum holds very interesting archives and photographs. See info@konglungkauai.com and additional story in later pages of this biography.

According to his WWII Registration Card, John Souza later worked at the Kilauea Sugar Plantation Company in Kilauea on the north shore of Kauai by July 30, 1918. John listed his height at 5' 8" tall, medium brown hair and dark brown eyes. He listed his mother, Mary Souza Bento, as his nearest relative so I believe his father, John Souza Bento, Sr., must have been deceased by that time.

---

[48] Dora told this story to her daughter, Dorothy Souza Petersen

John began courting Theodora, a young woman from the Spanish camp nearby, a woman he'd known for some time because the ethnic communities often spent time together in group entertainment and shared music-filled meals. The Silváns and Souzas spent a lot of time together during the growing season and shared vegetables and the fruits of their gardening labor.

The women often met in quilting circles, baking together, watching over the other children; it appeared to be a community unto their own. The older generation frowned on mixing the blood between ethnic communities, but it did not deter John. He procured both parent's permission and they became betrothed. By the spring of 1919[49], he married Teodora Silván Martin in St. Sylvester's Church in Kilauea.[50]

Their early married life is unknown other than the birth of their first child, Josephine in the spring of 1920. A census dated January 1920 shows their residence in Kilauea, Kauai.

It is believed that the Souza family wanted to immigrate to America to make a better life; their friends and some family members who had previously sailed to California from the islands encouraged and invited them to California, writing about their lives there.

John's older brothers had families with children ranging in ages from one and fifteen, eight in all. Mary Souza wanted to live near her children and grandchildren, so the group prepared to make another mass exodus just as the Silván family had ten years earlier from Spain. The Souza family left Portugal in the late 1800s. It was time to move again.

---

[49] This date is based on baptismal records for children of Manuel and Joe Souza who list godparents in couples except for John, who appeared to be single on March 15, 1919 and Josephine was born April 4, 1920.

[50] This is the church listed on six baptismal records for the Souza Bento family, so the church as the venue for their wedding is based on that documentation. No marriage records could be found at the Roman Catholic Church in the State of Hawaii's Chancery Office in Honolulu, the archdiocese in Kauai, or the vital statistic records.

John, Theodora and Josephine were the first to leave the islands.

Though the last name was listed as "Bento" – the name was changed to Souza upon arrival. I have found no records to indicate where the Bento name originated in this family so I can only assume the name rules are similar to Spanish = Souza was John's father's paternal name and Bento must have been his mother's paternal name. John Souza, Sr.'s secondary name is unknown by this writing but based on these naming rules it is safe to assume Maria's name was Maria Perreira (also seen noted as Pereira) Bento. (Copy of this census available upon request)

In May of 1921, just two months later, his brother, Joe Souza Bento and Maria Rosa (Pacheco) followed with their children, John and Joe, Jr. along with Manuel (Manuel's son/Joe's godson.)

The SS VENEZUELA left the Honolulu harbor on May 10, 1921 and arrived in San Francisco on May 18th. No destination city is listed on the ship's manifest like many others so we can only assume they were also destined for Oakland like his brothers and mother. The birth cities for Joe, his wife and all the children are listed as Honolulu but I believe that was their ship's port, not their birth city. All the other brothers and family members were born in Kilauea or Hanamaulu.

The baptismal records[51] I received shows a son named Luiz Bento born April 18, 1911 to Manuel Souza Bento and Crescéncia Pereira[52]. His godfather is Joe Souza Bento and godmother is Francisca Romualdo. He is not found on any ship's manifest which leads me to believe he may have died in Hawaii.

---

[51] See end of this chapter for copies of baptismal records for the Souza Bento children

[52] Perreira and Pereira are spellings I found on differing documents. Also, I questioned the name and wondered about the relationship between Maria Perreira (the mother) and Christina Pereira who married her son, Manuel.

Their widowed mother, Maria de Souza Bento sailed on the SS GOLDEN STATE from Honolulu harbor on May 11, 1921. She was 60 years old and it is unknown if she traveled with a friend or family member according to this ship's manifest and my knowledge of her extended family. Her final destination was listed as Oakland.

LIST OF UNITED STATES CITIZENS
(FOR THE IMMIGRATION AUTHORITIES)

Family Name	Given Name	Age	Sex	If native of United States give date and place of birth or turn annexed.	If naturalized, give name and location of court and date of papers	Address in United States
Souza Bento	Manuel	27	M	Garapuzdo Açui Jan 13 1894		Oakland Cal
Souza Bento	Christine	23	F	-"- Mar 14 1869		"
Evans Bento	Olivia	14	F	-"- May 30 1907		"
Souza Bento	Dewn	12	F	Kilauea Kauai Mar 3 1909		"
Souza Bento	Mary	9	F	-"- Mar 1 1914		"
Souza Bento	Bertha	4	M	-"- Mar 3 1917		"
Souza Bento	Margaret	1	F	-"- Aug 23 1920		"
Le Medina	Juan	53	M	Vizcain Mish Feb 18 1868		San Francisco
Cigarn	David	32	M	Las Torte D 1 Oct 16 1901		"
Ghogami	Manno		M	Maui 1 R Oct 11 1903		"
Austral	Lagano	14	M	San Juan P 1 Se t 7 1893		Waipehu Cal
Cigile	Maria	33	F	San Jose Porto Rico Mar 28 1888		"
Cigile	Raymond	10	M	Lau 1 R June 28 1901		"
Cigile	William	8	M	Kauai 1 R Dec 8 1908		"
Cigile	Pedro	7	M	Honolulu 1 R July 7 1914		"
Cigile	Pietro	32	M	Orfield P 1 Jan 27 1908		"

Four months later, Manuel Souza Bento and Crescéncia (Pereira) with their five children, Olivia, Rosa, Mary, Sophie and Margaret followed them to California aboard the SS EMPIRE STATE, leaving the Honolulu September 19, 1921 and arriving in San Francisco on September 25th. Their destination was Oakland. Afterward, they had two more children; Irene in 1924, Alfred in 1925.

Life in the close-knit Spanish community for Dora and John consisted of family gatherings and dance clubs. The local Spanish Club offered dances and dinners and despite the fact that Dora was not musically inclined and John's leg injury kept them off the dance floor at times, they enjoyed watching others. Although a quiet man, he made a few friends in the city, particularly a Portuguese man named Seraphim (Joe) Medeiros. It was at one of these dances they introduced Alice to Joe.

Nine years after their arrival, John Souza and his family are shown on the April 7, 1930 Census in Oakland, Alameda County, California. John was earning $3,500 per year and the family's address was 1428 - 99th Avenue in Oakland. It lists John (32), Dora (31), Josephine (10), Victor (8), Alfred (6), George (5), Dorothy (3) and Lillian (1/12, one month old).

My interview with John and Dora's daughter, Dorothy, included several memories; her father did not have a car until the children were older and he was a lumber grader at a wood mill. She could not remember her parents drinking much alcohol except for a glass of wine now and then and possibly during social gatherings and family functions.

Her father was distant and sometimes harsh with his children. The old country way of raising children did not include nurturing from their fathers. This often left scars on the children in later life as I heard in several stories from his descendants.

Others said he was just very quiet, sometimes barely talking at all. Nobody seemed to know the reason why.

Dora Silván Souza, John Souza Bento and Alice Silván Medeiros

When John Souza was 70 years old, he wanted to take Lillian, Josephine and Dorothy to Kauai to visit the place where he worked and lived in Hawaii. Lillian was living in Paris while her husband was stationed in the Navy so she couldn't go. Dorothy said the village was called Hanamaulu. I found it on a map just south of Kapaá on Kauai. John told them the Lihue Plantation was near an old country store and was happy it was still standing.

When he took his daughters inside the store, he was stunned when the old man remembered John. He remembered John Souza using a walking stick and limping from a machete injury on the plantation.

I must add one of the sweeter memories from one of his grandchildren, Cheryl Souza Edwards:

"My grandfather was a man of few words or no words at all. I remember after he retired, he spent his time gardening and would nap on an old covered swing with his pet rabbit on his chest. What made this memorable was that my grandparents always raised chickens and rabbits for food when the kids were growing up. He probably always loved his rabbits, but food was a necessity. I remember it sleeping and glad he got some pleasure from it then.

John Souza died just after his 77th birthday and is buried in Hayward at the Holy Sepulchre Cemetery. He died of a coronary thrombosis, a blood clot to the heart at Doctor's Hospital in San Leandro, Alameda County, California on October 17, 1973, just a few months after his brother in law, Joe Medeiros.

"Blessed are they that mourn: for they shall be comforted."
—St. Matt. V. 5

†

My Jesus have mercy on the Soul of
John Souza
October 17, 1973

PRAYER

LORD, make me an instrument of Your peace. Where there is hatred, let me sow love; where there is injury, pardon; where there is doubt, faith; where there is despair, hope; where there is darkness, light; and where there is sadness, joy.

O, DIVINE MASTER, grant that I may not so much seek to be consoled as to console; to be understood as to understand; to be loved as to love, for it is in giving that we receive; it is in pardoning that we are pardoned; and it is in dying that we are born to eternal life.

Santos - Robinson
160 Estudillo Ave.,
San Leandro, California

Outline Descendant Report for John Souza Bento

```
    1 John Souza Bento b: 1855 in , Portugal, d: Kilauea, Kauai, Hawaii
    + Maria Perreira b: 1860 in , Portugal
        2 Manuel Souza Bento b: 23 Jan 1883 in Hanamaulu, Kauai, Hawaii Territory, d: 03 Feb 1936
            in Oakland, California, USA
        + Christina Perreira b: 01 Aug 1889 in Honolulu, Hawaii, USA, d: 20 Oct 1937 in Oakland,
            California, USA
            3 Manuel Souza Bento b: 15 Jan 1906 in Hawaii, d: 17 Oct 1983 in Alameda, California
            + Beatriz Refugio de la Pena
            3 Olivia Souza Bento b: 14 May 1907 in Kauai, Hawaii
            + Richard Ferreira
            3 Rosa Souza Bento b: 03 Sep 1909 in Kauai, Hawaii
            + Arthur George Moniz
            3 Mary Souza Bento b: 01 Mar 1916 in Kauai, Hawaii
            + Andrew Ginnie
            3 Sophia Souza Bento b: 07 May 1917 in Kauai, Hawaii, d: 27 Jul 1995 in Alameda,
                California, USA
            + David Rodriques Gonzales b: 21 Dec 1915 in Hilo, Hawaii, USA, m: 31 Jul 1937 in
                Oakland, California, USA, d: 18 Jan 1991 in Alameda, California, USA
            3 Margaret Souza Bento b: 23 Aug 1920 in Kauai, Hawaii
            + Elwood Perry
            3 Irene Souza Bento b: 1924 in Oakland, Alameda County, CA
            + Harry Matthews
            3 Alfred Richard Bento b: 17 May 1928 in Oakland, Alameda County, CA
        2 Joe Souza Bento b: 27 Apr 1885 in , Hawaii
        + Mary Pacheco b: 10 Jan 1890 in , Hawaii
            3 John Souza Bento b: 12 Jan 1916 in Kauai, Hawaii
            3 Joe Souza Bento b: 19 Jul 1918 in Kauai, Hawaii
        2 John Souza Bento b: 10 Jul 1897 in Kauai, Hawaii, d: 17 Oct 1973 in Oakland, Alameda
            County, CA
        + Theodora Flesa Silvan b: 06 Sep 1899 in Fuentesaúco, Zamora, Castilla-Leon, Spain, d: 24
            Jul 1991 in Pleasanton, Alameda County, CA
            3 Josephine Souza b: 04 Feb 1920 in , Hawaii, d: 16 Nov 1996 in San Jose, Santa Clara,
                California, USA
            + Lazetera
            3 Victor John Souza b: 25 Jun 1921 in Oakland, Alameda County, CA, d: 01 Oct 1986 in
                San Jose, Santa Clara, California, USA
            + Charlotte Louise Sanford
            3 Alfred Souza
            3 George Souza b: 24 Jul 1925 in Oakland, Alameda County, CA
            3 Dorothy Souza b: 20 Mar 1927 in Oakland, Alameda County, CA
            3 Lillian Souza b: 26 Mar 1930 in Oakland, Alameda County, CA
```

The baptismal records[53] for several of the Souza Bento third generation children are shown on the next pages. Source: Catholic Church archives in Kauai, Hawaii. It appears that the Souza men used their father's maternal surname, BENTO. So, there are many Bento Souza family members. His mother was Bento Perreira and some men kept the Souza name, others used the Bento name. One ship's manifest listed Theodora as "Bento". She must have been bewildered in America when her paperwork was changed again = to Souza.

---

[53] NOTE: John's brother, Manuel Souza, was also born in Hanamaulu, Hawaii on 23 January 1884. He married Crescéncia Pereira about 1906 and their first child, Olivia, was born in 1907. The Souza family lived in Hanamaulu until they moved to Kilauea when their daughter, Rosa, was born in 1909 in Kilauea and no other child is documented that I could find again until 1 March, 1916, when Maria was born. Manuel and Crescéncia's children born in Kilauea, Kauai in 1909, 1916, 1917 and 1920 leads to the question of whether she had babies born who died between that six year time period. The only child who did not appear on the ship manifest was Luiz, born n 1911. So, that means from Luiz's birth in April of 1911, the next child wasn't born until Maria five years later.

NAME BENTO, Olivia de Souza

BAPTISM REF. 4/11/319
Date of Birth: May 24, 1907 — Place of Birth: Kilauea, Kauai
Date of Bapt.: May 23, 1907 — Place of Bapt.: St. Sylvester, Kilauea
Father: Manuel Souza Bento — Mother: Christina Pereira
Sponsors: Antonio Pacheco — and Luxandrinta Pacheco
Remarks: (Looks like "Oliver" in record, but request confirm "Olivia", Nov.13,'e — Priest: Fr. Julian Thiempont

FIRST COMMUNION REF. Date — Place

CONFIRMATION REF. Date — Conf. Name
Bishop — Place
— Sponsor

MARRIAGE REF. with — Priest
Date — Place
Witnesses — and
Remarks

DEATH REF. Date of Death — Place of Death
Date of Burial — Place of Burial

NAME BENTO, MARIA

BAPTISM REF. 4/20/593
Date of Birth: March 2, 1916 — Place of Birth: Kilauea, Kauai, Hawaii
Date of Bapt.: March 5, 1915 — Place of Bapt.: St. Sylvester's, Kilauea
Father: Manuel Souza Bento — Mother: Christina Ferreira
Sponsor: Joe Souza Bento — and Francisca Romaldo
Remarks — Priest: Fr. James, SS.CC.

FIRST COMMUNION REF. Date — Place

CONFIRMATION REF. Date: Sept. 21, 1919 — Conf. Name
Bishop: Libert Boeynaems, SS.CC. — Place
— Sponsor

MARRIAGE REF. with — Priest
Date — Place
Witnesses — and
Remarks

DEATH REF. Date of Death — Place of Death
Date of Burial — Place of Burial

NAME BENTO, MARGARET SOUZA

BAPTISM REF. 4/25/758
Date of Birth: July 11, 1920 — Place of Birth: Kilauea, Kauai, Hawaii
Date of Bapt.: July 18, 1920 — Place of Bapt.: St. Sylvester's, Kilauea
Father: Manuel Souza Bento — Mother: Christina Ferreira
Sponsors: Ben Iida — and Mary Iida
Remarks — Priest: Father Hubert Klijn, SS.CC.

FIRST COMMUNION REF. Date — Place

CONFIRMATION REF. Date — Conf. Name
Bishop — Place
— Sponsor

MARRIAGE REF. with — Priest
Date — Place
Witnesses — and
Remarks

DEATH REF. Date of Death — Place of Death
Date of Burial — Place of Burial

NAME BENTO, MANUEL

BAPTISM REF. 4/10/286
Date of Birth: January 15, 1906 — Place of Birth: Kilauea, Kauai
Date of Bapt.: February 4, 1906 — Place of Bapt.: St. Sylvester, Kilauea
Father: Manuel Souza Bento — Mother: Christina Pereira
Sponsors: Joao Cosmo — and Maria Cosmo
Remarks — Priest: Father Adalbert, SS.CC.

FIRST COMMUNION REF. Date — Place

CONFIRMATION REF. Date — Conf. Name
Bishop — Place
— Sponsor

MARRIAGE REF. with — Priest
Date — Place
Witnesses — and
Remarks

DEATH REF. Date of Death — Place of Death
Date of Burial — Place of Burial

NAME BENTO, LUIZ
BAPTISM REF. 4/14/415
Date of Birth   April 13, 1921   Place of Birth   Kilauea, Kauai
Date of Bapt.   April 22, 1921   Place of Bapt.   St. Sylvester, Kilauea
Father   Manuel Sousa Bento   Mother   Christina Pereira
Sponsors   Joe Sousa Bento   and   Francisca Romualdo
Remarks   Priest   Father Hermann, SS.CC.

FIRST COMMUNION REF.
Date   Place

CONFIRMATION REF.
Date   Conf. Name
Bishop   Place
                                            Sponsor

MARRIAGE REF.
with   Priest
Date   Place
Witnesses   and
Remarks

DEATH REF.
Date of Death   Place of Death
Date of Burial   Place of Burial

NAME BENTO, JOSE DE SOUZA
BAPTISM REF. 4/23/712
Date of Birth   March 2, 1919   Place of Birth   Kilauea, Kauai, Hawaii
Date of Bapt.   March 15, 1919   Place of Bapt.   St. Sylvester's, Kilauea
Father   Jose de Sousa Bento   Mother   Maria Rosa Pacheco
Sponsors   John Sousa Bento   and   Francisca Romualdo
Remarks   Priest   Fr. Hubert Mlija, SS.CC.

FIRST COMMUNION REF.
Date   Place

CONFIRMATION REF.
Date   Sept. 21, 1919   Conf. Name
Bishop   Libert Boeynaems, SS.CC.   Place   St. Sylvester's, Kilauea
                                            Sponsor

MARRIAGE REF.
with   Priest
Date   Place
Witnesses   and
Remarks

DEATH REF.
Date of Death   Place of Death
Date of Burial   Place of Burial

NAME BENTO, ROSA SOUZA
BAPTISM REF. 4/13/376
Date of Birth   September 4, 1909   Place of Birth   Kilauea, Kauai
Date of Bapt.   October 3, 1909   Place of Bapt.   St. Sylvester, Kilauea
Father   Manuel Sousa Bento   Mother   Christina Pereira
Sponsors   Joao Sousa Bento   and   Francisca Romualdo
Remarks   Priest   Father Julien, SS.CC.

FIRST COMMUNION REF.
Date   Place

CONFIRMATION REF.
Date   Conf. Name
Bishop   Place
                                            Sponsor

MARRIAGE REF.
with   Priest
Date   Place
Witnesses   and
Remarks

DEATH REF.
Date of Death   Place of Death
Date of Burial   Place of Burial

NAME BENTO, SOPHIA SOUZA
BAPTISM REF. 4/21/441
Date of Birth   March 7, 1917   Place of Birth   Kilauea, Kauai, Hawaii
Date of Bapt.   March 11, 1917   Place of Bapt.   St. Sylvester's, Kilauea
Father   Manuel Sousa Bento   Mother   Christina Pereira
Sponsors   Manuel Aguilar   and   Philomena Aguilar
Remarks   Priest   Fr. Juano, SS.CC.

FIRST COMMUNION REF.
Date   Place

CONFIRMATION REF.
Date   Sept. 21, 1919   Conf. Name
Bishop   Libert Boeynaems, SS.CC.   Place   St. Sylvester's, Kilauea
                                            Sponsor

MARRIAGE REF.
with   Priest
Date   Place
Witnesses   and
Remarks

DEATH REF.
Date of Death   Place of Death
Date of Burial   Place of Burial

FELISA (Alice) SILVÁN MARTIN (MEDEIROS)
November 6, 1904 - December 10, 1991
Married: Seraphim Andrew Medeiros

Felisa loved to dance. She was born at 10:00 a.m. in Fuentesaúco, Province of Zamora, Spain to Victorino Luciano Silván Hernández and Romana Martin Lorenzo on November 6, 1904, the second of four children. Her older sister was Teodora Silván Martin and her younger brothers were twins, Jacinto and Celestino Silván Martin.

She was seven years old when it was decided early in January, 1911 to emigrate from Spain. The short train ride was a curious adventure. The long walk afterward wasn't. But it was the only way the families could afford the travel necessary to reach La Linea in the south to Gibraltar where the ship waited.

The SS ORTERIC sailed from Spain at Gibraltar February 24, 1911 carrying her family, her uncle Juan Silván Hernández, aunt Rita, their children, aunt Crescéncia Silván, uncle Felix Gonzales and their boys. Also aboard were Martin family, cousins that included Juliana Martin.

She learned at a very young age how fragile life could be; on the ship, her little brother, Jacinto, contracted the measles and died during the voyage from Spain. Her heart ached when she learned he would be dropped into the choppy ocean; she was numbed by the burial at sea. Within a couple of weeks, her two-year old cousin, Simon Martin, followed her brother into his own watery grave.

Felisa spent the next ten years in Hawaii as her family worked in the sugar plantations. She haltingly began to read and write. She was excited to learn. Her cousin, Manuela, lasted one day but that's another story.[54]

Felisa always loved music and dancing, often tap...tap... tapping her feet when uncle Juan Silván and others played their instruments. She ached to dance la jota with the older girls, rarely keeping still when uncle Juan's drum beat out music. Her mother, Ramona, watched and smiled. She loved dancing also and knew her second daughter had music in her blood. After arriving in Hawaii, she

Ancestry.com - Honolulu, Hawaii, Passenger Lists, 1900-1953   Page 1 of

ancestry

Honolulu, Hawaii, Passenger Lists, 1900-1953

Name:	Feliza Silban Martinez
Age:	7
Gender:	Female
Birth Year:	abt 1904
Port of Departure:	Gibraltar
Departure Date:	24 Feb 1911
Ship:	Orteric
Port of Arrival:	Honolulu, Hawaii
Arrival Date:	13 Apr 1911
Ethnicity/Race/Nationality:	Spanish
Last Residence:	Spain

and her mother swooned over the native music and watched the new dance, the Hula. Felisa wanted to learn all the dances!

The Silván family lived in several villages as her father worked in the sugar plantations of Oahu and Kauai. By 1920, they lived near the Kilauea Sugar Plantation on the north coast of Kauai

---

[54] See Manuela Silván Trascasas

in Hanalei, Waianae County in the Territory of Hawaii. It would be a place she would always carry fond memories of.

With her parents, she and her brother sailed into San Francisco harbor sometime after June 1920[55], before her sister, Teodora and family left Hawaii. Felisa was sixteen years old. Her aunts and uncles and many cousins had already left the islands in January of 1918 and she was anxious to see them again.

Once in California, it wasn't long before she figured out the new land was not like Spain or Hawaii. Being a Spaniard appeared low class; she was disturbed by the way people treated her. When she began school in America at age 16, she felt her foreignness. The teacher, hoping to assimilate the immigrants into American culture, changed her name from Felisa to Alice, the English equivalent, so she became Alice.

By then, Alice stood 5 feet, 3 inches tall. She had large cocoa-brown eyes and an oval face framed by chestnut-colored hair with a small scar on her left cheek.

With great sadness, she had to drop out of school after elementary classes to pick fruit and later work in the cannery to earn money for their family. They wanted a house of their own, so she and Celestino worked hard to earn money for the family.

After a time, their dream was realty. Victorino and Ramona bought a large white house at 214 Dabner Street in San Leandro, California. The street was lined with old Victorian houses with wonderful verandahs surrounded by porch railings that could be reached after climbing a bank of steps. It was comfortable, clean and cozy. (It is unknown how Victorino earned money during his short life in California).

---

[55] Documents show them on the 1920 census in Hanelei, Kauai, but I cannot find the ship manifest showing them sailing from Hawaii to California. It is only through family stories that we know they settled in San Leandro, Alameda, California.

When Alice was about eighteen, her sister, Teodora, and brother in law invited her to a dance hall in Oakland. John Souza introduced his sister-in-law to his friend, Seraphim "Joe" Medeiros. Joe was quite popular with the other ladies and Alice was attracted to him at once. He was a good dancer and her feet tapped the floor and itched to be on the dance floor.... She danced the entire evening with Joe.

Soon afterward, when Joe traveled from his home in Oakland to visit Alice in San Leandro, her mother, Ramona Silván, sat in a corner of the room where they chatted. When he left, she told her daughter the man was not welcome at their home because his skin was too dark; he was Portuguese, after all.

But Joe was in love. And he did not allow Ramona Silván's announcement keep him away. Alice Silván knew Joe Medeiros was the man for her.

After a persistent two year courtship, Joe married Alice on May 5, 1924 in Alameda County.

Dora and their cousin, Manuela were witnesses in their finery.[56] It is unknown who was best man for

---

[56] The dress that her cousin, Manuela Silvan Trascasas (Ruiz) wore in Felisa's wedding currently hangs in her daughter's (Millie) closet in Woodland, California, still pristine and beautiful.

John Souza or his attendants.

Joe and Alice rented a little house in Oakland on the property of a Jewish Cemetery on Fairfax Avenue. The newlyweds welcomed their first child, Melvin Andrew Medeiros on June 2, 1925.

Felisa couldn't quite believe the blessings she received in the tiny little boy.

Photo: Alice with son, Melvin.

Her joy dimmed as her father grew more frail, his health condition worsening. By the time Mel was six months old, Victorino Silván died of a lung abscess and was buried in St. Mary's Cemetery. The funeral was held at their church, Saint Leander.

Five months later, just three days before Melvin's first birthday, his baby brother, Jerome Stanley Medeiros was born May 30, 1926.

She and Joe were happy and both doted on their boys. It is said their marriage was quite different compared to her older sister's.

Maybe it was the music? As a child, Felisa felt music flow through her and that musicality bloomed during her life in Hawaii whenever dancing or music was nearby. She couldn't keep her feet still and during the Roaring 1920s she and Joe could jive with the best of them. When everyone sat down to huff and puff, Felisa and Joe laughed and finished out the dance.

They often traveled two hours north to the Gonzales ranch in Winters to visit her aunt Christina Gonzales, uncle Felix and her cousins, uncle John Silván, aunt Rita and their children. They enjoyed big family gatherings at the Gonzales ranch and danced for hours as children slept, piled in corners to sleep the night away.

LEFT: This is a photo of Alice at the Gonzales Ranch. Felisa stands between Marie and Sally Gonzales, who were ten and seven years younger than she was. The cousins loved to dress up and oftentimes, María and Sally dressed alike, just as this photo shows.

BELOW: Alice at Gonzales Ranch in Winters with her sons and Gonzales cousins: María, Sally, Felisa (Mel and Jerome), Lena (Red Gonzales's first wife), Victoria, Theresa and Alfred "Dutch"

April 7, 1930 Census in San Leandro, California lists S. Medeiros, Alice, Jerome and Melvin (spelled Medora) with Romana and Celestino Silva(n) at 214 Dabner Street.[57]   In the mid 1930s, Alice and Joe bought property and Joe built her dream house at 4723 Fairfax Avenue in Oakland; a wonderful Spanish adobe-style, tri-level home where they raised both of their sons. They lived a few houses (4639 Fairfax Avenue) from Manuel Medeiros, (Joe's brother) and his wife, Shandra and two children, Raymond and Velma.

---

[57] It is Lynda Medeiros Ely and my assumption the Medeiros family lived with her mother, Ramona, and brother, Celestino, while their new home was being built on Fairfax Avenue.

LEFT: Mel has his arm around a cousin, a Souza cousin or a Gonzales cousin? Jerome Medeiros is sitting on the ground with their dog.Below: Melvin and Jerome Medeiros

Left to right: Melvin, Alice and Jerome 1936, Oakland, Alameda, California

World War II erupted and the world was in panic mode. Joe and Felisa managed to keep their jobs and their house, while war raged. They learned to live on less rubber, sugar, flour and nylons. Each family member received a Ration Book. She made it work for the boys through their high school years

and beyond.

Alice longed to become an American Citizen, BE American so she attended school and passed the citizenship test. On July 12, 1943 at age 38, she proudly received Certificate #73525 of Naturalization; an American citizen at last. Her sons were 17 and 18 years old.

A MONTH LATER, Felisa's first-born son, Melvin (Mel), enlisted in the U.S. Army on the 27th of August, 1943. In the midst of World War II, he soon earned the rank of PFC. Here is a photograph of PFC Melvin Medeiros standing next to his tiny abuela, Ramona (Martin) Silván.

MEL WAS KILLED in the Philippines less than two years later on April 27, 1945. He is buried in a military cemetery: Golden Gate Cemetery, 1300 Sneath Lane, San Bruno, CA 94066 in Section B, Site 473.

http://www.cem.va.gov/CEM/cems/nchp/goldengate.asp

Family information stated he died in combat in the Philippines so I researched his company and found the Battle of Manila was between February 3, 1945 and March 3, 1945. Mel died April 27. I believe he was injured and died two months later from those injuries. However, there is nothing to document this theory. The end of the particular battle brought America's control over the Philippines but sporadic fighting continued so Mel may have taken part in those military bouts.

Alice was devastated and never got over his death. What parent could? However, she was tenacious and strong; she forced one foot in front of the other. She had a husband to take care of; one who grieved along with her. And she had her younger son, Jerome, whom she focused on with ferocious mother love.

The following year, Jerome was besotted. When he brought Dorothy Felipa George to meet his family the first time, Alice was dumbstruck. She latched onto the girl and stared into her face.

"Is your mother's name Juliana?" she asked the girl urgently.

Juliana. The cousin and best friend who'd sailed on the SS ORTERIC with her family all those years ago. She saw Juliana Martin in the girl's face. And indeed it was. Juliana was Dorothy's mother. Felisa could hardly believe the wonder of finding her after thirty five years.

When Dorothy Filipa George came into her son's life and married him in 1946, it salved a bit of Felisa's brutal grief after losing Mel. Her aunt Christina Gonzales had just died also and Dorothy brought love and joy into the Martin family again. Juliana. She must have smiled, remembering how they'd played with each other as young girls; a melancholy reunion.[58] (Felisa Martin Silván and Juliana Martin Sesmilo were both born in Fuentesaúco, Spain.)[59]

And soon, she would be blessed with grandchildren. When Dorothy became pregnant, Felisa told her and Jerome if they brought home a little girl, she would pay the hospital bill. And she did. Lynda Diane Medeiros was the first child and only girl. Five sons followed; Melvin A., Martie G. and Montie[60], (twins), Ronnie J. and Johnny A. Medeiros.

Alice was grandmother to more children than just Jerome's; When Dorothy married Jerome, she brought a wealth of family along with her; her sister, Nellie George and her brothers. Dorothy's niece, Julie Elliott, (her sister Nellie's daughter) told me she loved Felisa as her grandmother and called her "Lita" which was short for abuelita, which means grandma. And of course, Joe was called "Lito" for the same reason, abuelito.

---

[58] See the story in *A Girl Immigrant*, a story about the Silván's trek from Spain to Hawaii and on to California

[59] Maria Dovales Alejo and Angel Silván Martin were Victorino Silván Hernandez's grandparents. They were also Juliana Martin Sesmilo's maternal grandparents. Source: Document for Enrique Martin used for immigration purposes dated January 24, 1911 listing children, Antonia, Juliana, Maria and Simon. Yes, they were cousins.

[60] Martie's twin, Monte, died as a baby

Alice spent a lot of time in her kitchen. She loved cooking and sharing dishes with guests; potato omelets (aka Tortilla Española) fava beans[61], garbanzo bean soup and especially Torrone candy[62]. On Sundays, with as many family members who could fit at the table, noodle soup first, then the beans etc, and a tiny glass of wine to wash it down. And don't forget the Olla.[63] And then there was Felisa's baking! No processed foods for her. She baked from scratch and rarely used a recipe! *Pineapple Upside Down Cake* was her son's favorite so she baked it for Jerome often. For her only granddaughter, Lynda, she baked *Lemon Meringue Pie*. For her grandsons, she baked huge *Chocolate Chip Cookies*. For Joe, she baked whatever he asked for.

When asked for recipes from some of the older Spanish women, including Juliana Martin, they were instructed through words and hand motions. The older generation couldn't write and didn't use recipes. "You'll know it is ready when it smells like it's ready" was a common direction.

Soap operas? Yes! Felisa was hooked on *All My Children*. Watching the soap probably helped her English as she rarely missed an episode.

---

[61] Fava beans are more Portuguese, but my Lito used to grow them in his garden. They are long (like 12 inch) pod beans. You have to shuck them and then boil the hell out of the beans with garlic and olive oil, and then you cool them and pop the beans out of their skins into your mouth. See recipe in THE GIRL IMMIGRANT book.

[62] Torrone is a delicious almond/nougat candy that is sort of like divinity. It's made in sheet pans, covered in edible rice paper, flavored with almond extract, chock full of almonds

[63] "My Lita (Juliana Martin) made "olla" or as we called it "cheechees" frequently. Again, I don't have a recipe, but I'll get it from my mom. It's basically a soup made with garbanzos, beef shanks, salt pork, fideo pasta, and a "tortilla" made from bread, garlic, eggs, and parsley fried and then reheated in the broth." Source: Julie Elliott.

And they always loved to dance! They often attended Holy Ghost celebration dances and once a month found them at various retirement parties at the General Motors plant, where Joe worked for many years. They danced their way through dance clubs. A cousin, Victorina Silván Gonzales Weber, remembers when Joe and Felisa came to their house in Winters, California. Music blared. She and her sisters (Sally and Marie), watched Alice jump up, reach for Joe's outstretched hand and say, "Come on, Saa[64]. Let's show them how it's done."

The gardens surrounding Alice and Joe's home in Oakland were always alight with color. She spent hours outside with her rhododendrons, roses, azaleas and philodendrons. She inherited her love of gardening and green thumb from the Silváns. In Spain, gardens fed them. In Hawaii, their small garden plots were shared with the Silván siblings; each child had their special little corner to grow what they wanted. Flowering trees, olives, grape vines and other flowers adorned the family's surroundings always; it was definitely in their Spanish blood.

Felisa's big catch!

But besides cooking, soap operas, dancing, gardening and children, she loved to fish, a pastime Joe introduced her to...

1968 was a terrible year; another tragic death. Felisa's daughter in law, Dorothy Felipa George Medeiros died of breast

---

[64] Saa was a nickname remembered by his granddaughter, Lynda Ely and Felisa's cousin, Victorina Gonzales. Neither knows where it originated but both remember him being called "Saa" rhyming with "Baa"..

cancer. Grief besieged her and Joe for the loss of a good woman and for the pain that overwhelmed their son and his children.

Then, on March 29, 1973, when Felisa was 69 years old, she became a widow when her beloved Joe died just after his 72nd birthday. He is interred in Oakland at the Holy Sepulchre Mausoleum. She sold the house on Fairfax Street some time afterward because she didn't want to live in their big house alone. In 1994, she lived at 8100 Hague Way in Elverta, California.

As it happened, her sister's husband, John Souza, died seven months later. The sisters had already drifted apart; when their mother died in 1955, they had a disagreement that was never resolved. Alice's granddaughter thinks it was because both girls wanted Ramona's belongings. A particular item of contention was a large trunk; it started its life in Fuentesaúco, bumped along the train tracks through Spain, road the waves in the ORTERIC and later held their possessions all the way to California. An empty trunk filled with nostalgia. After the uproar, Celestino gave the trunk to Alice's only granddaughter, Lynda, and there it resides. Others[65] believed the sisters became estranged after their brother, Celestino, died. Both stories may be true and both stories may surround this wonderful old trunk.

When Alice Silván Hernández Medeiros died on December 10, 1991 in Alameda County, she was buried near her husband, Joe, in the Holy Sepulchre Mausoleum in unit 142-5A.[66]

---

[65] Source: Dorothy Souza Petersen
[66] The cemetery document lists her maiden name at "Sylban" and her mother's maiden name as Martin.

HUSBAND OF FELISA SILVÁN MARTIN:
SERAPHIM (JOE) ANDREWS MEDEIROS
12 March 1901 – 29 March 1973

Joe Medeiros loved to dance and spent many years proving it. He was born March 12, 1901 in the Territory of Hawaii to parents who emigrated from Portugal to Hawaii in the late 1800s. I was also told "Joe" was Filipino but I found no documents to prove his birth in either country. I am told he was born in Kaia, Hawaii but researching the town name lists only baby's names.

Joe bought property on Fairfax Avenue and proceeded to build Felisa her dream house, a Spanish adobe tri-level home to raise their sons.

His granddaughter, Lynda, said Joe loved baseball; he played ball for many years on a semi-pro team in San Leandro sponsored by the Risdon Bakery. He often took his sons, Melvin and Jerome, to the baseball park to watch their father play ball, making it a family affair.

Seraphim Medeiros - SemiPro 1920-30s

Joe Medeiros also loved to fish and shared his enjoyment with Felisa. They were always off on fishing trips and sometimes treated their grandchildren by taking them along.

In the early 1960s, they bought a small cabin cruiser and named it the *Lynda M.* after their only granddaughter.

He worked as an auto mechanic and later the foreman at the Durant Auto Company, a Chevrolet assembly plant. His brother, Manuel Medeiros, also worked there, supplying the west coast with automobiles.

His nephew, Fred Souza, put wheels on cars so the car rolled off the track on its own wheels. Joe Medeiros and Fred Souza did not get along very well but Fred was glad to have the job just after he was released from the US Army.

Joe is buried next to his wife at Holy Sepulchre Mausoleum. Memorial 84263848 www.findagrave.com

Seraphim (Joe) Medeiros with sons, Mel and Jerome

Descendants of Felisa Silván Martin and Seraphim "Joe"Medeiros:

Family Group Sheet for Jerome Stanley "Babe" Medeiros

Husband:		Jerome Stanley "Babe" Medeiros
	Birth:	30 May 1926 in San Leandro, Alameda, California USA
	Death:	27 Sep 2006 in Modesto, Stanislaus, California, USA
	Burial:	Hayward, Alameda County, California, USA
	Marriage:	1945 in Oakland, Alameda, California, USA
	Father:	Seraphim Andrews (Joe) Medeiros
	Mother:	Felisa (Alice) Martin Silvan
Wife:		Dorothy Filipa George
	Birth:	27 Aug 1927 in California
	Death:	27 Jan 1968 in San Lorenzo, Solano, California, USA
	Father:	Candido Isidore Jorge
	Mother:	Juliana Martin Sesmilo
Children:		
1 F	Name:	Lynda Diane Medeiros
	Birth:	30 Sep 1947 in San Lorenzo, Solano, California, USA
	Marriage:	19 Dec 1972 in Alameda, Alameda, California USA
	Spouse:	Rodger W. Ely
2 M	Name:	Melvin Andrew Medeiros
	Birth:	13 Dec 1948 in San Lorenzo, Solono, California
3 M	Name:	Montie Seraphim Medeiros
	Birth:	28 Sep 1950 in San Lorenzo, Solono, California
	Death:	08 Dec 1950 in Alameda, California
4 M	Name:	Martie G. Medeiros
	Birth:	28 Sep 1950 in San Lorenzo, Solono, California
5 M	Name:	Ronnie J. Medeiros
	Birth:	30 Jun 1957 in Alameda, California
6 M	Name:	Johnny A. Medeiros
	Birth:	14 Mar 1960 in Alameda, California

JACINTO MARTIN SILVÁN (SILBAN)
July 19, 1906 – Died between February 24th - April 14th, 1911
On the SS ORTERIC

Seal of Spain

Victorino Silván Hernández and Ramona Martin Lorenzo's youngest children were twin boys, Celestino and Jacinto. Jacinto was the first son, born at 11:00 p.m. on July 19, 1906 in Fuentesaúco, Zamora, Spain. When they left Fuentesaúco, he was four months shy of turning five years old. The brothers were inseparable and loved playing jokes on others.

He contracted measles and died on the S.S. ORTERIC during the long ocean voyage from Gibraltar to Honolulu, Hawaii. During the forty eight days at sea, many children were buried at sea, trussed up in linen shrouds and silently, prayerfully slipped over the side of the ship off a plank.

This boy's death burrowed a hole in the hearts of the Silván family as their ship trundled across an ocean seemingly without end as they tried to console each other and adjust their spirits to think of a future without little Jacinto in their midst.

No laughter or jokes between little boys filled the sleeping area or the deck of the ship after he died and the deaths kept coming. Another cousin of the Martin family succumbed shortly thereafter and he was also slid into the choppy waters of the ocean.

I found no photographs of this child. I can only assume he was a mirror image of his twin brother, Celestino. We will probably never know as no photos have surfaced in all my research the past few years. We heard the stories and as long as he is remembered, he will stay with us.

CELESTINO MARTIN SILVÁN (SILBAN)
"The Sheik"
[67]July 20, 1906 – July 1, 1983

They called him "the Sheik" around San Leandro, California because of his stark resemblance to Rudolph Valentino in the 1921 silent movie titled, The Sheik. He was soft spoken and kind.

Celestino was born one hour after his twin, Jacinto Silván, to Victorino Luciano Silván Hernández and Ramona Martin[68] just past midnight on July 20, 1906 in Fuentesaúco, Zamora, Spain. When they left Fuentesaúco, he was almost five years old. The twin brothers were very close; where you saw one, you saw the other.

Celestino Martin Silván was a shadow of himself after his twin, Jacinto, died on the S.S. ORTERIC during the long ocean voyage from Gibraltar to Honolulu, Hawaii. He must have felt lost for months and years afterward.

After the ORTERIC sailed into the port at Honolulu and the families chose the sugar plantations they would spend the next few years in Hawaii, their lives changed dramatically. Employment, schools, available medical and land to grow their own food in an

---

[67] Despite the death certificate listing birth date as July 17, the Civil Registry document from 1911 states "**Celestino Silban Martin** natural son of **Victorino Silban Hernandez** and **Romana Martin Lorenzo,** granddaughter of the aforementioned couples, was born in this village on 20 July 1906 as recorded on volume 12, page 30, column 76."

[68] Jacinto was born at 11:00 p.m. July 19, 1906, a little over an hour before Celestino

island paradise helped to add fresh air and a new peace to their loss and memories of a seaboard funeral.

Young Celestino ran barefoot, husked coconuts and ate bananas; he played with a guitar and jumped warm, turquoise waves along Kauai's beautiful, sandy beaches. And he learned at a very young age that time was money, earning wages with odd jobs for the household, keeping only a few coins. He grew from a child to a teenager in a paradise he would always remember.

His oldest sister, Theodora, married John Souza Bento, a Portuguese man who had become family friends during the plantation experiences on the island of Kauai by the spring of 1919. The following year, her baby Josephine was born on February 20, 1920 in Hanalei, Kauai.

He was delighted to be an uncle. He was thirteen years old. At that time, he lived with his parents and sister, Felisa, near the Kilauea Sugar Plantation on the north coast of Kauai in a small village called Hanalei, Waianae County in the Territory of Hawaii. His father was fifty-two years old, struggling with plantation work, often pushing himself beyond endurance. Celestino watched his father age, move slower and become ill.

His uncle Juan, aunt Rita, aunt Crescéncia and uncle Eusebio had already left Hawaii two years earlier, settling in California. He missed them and his cousins too. He was torn when talk of moving to California to join them became serious. He would miss Hawaii and knew his parents were slow to leave because Theodora and her husband, John Souza, still remained. And they disliked leaving their grandchild but Victorino's health dictated the emigration. He wanted Ramona and his children near other family members if something should happen to him. California called.

The 1930 San Leandro census lists Celestino Silva(n) 22, Ramona Silva(n) 67, Alice 24, S. Medeiros 28, and their two sons living at 214 Dabner Street House. [69]

---

[69] I believe Felisa and Joe Medeiros lived there during the construction of their new house on Fairfax Street.

Celestino Silván stood 5 feet, 8 inches tall, his pencil-thin mustache trimmed to perfection, his thick brown hair neat above soft brown eyes. He was 33 years old and 134 pounds when he received his citizenship papers in Oakland, California on July 21, 1939. His residence was listed at 214 Dabner Street in San Leandro. He never married.

He enjoyed being uncle to his three nieces (Josephine, Dorothy and Lillian) and seven nephews, (Jerome #1, Melvin, Victor, George, Alfred, Bobby and Jerome #2). [70]

---

[70] Theodora (Dora) Souza and Felisa (Alice) Medeiros both named sons Jerome.

This is a photo of Celestino with his great niece, Lynda Medeiros Ely about 1952 when she was five years old and he was about forty six. Her father was Jerome Medeiros, son of his sister, Felisa Silván Medeiros.

He bought a great old Victorian house next door at 270 Dabner Street when his mother became ill. Years later, Lynda Ely moved into the big house to care for him; her Uncle Celestino lived in a shack at the rear of the house.

He loved gardening and his tanned face reflected it. Lynda remembers seeing him stand on a high ladder proudly reaching the top of his fifteen-foot green-bean stalk.

He always rode a bicycle with a basket full of his home-grown vegetables to sell around town to the locals. Celestino also worked as a laborer at the Colorado Fuel and Iron, a wire manufacturing company in San Leandro, California from 1978 until his death in 1983.

He never got his driving license, nor drove an automobile. His mode of transportation was a bicycle and remained so until his death sixteen days before his 77th birthday. He was hit by an automobile while riding his bicycle home from a bar called BJs on Davis Street. His leg wound festered but he refused a doctor's treatment, so they wrapped his leg and his nephew, Bob Souza, took him home.

The wound was indeed infected. When his nephew, Bob,[71] begged Celestino to see a doctor, his uncle chased him away.

Lynda said she tried to keep his wound clean but he would not let her change the bandages. After awhile, Lynda forced the issue, but by then, the wound was covered in maggots and he later died in his bedroom. The family believed his death was caused from the horrible infection from his leg wound but the death certificate lists cause of death as *Cardiac Failure* and *Coronary Atherosclerosis*. [72]

Celestino is buried in the common plot with his parents, Victorino Silván Hernández and Ramona Martin Lorenzo Silván in St. Mary's Cemetery at 4529 Howe Street, Oakland, California on July 6, 1983. (Santos-Robinson Mortuary).

Theodora Souza's son, Bob Souza, was the informant for his uncle Celestino's death certificate.

Celestino left the big house to his great niece, Lynda Medeiros Ely, where she raised her children. However, after the 1989 earthquake in San Francisco, the house was damaged beyond repair and she was forced to sell the grand old Victorian.

---

[71] Bob Souza

[72] Dorothy Souza Petersen told me, "Uncle Celestino Silván was an alcoholic with diabetes. He was always riding the roads on his bicycle and eventually died from a bicycle accident."

STATE OF CALIFORNIA
CERTIFICATION OF VITAL RECORD

OFFICE OF RECORDER

COUNTY OF ALAMEDA

OAKLAND, CALIFORNIA

CERTIFICATE OF DEATH
STATE OF CALIFORNIA

6097   4279

Celestino	M.	Silvan	7/1/83		fd.1900	
Male	White/Spanish	Spanish	July 17, 1906	76		
Spain	Victorino Silban	Spain	Romana Martin	Spain		
U.S.A.		Never Married				
Laborer		Colorado Fuel & Iron	Wire Mfg:			

USUAL RESIDENCE: 270 Dabner Street

Alameda   California   San Leandro

PLACE OF DEATH: 270 Dabner Avenue Rear   Alameda

Bob Souza (Nephew)
12 Cambridge Way
Piedmont, Ca. 94611

270 Dabner Avenue Rear   San Leandro

CAUSE OF DEATH:
IMMEDIATE CAUSE (A) Cardiac Failure

(B) Coronary Atherosclerosis

Investigation

Burial   7-5-83   St. Mary's Cemetery   Oakland, Ca.   6465

Santos-Robinson Mortuary   F-81

Deputy Coroner   7/3/83

Guy L. Dilling

JUL 5 1983

INFORMATIONAL - NOT A VALID
DOCUMENT TO ESTABLISH IDENTITY

CERTIFIED COPY OF VITAL RECORD
STATE OF CALIFORNIA, COUNTY OF ALAMEDA
This is a true and exact reproduction of the document officially registered
and placed on file in the office of the Alameda County Recorder.

002045729

PATRICK O'CONNELL
ALAMEDA COUNTY RECORDER

DATE ISSUED   APR 23 2015

This copy is not valid unless prepared on an engraved border displaying the date, seal and signature of the Recorder.

DECENDANTS OF:
Juan Francisco Silván Hernández
(Eustoquia Rita Trascasas Marzo)

Manuela, Rita, María[73], José, Juan and Agustín

---

[73] Manuela Silván Trascasas Ruiz was adamant that the child in her mother's arms was not her sister, María Silván (Cuellar). Manuela told the bittersweet story, "this child is my cousin, my aunt's child, María."

The story: Rita Silván refused to sit for the portrait empty arms; her recent baby had been stillborn. Rita looks pregnant in this photo and Manuela looks to be about 12, probably late 1913. This baby appears about two years old. With careful research, I believe Manuela's "aunt" was Crescéncia Silván Hernandez Gonzales… and her cousin was Maria Gregoria Gonzales, born in May 18, 1912.
Manuela's sister, Maria (Mary) Silván was not born until April of 1914.

Manuela Trascasas SILVAN

View relationship to me

Birth 24 June 1901 in Fuentesauco, Province of Zamora, Spain
Death 21 Apr 2001 in Woodland, Yolo, California, United States of America

Bernardo Romero Ruiz
1896 – 1962

Francisco Silvan Ruiz
1920 –

Juan Silvan Ruiz
1922 –

Rosa Silvan Ruiz
1923 – 2005

Bernardo (Benny) Silvan Ruiz
1925 – 1927

Michael Silvan Ruiz
1926 – 2006

Maria (Mary) Silvan Ruiz
1928 –

Manuela (Millie) Silvan Ruiz
1930 –

Jose Silvan Ruiz
1931 – 2008

Dolores (Lola) Silvan Ruiz
1933 – 1938

Rita Christina Silvan Ruiz
1934 –

Antoinette Silvan Ruiz
1936 –

Josephine Augustina Silvan Ruiz
1937 –

Antonio Augustin Silvan Ruiz
1938 –

Encarnation Veronica Ruiz
1941 –

Benarda Silvan Ruiz
1943 – 1943

MANUELA SILVÁN TRASCASAS
25 June 1901- 21 April 2001
Married: Bernardo Ruiz Romero

Manuela always believed her birthday was June 24, 1900 and celebrated it on that date. Hence, she celebrated her 100th birthday when she was 99 years old.

She could not read or write but she learned to draw her initials; MSR = Manuela Silván Ruiz. She sparked one's imagination; at age nine, she was ripped from her home in Fuentesaúco with her extended family, rode a train, walked twelve days, boarded a ship that sailed from Gibraltar to Hawaii and created stories to tell her descendants for years afterward.

She was the first living child of Juan Francisco Silván Hernández and Eustoquia Rita Trascasas Marzo, born in northern Spain in the Province of Zamora, southwest of Madrid.

She was precocious, loving, musically inclined and could squeeze pennies from a dollar. She cooked, sewed, crocheted, sang and hugged grandchildren. When I took my 2-year-old daughter, Christina, to meet her in Vacaville in 1972, the first thing abuelita did after hugging and kissing her was reach for my child's hand and lead her to flower beds so she and Chrissy could smell her roses. To me, she was the epitome of grand-motherhood.

B. 7.821.474*

6/25/1901/

Translation of Document B. 7.821.474[74]

Don Emilio Ladron de Cegama, Attorney and Deputy Municipal Justice for the district of this village of Fuentesaúco and administrator of the Municipal Civil Registry of said district certifies to the following:

Certificate: That according to the entries recorded in the archives of the Civil Registry.

Juan Francisco Silban Hernández, native and resident of this village, natural son of **Celestino Silban** and **Agustina Hernández,** married **Eustoquia Rita Trascasas Marzo** a native and resident of the the village of Toro, natural daughter of **Manuel Trascasas** and of **Manuela Marzo.** The marriage ceremony took place at the parochial church of *Santa Maria* in the same village on 23 of April in 1900 at 8:00 a.m. as recorded in the matrimonial volume 7, page 149, column 12 of the Registry.

That **Manuela Silban Trascasas** natural daughter of **Juan Francisco Silban Hernández,** a native and resident of this village and **Eustoquia Rita Trascasas Marzo,** a native and resident of the village of Toro, and paternal granddaughter of **Celestino Silban** and **Agustina Hernández,** maternal granddaughter of **Manuel Trascasas** and **Manuela Marzo,** was born in this village at 3:20 p.m. on 25 June 1901 as recorded in the birth volume 93, page 346, column 15.

I grant this statement at the request of **Juan Francisco Silban Hernández** for immigration purposes. The Municipal Justice of Fuentesaúco has affixed his Seal of Office on this 27th day of January, 1911.

Signed: Julio Corrales   The Secretary

---

[74] See certificate for four children of Victorino Silban Hernandez and Romana Martin Lorenzo in picture pages

A good friend once described his grandmother to me and I never forgot his words because they depicted my own abuelita-memories, He said, *"I associate my grandmother's softness with the sounds. Her touch, her spoken word, her being -- there was a softness, a caress about her -- she was amazing to me. When I sat with her and held her hand, uncharacteristically warm to the touch, raising her palm to my cheek to wipe away my tears, I don't think she understood that she was one of the most important people in my life. She would say to me "tranquillo" when I was upset -- "tranquillo" was her way. She probably never ever heard the prayer,* **God, Grant me the serenity to accept the things I cannot change, change the things I can, and the wisdom to know the difference.** *That was my grandmother's philosophy of life."*

Manuela Silvan faced extremely hard times and sometimes those pieces of her life created friction in her relationships with family, but never with me. With me, she was a sense of wonder and I miss her still.

An excerpt from *The Girl Immigrant*, their immigration story that was mostly written from the child-Manuela's point of view:

Nine-year old Manuela was brown-eyed with a small sun-drenched face. She hadn't had time to be a child. Her little brothers needed her to do any number of chores for them. Despite her age, she helped with their breakfast, learned how to cook and mix and knead bread. She'd milked goats, chased pigs, emptied buckets of kitchen garbage and learned to wash laundry and crochet pretties without a pattern.

In spite of the work load, she still found bits of time for music and dancing. Her mother, Rita, and her aunts, Ramona and Crescéncia, were her best teachers. Pulling her skirts to her shins and swaying to the beat of her father's drum, she'd learned to dance beside the women and the memories of those sweet days lingered. Tia Ramona danced at every opportunity so where there was music, she knew there would be dancing. And

Ramona's younger daughter, Felisa, was right there beside them, watching, smiling and dancing. She left her sister, Teodora in the dust, who seemed disinclined to lose herself in music.

The dancing and music couldn't change. Manuela's mind rattled the words as she gazed sideways at the women quietly gripping bags and nudging children.

~

After living in Hawaii for seven years during the sugar-plantation commitment with her family, Manuela traveled to California aboard the SS HERMAN GOVERNOR at the age of 16 ½. Her father and very-pregnant mother, two brothers and one sister landed in San Francisco in January of 1918 on a military cruiser to begin their life in America. She hadn't wanted to leave Hawaii any more than she'd wanted to leave Spain, but for a young girl in 1918, she had no choice. She loved the flowers, the freedom to run through the sand and dust with bare feet and the muumuus that swayed around her small frame. In California, muumuus and flowers were a mainstay for the rest of her life. Sometimes she wore flowers in her hair and created garden borders with a multitude of anemone shells. She always missed Hawaii.

Her first job in California was at the California Cotton Mills Co. Factory located at 1091 Calcot Place in Oakland, just outside San Lorenzo where she rolled cotton thread. The Del Monte Fruitvale Plant hired her later to sort, clean and inspect peaches.

She fell in love with Bernardo RUIZ Romero after becoming reacquainted in California when the Silván and Ruiz families followed the summer crops. By then, his name changed to Bernardo Ruiz with Romero as his middle name; the American way. By October of 1919, they decided to marry.

By the end of September as the fruit harvests slowed, Ben and Manuela planned a wedding trip to Esparto on the train. Juan and Rita approved the match although they wished they would wait another year. Ben was twenty three. Manuela, eighteen. But they didn't want to wait.

In early January, Ben did the best that he could; they moved into an apartment at 292 Foothill Blvd., in the Hayward Park area of Alameda County with his brother, Miguel Ruiz Romero.

The brothers both had jobs in the shipyard; they made a pact to share expenses and though Manuela also worked outside the home, she was thrilled to be away from the big family.

Making it their home was appealing to Manuela and added a new confidence she enjoyed; cooking for both men was an achievement she could be proud of. They ate everything put in front of them. She cooked Ben stewed tomatoes and garbanzo soup and Tortilla Española with peas.

Her first child, Francisco, was born in September, 1920 after each of their fathers. After "Frank" was born, there followed fourteen more children by the time Manuela was forty two years old. She buried two; Benny was a toddler and Lola was nearing school age. One was a stillbirth. Twelve Ruiz children grew to adulthood.

By the 1930s, her parents had a 50-acre ranch on the hill roads in the Olive District off Pleasant Valley Road in Solano County and Ben and Manuela eventually lived on a ranch called *El Rancho de los Coyotes* just three miles from Olive School, where the Ruiz children attended along with their Martin and Gonzales cousins. The ranch grew fruit trees such as plums, apricots, peaches, figs and grapes.

The April 12, 1930 Federal Census lists John, Rita, Joe, Mary, Juanita and Celestino along with Ben, Mildred (Manuela), Frank, John, Rosie, Mike and Mary plus August, María and John Ruiz in Silveyville, Solano County, California.

She also worked hard in the apricot sheds and canneries; her hands blurred as she picked up an apricot, halved and pulled the seed out quickly before laying the halves into a tray. They earned their money by the lug of peaches and apricots; fast was money. The filled trays were placed in a small shed and sulfur was filtered over the fruit to kill bugs, and then later left in the sun to dry.

Manuela was frugal like her mother and saved every penny. She loved the big family parties; food was laid out, everyone sang, danced and she could yodel! She sewed her daughters' dresses out of flour sacks with her Singer foot-pedal machine. She made soups with garbanzos and peas. She made bread, chorizo and more soup.

Manuela's daughter, Mary Ruiz Sanderson, remembers when her grandfather (John Silván) came to visit, she and her siblings always knew he was on his way because he arrived in his horse and buggy. It made the clop, clop, clop sound before he tied his horse to a post in front of the house and they had a visit.

WM

COMPARED

DEED OF GIFT

THIS INDENTURE made this 27th day of March, 1951, by and between MANUELLA S. RUIZ, the party of the First Part, and BEN RUIZ, the party of the Second Part,

W I T N E S S E T H :

That the party of the first part, for and in consideration of the love and affection which she has for the party of the second part, does by these presents, give and grant unto the said party of the second part, and to his heirs and assigns forever, all that certain piece or parcel of land situate, lying and being in the County of YOLO, State of CALIFORNIA, and more particulary described as follows, to-wit:

Lots numbered 88, 89 and 90 of Haven's Addition to Winters, according to the map thereof filed for record in the Office of the County Recorder of the County of Yolo, on June 4th, 1913, in Book 2 of Maps at page 78.

Together with the tenements, hereditaments and appurtenances thereunto belonging or appertaining and the reversions, remainders, rents, issues and profits thereof.

TO HAVE AND TO HOLD the said premises, together with the appurtenances unto the said party of the second part, and to his heirs and assigns forever.

IN WITNESS WHEREOF, the party of the first part has hereunto set her hand the day and year first above written.

MANUELLA S. RUIZ

STATE OF CALIFORNIA)
) SS.
COUNTY OF YOLO   )

On this 27th day of MARCH, 1951, before me, L. M. IRELAND, a Notary Public in and for the said County of Yolo, State of California, personally appeared MANUELLA S. RUIZ, known to me to be the person whose name is subscribed to the foregoing instrument and acknowledged to me that he executed the same.

IN WITNESS WHEREOF, I have hereunto set my hand and affixed my official seal the day and year in this certificate first above written.

(SEAL)   L. M. IRELAND Notary Public

in and for the County of Yolo, State of California. My commission expires 3/4/1955.

Recorded at Request of YOLO COUNTY TITLE ABSTRACT CO. APR 4 1951 at 33 min. past 11 o'clock A.M.

DOCUMENT NUMBER 2219   NILE I. FISHER RECORDER

Manuela's daughter-in-law, Neyda Hubbard Ruiz (Bettencourt), said, "Mom could crochet without watching her needle! She looked at you while talking and her crochet needle never stopped clicking. Mom taught me to crochet and I taught her how to create doilies from a pattern. She couldn't read, so after studying a pattern, I showed her special stitches. Instead of straight crochet stitches, she was delighted to crochet fancy edgings called a *picot*. Mom called them *picitos*."

In essence, they taught one another the intricacies of crochet.

By March of 1951, Manuela and Ben chose to live separately and she signed over a *Deed of Gift* to Ben Ruiz for their house and property listed as Haven's Addition in Winters on Abbey St.

VOL. 512 PAGE 148   3338   **Deed**   APPLICATION No. 18978

JOHN S. RUIZ and ROSELYN M. RUIZ, his wife, and MANUELLA RUIZ, all as Joint Tenants,

the first part ies , hereby Grant to   WOODLAND TITLE GUARANTY COMPANY, a California Corporation,

the second part y , all the real property situated in the City of Woodland,   County

of Yolo,   State of California, described as follows:

The South 30 feet of Lot 3 and the North 30 feet of Lot 4, of Block 2, Bynum's Addition, as shown on the Map or Plat thereof, filed for record in the Office of the County Recorder of the County of Yolo on May 2nd, 1872, in Book M of Deeds, at Page 152.

WITNESS our hand s this 26th day of APRIL , 19 57

John S. Ruiz
Roselyn M. Ruiz
Manuela Ruiz

For Recorder's Use Only

STATE OF CALIFORNIA
County of Yolo
On APRIL 26 , 19 57
before me, A. W. Potts
a Notary Public, in and for said County and State, personally appeared John S. Ruiz, Roselyn M. Ruiz, and Manuella Ruiz known to me to be the person s whose name s are subscribed to the within instrument, and acknowledged to me that the y executed the same.

Notary Public
My commission expires May 30, 1957

VOL. 512 PAGE 148
OFFICIAL RECORDS
RECORDED AT REQUEST OF
WOODLAND TITLE GUARANTY CO.
APR 29 1957
AT 16 MIN. PAST 1 O'CLOCK P.M.
YOLO COUNTY, CALIFORNIA
2.00
RECORDER

INDEXED

3338

WOODLAND TITLE GUARANTY COMPANY
519 Main Street, Woodland, California

Manuela purchased a Victorian house with a big bay window in Woodland just a few miles east of town for $5,000 at 745 First Street.   More flowers, more abalone shells and more grandchildren. It was here that I watched her brush and coil her long hair, learned to love cooked rice with cinnamon, sugar and warm milk. I learned abuelita's songs, played in her flower beds and napped by the stove where she pulled a steel cover off with a handle to drop wood inside to make the room cozy and warm for me and my cousins while our mothers worked.

By April of 1957, Manuela signed another Deed showing herself as joint tenants with John Silván Ruiz and his wife Roselyn (Dolly).

Manuela later purchased a house in Vacaville at 125 Laurel Street, to be nearer her sister, Mary Silván Cuellar.

Her son, Michael, took her to Spain in 1973. Searching genealogy, he'd found her long-lost cousin, Manuela Marzo in Toro, where her grandmother was born; she was thrilled to see her and touch Spanish soil once again.

Her niece, Rose Marie Cuellar, remembers her as happy. She loved fig bars, soap operas, Spanish music, John Wayne movies. Manuela told Rose Marie that she resembled her mother, Rita Trascasas Marzo. Rose Marie said she loved her tia Manuela dearly.

Manuela loved her grandchildren ---

Patricia (me) and abuelita[75]

---

[75] This photo was taken in 1947 when I lived in a tiny house with my parents just down the street in an alley that abuelita Manuela had previously purchased for her in-laws, Frank and María Ruiz in Winters, California

Manuela and Ben – 1940s
Manuela and children Josephine, Antoinette, Tony and Rita Ruiz 1944
Both photos were taken in Winters, Yolo Co., California

Manuela Trascasas *SILVAN* Ruiz [Edit Name]

| Memorial | Photos | Flowers | | Share | Edit |

Learn about upgrading this memorial...

[Transfer Management] [Edit] [Dele

Birth: Jun. 25, 1901
        Zamora
        Castilla y Leon, Spain
Death: Apr. 21, 2001
        Woodland
        Yolo County
        California, USA [Edit Dates]

Added by: Patricia Steele

Manuela SILVAN Trascasas was born in Fuentesauco, Province of Zamora, Spain to Juan Francisco SILVAN Hernandez and Eustoquia Rita Trascasas Marzo. At the age of 9 years old, she traveled with her parents, two brothers (Agustin & Jose), aunts, uncles and cousins to the Rock of Gibraltar where they sailed to the sugar fields in Hawaii aboard the SS ORTERIC in February 1911. After seven years, her family migrated to California where she married Bernardo RUIZ Romero and they had 15 children. Two died very young and one died stillborn. Twelve children grew to adulthood. She was a wonderful, loving woman and the grandmother of more children than I can count.

Her BIRTH CERTIFICATE LISTS JUNE 25, 1901 BIRTH DATE AND NAME SPELLED AS "MANUELA"

[Edit Bio]
Family links: [Edit]
 Spouse:
  Bernardo Romero Ruiz (1896 - 1962)*

 Children:
  Bernardo Ruiz (1924 - 1927)*
  Michael Silvan Ruiz (1926 - 2006)*

*Calculated relationship

[Add Marker Transcription]
Note: died in Woodland, Ca. 100 yrs old -Kraft Bros- Kin Josephine Ruiz
[Edit]

Burial: [Edit]
Winters Cemetery
Winters
Yolo County
California, USA
Plot: Sec 7 Office Walk-NWQ [Edit Plot]

Added by: Patricia Steele

Cemetery Photo
Don't show cemetery photos
on this memorial [?]

The summer of 1995, abuelita Manuela told me she wondered why she was still alive after losing all her siblings when she was the oldest child of her family. She had osteoporosis so bad, she walked nearly bent at the waist and she did not laugh much in the end. She died in Alderson's Convalescent Hospital two months before her 100th birthday of arteriosclerosis in 2001.

Her memorial was held at the St. Anthony's Catholic Church on Main Street in Winters, California. She is buried at the Winters Cemetery next to her husband, Bernardo Ruiz Romero.

HUSBAND OF MANUELA SILVÁN TRASCASAS:
BERNARDO *RUIZ* ROMERO
9 February 1896– 16 February 1962

Ben Ruiz looked more Irish than Spanish with his blue eyes and light complexion. He was the fourth and last child born to Francisco RUIZ Garcia and Rosa de la Santísima Trinidad ROMERO Ruiz near Málaga in Arroyos de Los Olivas near Campanillas, Spain.

Sadly, his mother[76] died when Bernardo was young, leaving his father a widower with four children. The reason for Rosa's death is unknown.

Ben was baptized at *Parroquia de Nuestra Señora del Carmen* in Campanillas, Málaga, Spain. This video,[77] Procesión Virgin Del Carmen De Campanillas, Málaga 2013 walks you down the streets of this village…

---

[76] Rosa was born in Alora, Malaga, Andalucía, Spain and baptized in la Iglesia de San Pablo, Málaga Calle Trinidad, 35, Málaga 29009 This is a Neo-Gothic style church, designed by Jerónimo Cuervo and built between 1874 and 1891. The original church has been demolished.

[77] http://www.youtube.com/watch?v=snbTPSbbXAA

Bernardo's mother was born in Álora. My brother, Steven, and I explored Álora and its tiny, convoluted streets. We asked where the cemetery was located and were told people were rarely buried because it is a hill town. Instead, they were cremated and their ashes were placed in small crypts in the old castle wall.

The small town of Álora is situated 25 miles north of Málaga by the road to Antequera. From a distance, it is a typical pueblo blanco; a whitewashed village nestled between three rocky spurs topped by the ruins of a magnificent castle.

This is a photo of Bernardo's mother (Rosa). Both Rosa and father, Miguel Romero, were born in Álora, Málaga, Spain. I can only assume she and her parent's ashes are interred inside the old Álora castle walls. In this photo, Rosa Romero Ruiz is holding her first child, María, Ben's oldest sister.

When Ben was about six, his widowed father remarried a woman named María Carmen Rey Garcia, a widow with a young child named Isabel Morales Rey.

María was a loving step-mother to Ben, Juan, Miguel and María. Her daughter, Isabel, was embraced as a true Ruiz sibling.

After the marriage, Diego Ruiz Rey and Josefa Ruiz Rey were soon born in or near Almogia in Colmenar in Spain.

In February 1912 when Ben was sixteen, he and his family sailed from Gibraltar on the SS HARPALION to Hawaii. At that time, Ben stood 4' 8" tall, had fair skin, brown hair and blue eyes. The ship manifest listed in comments, that Ben had a scar on the top of his head.

His father, Francisco Ruiz, was 5' 5" with fair skin, gray hair and blue eyes. He joined the exodus of Spaniards by committing to work in the sugarcane fields in exchange for travel fare, schooling for his children, medical attention and a house to live until they could continue on to California. He left a position as a math tutor in Almogia at the time of their emigration. Some of Francisco Ruiz's siblings immigrated to Hawaii also. See next book, Ruiz Legacies.

Diego was 8 and Josefa, 5, when they sailed to Hawaii on the SS HARPALION. During their life in Hawaii, Delores (Dee) Ruiz Rey was born in Honolulu[78].   Antonio (Tony) Ruiz Rey, Manuel (Ray) Ruiz Rey and Encarnacion (Connie) Ruiz Rey were all born after they arrived in California. All told, Ben had nine siblings plus Isabel to make ten.

We know the Ruiz family moved to Kauai after Delores' birth because that is where Bernardo met Manuela soon afterward. The Kilauea Sugar Plantation on the north shore of Kauai is where they lived in the Spanish Camp near a small stream. The Ruiz and Silván families and everyone else in the ethnic camps were like a large family, holding their culture together by keeping Spanish traditions, playing cards and sharing music.

---

[78] Since Delores was born in Honolulu, Hawaii, I believe the Ruiz family may have worked on the Ewa Plantation during that time before they moved to another plantation in Kauai.

The romance between Ben and Manuela didn't become serious until two years later after both families were settling into their lives in California[79].

This is an example of a contract the immigrant Spaniards signed to work on the plantations. The photo below is the Kilauea Sugar Plantation in Kilauea, Kauai in the Territory of Hawaii as it was known at the time before it became a state.

---

[79] See The Girl Immigrant for their story

Five years after arriving in Hawaii, Ben left for California aboard the SS VENTURA April 23, 1917 with his brother-in-law, Antonio Rodriguez Acedo, married to his sister, Mary Ruiz Garcia.
Top manifest: SS VENTURA 1917
Bottom manifest: SS HARPALION 1912

This Alien Certificate was a "ticket into the United States" because it showed the immigrant had already gone through inspection when he or she first arrived from Spain into Hawaii. The immigrant was able to avoid being detained in the arrival port, such as Ángel Island, once they arrived in California. This certificate was dated April 23, 1917 and shows it was surrendered to the San Francisco inspector named Nichols on May 1, 1917.

Registrar's Report lists Bernardo Romero Ruiz registered in Pleasanton, Alameda, California, June 5, 1917. He is listed as short, medium build, gray eyes, brown hair. (But…his eyes were blue, not gray.)

Ben's life continued to revolve around the agricultural industry. After he and Manuela married and their children started arriving, his work in the fields improved as he later pruned trees and sold vegetables and fruit to the farmer's markets in Sacramento. His daughter, Millie, helped him by coding the sale tags.

Ben was diagnosed with Tuberculosis in 1933. His brother in law, Joe Silván, drove him to the clinic where he was admitted to the Bushnell Sanatorium located outside Colfax, California for a short time[80]. His daughter, Delores "Lola" Ruiz died shortly after he was admitted to the clinic. She was not quite six years old.

He was proud to be a Red Cross volunteer during WWII in Winters, California where he was an Air Raid Warden. He notified residents to turn off lights during black-out periods. His daughter, Millie, still has the little Red Cross booklet in her possession. She remembers helping him read the book of instructions; he understood what was expected of him.

The old Spanish ways made a mark on Ben. Sometimes his old-world values clashed with the American Dream. He made some bad choices in his life but is remembered as being a jolly guy; smiling and card playing with his friends (often with the Jimenez brothers) in the Buckhorn Bar in Winters. He was not a drinker. One very sick hangover shortly after his marriage was all it took.

He continued to grow his vegetables and selling his produce in Sacramento. His children helped work on the ranch and went to school in Winters.

By 1956, Ben and Manuela grew apart and life for them changed. Ben stayed in Winters and Manuela bought a house in Woodland at 745 First Street.

They tried to live together a few times afterward but sadly, their lives no longer meshed as one.

---

[80] The Bushnell Sanatorium was later renamed Weimar Institute.

Ben lived with his daughter, Millie, and her family for short periods of time during 1956 and 1962 on Frost Drive in Woodland.

Millie remembers the day in 1962 when her father played with her sons while he laid on her couch and she wondered why he was so quiet all day. That night, when Millie's husband (Fred Cortopassi) arrived home from work, Ben asked Fred to drive him to the hospital. Her eyes misted as she recalled that day. "He didn't complain about his intense pain so we didn't know how sick he was," she said. He died just seven days after his 66th birthday.

The good news at the end of this story was learning that Ben and Manuela found each other, full circle, again before he died and his children tell me that was a good day. She forgave him for the sadness in their lives; she lived nearly forty years after Ben's death.

This house is where Bernardo Ruiz Romero was born, located in the *Arroyo de Los Olivas* near Málaga. Although it has been renovated a few times since his birth in 1896, it still sits on the original foundation.

Photo is courtesy of cousin, Angela Ruiz Fernandez, Los Nunez, Spain.

This is how I remember my grandfather: smiling.

Bernardo Romero "Ben" RUIZ [Edit Name]

Memorial | Photos | Flowers | Share | Edit

Learn about sponsoring this memorial...

[Transfer Management] [Edit] [Dele

Birth: Jan. 10, 1896
         Málaga
         Andalucia, Spain
Death: Feb. 16, 1962
         Woodland
         Yolo County
         California, USA [Edit Dates]

Added by: Patricia Steele

Bernardo RUIZ Romero was born in
Campanillas, outside Malaga in the Province of
Andalucia, Spain to Francisco RUIZ Garcia and
Rosa ROMERO Fernandez. He was the 4th and
youngest child of this union. His mother, Rosa,
died when he was about five years old.

A few years later, his father married Maria
Carmen Rey Garcia, who was a loving
stepmother and the mother of his six
subsequent siblings.

Ben Ruiz emigrated from Los Nunez, Almogia
near Malaga with his father, step mother and
siblings in 1912 from Gibraltar to Hawaii on the
immigrant ship, SS HARPALION and later to
San Francisco in 1917 with his brother in law,
Antonio Rodriguez. He married Manuela Silvan
Trascasas October 15, 1919 and they raised
their family in Winters, California.

Added by: Patricia Steele

He was an air raid warden in Winters in 1941
and an orchardist all his life.
[Edit Bio]
Family links: [Edit]
Spouse:
  Manuela Trascasas *SILVAN* Ruiz (1901 - 2001)

Children:
  Bernardo Ruiz (1924 - 1927)*
  Michael Silvan Ruiz (1926 - 2006)*

*Calculated relationship

Inscription: [Edit]
Benaldo - misspelled because of it's
pronounciation. The Spanish "R" is rolled to
sound like an "L", hence Benaldo vs. Bernardo

Note: 68 yrs old

Cemetery Photo
Don't show cemetery photos
on this memorial [?]

232 | Page

AGUSTIN (Gus) MARZO SILVÁN
29 March 1908 - 3 September 1994
Married: María Ernestasia Fernandez (divorced)
Married: Ruby Clinton

This man loved to fish; he caught the biggest fish of his life on the day he died. It was the best and worst of days for Gus. He was wheeled down to the pier in Homer, Alaska by his nephew by marriage, Jerry Potter. Feeling ebullient, he watched his family clean that huge fish and a heart attack took his last breath away – on a smile.

He was my mother's favorite uncle by marriage and combining her memories with nieces, nephews and documents, I pieced together his story.

Agustín was born in Spain, took his first train ride and sailed across the ocean by the age of three. He looked up to his sister, Manuela, and took care of his younger siblings as his life moved from Spain in 1911 and then from Hawaii to California in January of 1918. He loved fishing and baseball; especially the San Francisco Giants ball team. His occupation during the early years was building houses and he paid his nephew, John Hyatt, to paint his buildings during his summer vacations from school.

Agustino Marzo Silvan

View relationship to me

Birth 29 Mar 1908 in Fuentesauco, Province of Zamora, Spain
Death 3 Sep 1994 in Homer, Kenai Peninsula, Alaska, United States of America

Spouse & Children ▼

Maria Ernestasia Fernandez
1914 –

John Alexander Silvan
1929 –

Ruby Clinton
1899 – 1987

Two stories surround Gus's marital life; Gus married 16-year old María Ernestasia Fernandez (her second surname sounded phonetically like *Rebeccia*) in 1929. They lived in Winters with their son, John Alexander Silván[81] who was born in January of 1930. The information on the April, 1930 census from Silveyville in Solano County lists Gus, María and John living with his parents, John and Rita Silván. The couple's marriage ended in divorce.

A second version of the story is from Victorina Gonzales Weber, his first cousin (daughter of Christina Gonzales). She knew Gus well and told me María was already pregnant with another man's child. She did not think Gus married her. Gus did not raise the boy, nor did he play any part in his life. This may be why his son, Johnny Silván used the Fernandez name.

Gus built houses, sometimes buying old houses and renovating them with his brothers, Joe and Celestino. He resided in San José and later lived in Benicia and Napa. His niece, Carnie, told me he met his next wife while he was driving his truck. Ruby Clinton, nine years his senior, was hitch hiking with two suitcases.

---

[81] Source, Rose Marie Cuellar Dugger: The paternity story. Also, she said that Johnny died in an automobile accident as an adult. I could not find information about a marriage or his children. He took his mother's maiden name, Fernandez.

He stopped to give her a ride and they later married. They had no children.

Residences were 320 Raymond Avenue and 357 Rutland Avenue both in San Jose, California.

In the fall of 1960, Gus Silván proudly became a U.S. Citizen and posed for this photo.

It is unknown why Gus used the Marzo (aka March) name instead of his mother's surname, Trascasas… but he is clearly listed as *August March Silván* on the document below.

No. **8182813**

Name SILVAN, August March

residing at 357 Rutland Ave., San Jose, Calif.

Date of birth MAR 29 1908   Date of order of admission SEP 6 1960

Date certificate issued SEP 6 1960 by the

U. S. District Court at San Francisco, California

Petition No. 143510   Alien Registration No. 2 864 070

M.E.   August March Silvan
(COMPLETE AND TRUE SIGNATURE OF HOLDER)

Over the years, he retained a close relationship with his siblings. By 1996, when his niece, Carnie Ruiz Potter and her husband, Jerry, invited him to live with them in Alaska. His only living siblings were Manuela and Mary. He hated leaving them but he could fish! He lived with them in Alaska for eight years until his death in 1994.

During his life with Carnie and Jerry Potter in beautiful Homer, Alaska, Gus enjoyed the last years of his life on the stunning Kachemak Bay at the end of the Sterling Highway, 250 miles south of Anchorage, surrounded by wilderness and ocean.

Homer is a home base for great fishing, known as "The Halibut Fishing Capital of the World."

The Homer Spit ("spit" is a geological landform term) is the second longest in the world, and was recently named one of the best 100 beaches in the United States for its incredible views and variety of wildlife along the wonderful 4.5 mile multi-use trail that runs from its base to its tip – the true end of the road on Alaska's Highway 1.

It was here that his nephew wheeled him down to the pier in his wheelchair to pull in that last big fish. And it was there that his niece, Carnie, remembers how excited he was when he realized it was the biggest catch of his life. And it was here that he died, doing what he loved best.

Agustín Silván was cremated. Carnie Potter told me her uncle went fishing in the San Francisco, Bay every year with a group of his friends. A special memorial for Gus took place on a boat under the Golden Gate Bridge. His old fishing buddies and a few family members enjoyed the day fishing just like Gus would have imagined while their memories of Gus slid among them. Afterward, his ashes were tossed into the Bay under that great bridge along with their whispered prayers.

Gus (left), Ensenada, Mexico

Left to right: Juanita, Mary, and Manuela with Gus

JOSE MARZO SILVÁN
8 June 1910 - 17 August 1979
Married: Encarnacion "Carnie" Alva

Joe always wanted to be a farmer and it took him fifty years to realize that dream.

His parents were Juan Francisco SILVÁN Hernandez and Eustoquia Rita Trascasas Marzo. He was born in Fuentesaúco, Zamora, Spain.

He and his family left Spain in 1911 before he was a year old from La Linea, Spain at Gibraltar. The ORTERIC sailed to the sugar fields of Hawaii. Later, he sailed to San Francisco in January, 1918 on the HERMAN GOVERNOR.

He was a sickly baby which may have been one of the reasons his parents left Spain besides the political unrest and flooding. It is believed he may have had Rickets as a young child, which stunted his growth and weakened his bones. The main cause of Rickets is a lack of vitamin D and calcium. Rickets affects mainly children and in most cases, the child suffers from severe and long-term malnutrition, usually during early childhood.

During his youth in Winters, California, he assisted his father on their ranch learning orchardry. Joe worked hard and despite health problems, he persevered and did not let it slow him down or allow it to control him.

He grew up working hard on the ranch but also learned woodworking and worked with his older brother, Gus for several years south of Winters in a town called Benicia, California.

When he visited friends in Rocklin, California, he was charmed by Encarnacion (Carnie) Alva, whom he married in Reno, Washoe, Nevada shortly thereafter. I am told the Boiza family, who were friends of the Silvans in Fuentesaúco, introduced the couple.

They made their first home in Winters but later moved to Benicia where his elderly parents lived at that time.

Joe Silván worked at the army arsenal with his brother, Gus, and the spouse of a Gonzales cousin.

A few months after the end of World War II, their only child, Joe Alva Silván, Jr. was born on December 30, 1945 in Benicia, Solano County, California.

Sometime later, Joe moved his family to San Jose near his brother, Gus, building houses until his health slowed him down and they returned to Benicia. In later years, they lived in Sacramento where he worked at McClellan Air Force Base.

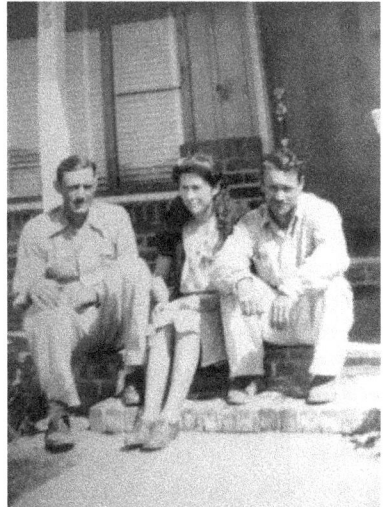

Photo: Gus Silván, Carnie Alva Silván and Joe Silván – San José, California

Jose Marzo Silvan

View relationship to me

Birth 8 Jun 1910 in Fuentesauco, Province of Zamora, Castilla-Leon, Spain
Death 17 Aug 1979 in Sacramento, Sacramento, California, United States

Spouse & Children ▼

Encarnacion 'Carnie" Alva
1913 – 1994

Joseph Alva Silvan
1945 –

BELOW Left: Joe Silván, Jr. with his uncle Celestino Silván
Right: Joe Silván, Jr.

But by the time he neared his fiftieth birthday, he wanted to make his next dream a reality; he purchased a peach orchard in 1959 against his wife's wishes and commuted back and forth from Sacramento to make it work.

With the help of his son and other relatives, it was eventually converted to prunes. His son, Joe, reminisced about his father, saying he'd always dreamed of being a farmer and those years were very sweet for him.

His son also remembers hand-planting those prune trees… and he decided farming wasn't for him.

Joe Marzo Silván is remembered as a fair, kind man who was respected by those who knew and worked with him. Joe died when he was 69 years old while living in Sacramento and is interred at the Calvary Catholic Cemetery and Mausoleum in Sacramento, Sacramento County, California.

www.findagrave.com #84170045

Jose Marzo "Joe" Silvan [Edit Name]

Memorial | Photos | Flowers   Share | E

[Transfer Management] [Edit] [De

Birth: Jun. 8, 1910
            Zamora
            Castilla y Leon, Spain
Death: Aug. 17, 1979
            Sacramento
            Sacramento County
            California, USA [Edit Dates]

Joe Silvan was the 3rd of 7 children born to
Juan Francisco SILVAN Hernandez and
Eustoquia Rita Trascasas Marzo Silvan in
Fuentesauco, Province of Zamora, Spain. He
and his family emigrated in 1911 before he
was a year old. He traveled with his parents,
his sister (Manuela) and brother
(Agustin)along with uncles, aunts and cousins
Gibraltar on the SS ORTERIC sailing to the
sugar fields of Hawaii and later to San
Francisco in January of 1918 where he went
to school and grew up in Winters, California.
He helped his father on the ranch as an
orchardist.

Added by: Patricia Steele

He married Encarnacion Alva from Rocklin,
California in 1939 and they had one son, Joe
Alva Silvan, Jr.

They moved to Benicia where his parents lived
and worked at the army arsenal with his
brother and cousin. They later moved to San
Jose near his brother, Gus, building houses
until his health slowed him down. In later
years, they lived in Sacramento where he
worked at McClellon Air Force Base and later
purchased a peach orchard in 1959 and
eventually converted it to prunes with the
help of his son, Joe and several relatives. He'd
always dreamed of being a farmer and those
years were sweet for him.

Added by: Patricia Steele

He was remembered as a fair, kind man who
was respected by those who knew and
worked with him. Joe died when he was 69
years old in Sacramento. His wife, Carnie,
lived for another fifteen years.
[Edit Bio]
Family links: [Edit]
 Parents:
  Juan Francisco SILVAN Hernandez (1875 -
1945)
  Eustoquia Rita Trascasas Marzo Silvan (1880 -
1953)

WIFE OF JOSE MARZO SILVÁN:
ENCARNACION **ALVA** ZAMORANO
Rocklin, Placer, California
2 August 1913 - 7 May 1994

She was called Carnie.
Encarnacion Alva was one of seven children born to Telesforo Alejano Alva and Marcelina Zamarano. Her parents (with her older sister, Gala Alva) emigrated from Fuentesauco, Zamora, Spain after riding in a wagon to Gibraltar and boarding the SS WILLESDEN in 1911 to sail to Hawaii where they worked in the sugar plantations for two years before sailing on to California in 1913.

Like many Spaniard immigrant families, they earned their livelihoods from the fruit harvests. Traveling from one orchard to the next, where the fruit pickers could earn their money, they chose Rocklin as their home. When the Alva family settled in Rocklin, they eventually had their own fruit ranch.

A park is dedicated to their families, called the Corral-Alva Park in Rocklin.

It is said Carnie was born under a peach tree in a tent during summer harvests in Fowler, California, later baptized in Santa Clara, California[82]

---

[82] Source: story by her niece, Frances Corral Pugliese

Her siblings were Gala, Julia, Bicenta (Barbara), Francisco (Frank), Dolores (Laura), and Mercedes (Irene)Carnie grew up in Rocklin and married Joe Marzo Silván on November 11,

They began their new life together in Benicia, California where their only son, Joe Alva Silván, Jr., was born.

In 1952 or 1953, they moved to Sacramento and later to Roseville before she died in Carmichael fifteen years after her husband's death. She is interred at the Calvary Catholic Cemetery and Mausoleum in Sacramento, Sacramento County, California next to Joe.

www.findagrave.com - Memorial# 84662433

MARIA (Mary) TRASCASAS SILVÁN
7 March 1914 - 10 July 1997
Marriage: Frank Pareja Cuellar

Mary learned a hard lesson while still living in Kauai where, as a toddler, she waded through water where hot lava flowed beneath its surface. Her legs were badly burned from the knees down.

Mary was the only living[83] Hawaiian- born child of Juan Francisco Silván Hernández and Eustoquia Rita Trascasas Marzo. Her birth certificate lists place of birth as Kapa'a. Their residence was listed as Kealia,[84] which is a community near Kapa'a and the informant was Francisco Linares.

Her parents emigrated from Spain with her three older siblings, Manuela, Agustín (Gus) and José (Joe) three years before her birth. She was a precocious four-year-old and followed her sister and brothers around like a shadow. It was an adventure when her family sailed on the military ship to California in January 1918 during World War I.

---

[83] María Silvan was the second María born to Rita Silván. The first Maria died and Rita Silvan was adamant about naming one of her children, María.

[84] Kealia, literally "the salt encrustation" in Hawaiian), an unincorporated community on the island of Kauai in Kauai County, Hawaii, United States. Its elevation is 16 feet. The Board on Geographic Names officially designated it "Kealia" in 1914, the same year María was born.

Maria Trascasas Silvan
View relationship to me

Birth 7 Mar 1914 in Kapaa, Kauai, Hawaii, USA
Death 10 July 1997 in Vacaville, Solano, California, United States

Francisco Pareja Cuellar
1907 – 1995

Frank Cuellar, Jr.
1933 –

Fred Silvan Cuellar
1934 – 1999

Rose Marie Cuellar
1936 –

Helen Lucille Cuellar
1937 –

Certificate courtesy of her son, Frank Cuellar, Jr.

Mary grew up working in orchard agriculture, kneading bread for her mother before school, playing baseball on the boy's teams, caring for sick animals and whistling shrilly with a finger between her lips. Her life defined the young woman she became and Frank Cuellar noticed. And he couldn't resist her charms. Mary's sister, Manuela and her husband, Bernardo Ruiz often chaperoned the couple which was a tradition the Spaniards did not let slide.

At age 17, Mary Silvan married Frank Pareja Cuellar in the court house at Sacramento, California on Christmas Eve, 1931 with Manuela Silván Ruiz and Bernardo Ruiz as their witnesses. Mary and Frank Cuellar were married sixty two (62) years.

She worked on fruit farms during World War II and Frank worked at the Benicia Arsenal. She sorted and packed baskets of fruit and candy during the holidays. Later, Mary worked at the Basic Vegetable Company where she sorted onions and garlic powder, wearing a blue uniform and white hat with a net. Her daughter, Rose Marie, tells me her mother always "had a special onion fragrance when she came home…"

The 1940 U.S. federal census for Silveyville[85], Solano County, California, lists Frank (33), Mary (27) and their four children, Frank, Jr. (7), Fred (6), Rose Marie (4) and Helen L. Cuellar (2). The occupation listed for Frank Cuellar was "foreman" on a ranch.

As her children grew, the family picked prunes and Mary was quick to notice rattle snakes around the trunk of trees where husband Frank would quickly kill it and work would continue.

Her children listened for her loud whistle and knew it was time to get home.

---

[85] The township of Silveyville was located in the uppermost northern section of Solano County. At the time of its development, its boundaries ran along the Rio Los Putas and Yolo county on the north, Tremont Township on the east, Maine Prairie and Elmira Townships on the south, and on the west by Vacaville Township. Today, Silveyville is no longer a spot on a map, but its name still appears on a few Dixon cemeteries, schools and streets memorializing this original settlement.

Mary loved playing nickel, dime and quarter machines at Reno and Lake Tahoe in her later years as well as enjoying trips with the Spanish Club or playing cards at the senior center. And she loved eating "out." She loved staying busy and is often remembered with a broom in her hands.

Mary Silván Cuellar and her sister, Manuela Silván Ruiz, remained very close all their lives and she welcomed Manuela to Vacaville in the late 1950s after she moved to 125 Laurel Street. They liked visiting often and kept their families close.

Joe Silván, Jr. tells me he spent many happy hours with his Cuellar cousins. Living near Rocklin, he purchased a copy of *Memories of Spain* by Anne Aguilar Santucci, for aunt Mary. After her death, her daughter, Rose Marie Cuellar Dugger inherited the book. When I heard the story from Joe, I called Rose Marie. She happily shipped it to me overnight for my research. I had never met her! The book was given in love, shared in love and continues to connect puzzle pieces in Spanish history.

Photo: Mary with brother, Gus Silván

Mary Silvan and her mother, Rita Trascasas Marzo Silván
(love those shoes!)

1940 Federal census: Top: Frank and Mary; Bottom: children
Silveyville, Solano County, California
142 Linda Street was their home later – in Vacaville, California

Mary and Frank Cuellar celebrate their 50th wedding anniversary, December 1981.

To Remembrance

The Lord is my shepherd;

I shall not want.

He maketh me to lie down in green pastures;
He leadeth me beside the still waters.

He restoreth my soul: He leadeth me in the
paths of righteousness for His name's sake.

Yea, though I walk through the valley of the
shadow of death, I will fear no evil;
for Thou art with me;
Thy rod and Thy staff they comfort me.

Thou preparest a table before me
in the presence of mine enemies;
Thou anointest my head with oil;
my cup runneth over.

Surely goodness and mercy shall follow me
all the days of my life; and I
will dwell in the house of the Lord forever.

THE TWENTY-THIRD PSALM

IN MEMORY OF

Mary Cuellar

BORN
Hawaii
March 7, 1914

ENTERED INTO REST
Vacaville, California
July 10, 1997

AGE
83 Years 4 Months 3 Days

FUNERAL SERVICE
McCune Garden Chapel
July 14, 1997
10:00 A.M.

OFFICIATING
Pastor Lester Seto
Bethany Lutheran Church

INTERMENT
Vacaville Elmira Cemetery
Vacaville, California

Mary *Silvan* Cuellar

| Memorial | Photos | Flowers | | Share | Edit |

Learn about removing the ads from this memorial...

Birth: Mar. 7, 1914
            Kapaa
            Kauai County
            Hawaii, USA

Death: Jul. 10, 1997
            Vacaville
            Solano County
            California, USA

Mrs. Mary Cuellar died Thursday, July 10, 1997, in Vacaville CA. A native of Hawaii, she lived in the Vacaville area for 70 years. She was an assembly line worker for Basic Vegetable for 25 years and a homemaker for 60 years. Memberships included the Spanish American Club in Woodland CA and the Senior Citizen Center. Mrs. Cuellar enjoyed bingo, trips to Reno, and was an avid gardener. Survivors include 2 sons, 2 daughters, a sister, 12 grandchildren, and 19 great-grandchildren.
(Fairfield Daily Republic, Fri, July 11, 1997)

Family links:
 Spouse:
  Francisco Pareja Cuellar (1908 - 1995)

Burial:
Vacaville-Elmira Cemetery
Vacaville
Solano County
California, USA

Edit Virtual Cemetery info [?]

Created by: M Roberts
Record added: Mar 01, 2011
Find A Grave Memorial# 66344031

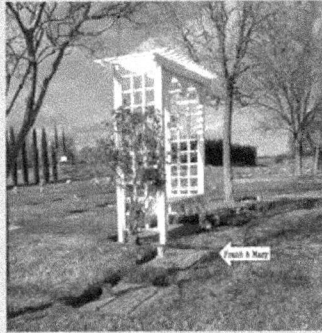
Added by: Kristie Mudgett Dovel

CUELLAR
FRANK P.   MARY S.
1907 -- 1995   1914 -- 1997
Added by: Kristie Mudgett Dovel

Added by: Patricia Steele

www.findagrave.com Memorial #66344031

HUSBAND OF MARÍA SILVÁN TRASCASAS:
FRANCISCO (Frank) PAREJA CUELLAR
Ewa Mill, Honolulu, Territory of Hawaii
26 January 1908 - 3 October 1995

He was one of seven children born to *Antonio Cuellar Guerrero*[86] and *María de los Delores Pareja Rodrigues* who were married in Santa Fe, Spain on July 1, 1899 based on a record found on www.FamilySearch.org [87]

In 1907, Antonio and his family lived in Santa Fé, Spain in the Province of Granada, a village with an agricultural background

---

[86] Frank and his brothers and sisters intervened and gave their father an ultimatum: Stop abusing mama or go back to Spain. Antonio Cuellar chose Spain; they shipped him back to the old country and they never saw him again (per Frank Cuellar, Jr.)

[87] Name: Antonio Cuellar Guerrero
Event Type: Marriage
Event Date: 01 Jul 1899
Event Place: Granada, Spain
Gender: Male
Spouse's Name: Maria de los Dolores Pareja Rodrigues
GS Film number: 1880815
Image Number: 110

Citing this Record: "España, Provincia de Granada, expedientes de informaciones matrimoniales, 1556-1899," index, FamilySearch (https://familysearch.org/pal:/MM9.1.1/XPP4-5T5 : accessed 03 Feb 2014), Antonio Cuellar Guerrero and Maria de los Dolores Pareja Rodrigues, 1899.

near Málaga in Andalucía.   Antonio, like the other multitude of Spanish immigrants, wanted a better life.   He was a marine blacksmith in Spain but chose to move his family to Hawaii and for work in the sugar cane. The Heliopolis sailed from Malaga on March 10, 1907 arriving in Honolulu April 26, 1907.

Cuellar, Antonio	M	33	Santa Fe
Pareja, Dolores	F	28	Santa Fe
Cuellar, Jose[88]	M	11	Santa Fe
Cuellar, Manuela[89]	F	4	Santa Fe
Cuellar, Josefa	F	2	Santa Fe

Nine months after the Heliopolis docked in Honolulu, Frank Pareja Cuellar was born on the island of Oahu where his parents worked on the Ewa Sugar Plantation.   His name was listed as Francisco Coelho Guerrero, later corrected from Coelho to Cuellar. I was unable to find a ship manifest bringing the family to California.

There were other Cuellar children born after arriving in Hawaii and later in California: Juan (John) Pareja Cuellar, Antoinette (Ann) Pareja Cuellar, Lucille Pareja Cuellar and Emilio Pareja Cuellar.

Francisco became *Frank* in America like so many other Spanish families; they wanted to assimilate with American names. Despite being pushed to quit school after the 8th grade to earn money for the family, he became a very good carpenter.   Self educated, he was a good provider, a good friend to many people and a good man.

---

[88] The ship manifest for the Heliopolis lists their oldest son, Jose, as eleven, so my assumption is Antonio had been married previously and this was a child from the first marriage. Dolores was born in 1879 and José, the child, was born in 1886.

[89] Frank Cuellar, Jr. thought this siblings name was Manuel but the image shows a female named Manuela.

The original certificate listed his father's surnames as "Coelho Guerrero" when it should have been "Cuellar Guerrero." As most of the Spaniards did at that time, his mother's maiden name was his middle name. His name was Francisco Cuellar Pareja in Spain.

Delayed Certificate of birth is courtesy of Frank Cuellar, Jr.

DELAYED CERTIFICATE OF BIRTH

STATE OF HAWAII
DEPARTMENT OF HEALTH
RESEARCH AND STATISTICS OFFICE

FILE NUMBER DB 7 01977

1. FULL NAME OF REGISTRANT	a. First FRANK ~~FRANCISCO~~	b. Middle PAREJA	c. Last CUELLAR ~~COELHO GUERRERO~~	Altered MAR 30 1937
2. SEX	Male	3. THIS BIRTH—Single, Twin, Triplet, etc. (Specify) Single	4. DATE OF BIRTH (Month, Day, Year) January 26, 1908	dated SEP 19
5. PLACE OF BIRTH	a. City or Town Ewa	b. Island Oahu	c. County Honolulu	
6. FULL NAME OF FATHER	a. First Antonio	b. Middle	c. Last Coelho Guerrero	7. STATE OF BIRTH (if not in U.S.A., Name Country) Spain
8. FULL MAIDEN NAME OF MOTHER	a. First Dolores	b. Middle	c. Last Parea	9. STATE OF BIRTH (if not in U.S.A., Name Country) Spain

10. I DECLARE UPON OATH THAT THE STATED INFORMATION IS TRUE AND CORRECT TO THE BEST OF MY KNOWLEDGE.

10a. SIGNATURE of Affiant   *Francisco Coelho Guerrero*

10b. RELATIONSHIP to Registrant   Self

11. CURRENT (Number & Street, RFD or P.O. Box; City or Town; State; Zip Code) ADDRESS   142 Linda Street, Vacaville, CA 95688

12a. OFFICIAL SEAL DAVID P. LUCCHESI NOTARY PUBLIC - CALIFORNIA PRINCIPAL OFFICE IN SOLANO COUNTY My Commission Expires March 18, 1983	12b. State of California County of Solano SUBSCRIBED AND SWORN TO BEFORE ME ON August 14, 1979	12c. Signature 12d. [X] Notary Public _____ Judicial Circuit My commission expires March 18, 1983 [ ] Health Department personnel authorized to administer oaths. Act 62, S.L. 1975

13. ABSTRACT OF DOCUMENTARY EVIDENCE — TO BE COMPLETED BY REGISTRAR

a.	Type of Document	Baptismal cert., The Immaculate Conception Church, Ewa	Date Established Feb. 9, 1908
	Date of Birth or Age	January 26, 1908	Place of Birth Ewa Mill
	Father's Name	Antonio Coelho Guerrero	Mother's Name Dolores Parea
b.	Type of Document	California marriage license	Date Established Dec. 24, 1931
	Date of Birth or Age	24	Place of Birth Hawaiian Islands
	Father's Name	not shown	Mother's Name not shown
c.	Type of Document	California birth record of daughter	Date Established July 24, 1937
	Date of Birth or Age	29	Place of Birth Hawaii
	Father's Name	not shown	Mother's Name not shown
d.	Type of Document		Date Established
	Date of Birth or Age		Place of Birth
	Father's Name		Mother's Name

14. SUPPLEMENTARY ENTRIES

Francisco Pareja "Frank" Cuellar

Memorial | Photos | Flowers   Share | E

Learn about sponsoring this memorial...

Birth: Jan. 26, 1907
                Hawaii, USA
Death: Oct. 3, 1995
                Vacaville
                Solano County
                California, USA

Note: California Death Records indicate birth
year 1907; SSDI says 1908.
Mother's Maiden Name: Pareja

Mr. Cuellar, 88, died at VacaValley Hospital
after a brief illness. A native of Hawaii, he
lived in Vacaville CA for the past 56 years. He
was a carpenter for many years.
Survivors include his wife, Mary S. Cuellar
(deceased 1997); two sons and two
daughters, two sisters, one brother, and 12
grandchildren.
(Source: Fairfield Daily Republic, October 6,
1995)

He was the son of Antonio Cuellar Guerrero
and Maria de los Delores Pareja Rodrigues from
Spain.
(Source: F.A.G. Contributor, P. Steele)

Family links:
 Spouse:
  Mary *Silvan* Cuellar (1914 - 1997)*

*Calculated relationship

Burial:
Vacaville-Elmira Cemetery
Vacaville
Solano County
California, USA

Edit Virtual Cemetery info [?]

Created by: M Roberts
Record added: Jan 15, 2011
Find A Grave Memorial# 64220445

Added by: Kristie Mudgett Dovel

Added by: Kristie Mudgett Dovel

CUELLAR
FRANK P   MARY S
1907 - 1995   1914 - 1997

Added by: Patricia Steele

www.findagrave.com Memorial# 64220445

JUANITA (Jenny or Nita) TRASCASAS SILVÁN
7 March 1918 - 13 January1981
Marriages: See marriages listed below

Juanita Silván was born six weeks after her parents arrived in California from Hawaii; the 5th of 7 children born to Juan Francisco SILVÁN Hernandez and Eustoquia Rita Marzo Trascasas Silván. Her parents immigrated from Fuentesaúco, Zamora, Spain in 1911 with her sister (Manuela) and brothers (Agustín and Jose) along with uncles, aunts and cousins at Gibraltar on the ORTERIC sailing to the sugar fields of Hawaii and later to San Francisco in January of 1918.

Nita loved to crochet; her fingers moved with lightning speed, just as her mother and grandmother before her. She crocheted beautiful bedspreads with tiny thread, doilies and baby clothes. She loved to dance and play cards. She enjoyed cooking, baking and gardening. She loved her grandchildren and had fun with them. Nita had a good sense of humor and liked to tease. She would have liked to travel more often. She raised poodles, and loved little dogs, such as Chihuahuas.[90]

My personal memory of Aunt Juanita is brief, but deeply etched as she taught me and my brother, Rick, a prayer, "Come Lord Jesus, be our guest. And to us this food we bless. God bless everybody. Amen."

Juanita had three children: Theresa, Roberta and John.

Husband#1: Juanita Silván married **Eugene Vidept Watkins** - 28 Oct 1932

Child: *Theresa Marie (Terry) Watkins Hyatt*, (adopted by Robert Hyatt)
Born: 9 December 1934 Solano Co., CA
Married: 26 April 1957 Orville Frederick Hayes / Raton, N.M. (1935-2004)
Died: 29 April 2005 (Resthaven Memory Gardens, Fort Collins, Larimer, Colorado)
www.findagrave.com – Memorial #23643897

Husband #2: Juanita Silván married **Manuel Castelar** - 16 July 1935 – Divorced
They lived in Benicia, California and cared for Grandpa & Grandma Silván
No children born from marriage; Stepson: Albert

Husband #3: Juanita Silván married **Robert Edgar Hyatt** - 24 April 1946 -1956 in Reno, NV;

---

[90] Memories from Linda and John Hyatt

Child: _Roberta Rose (Bobbi) Hyatt_
Born: 10 January 1948, Fort Collins, CO
Married: Jack Kelley
Died: 07 March 1984 (Hydrotropic Cardiomyopathy)
Bobbi died at age 36 from a heart attack, leaving her only child, Tandrea Dare Kelley who was later adopted by Joshua Mathison when she was 14. Tandy died Feb 11, 2014, possibly from the same medical condition.

Child: _John Carl Hyatt_
Born: 3 Oct 1949
Married: 12 Mar 1970, Linda Pfalzgraff Keefauver

John has his great grandfather John Silván's blue eyes and resembles his uncle Celestino Silván.

Below: John Carl Hyatt and Roberta Rose Hyatt

Husband #4: Juanita married **Albert Royal Schaeffer** 14 Aug 1957 (d. 1969)

Husband #5: Juanita married **Albert Rolland Hansen** 1980 (d. 1982)

Top: Juanita with Roberta & John

Bottom Left: Juanita (left) with John Silván and sister, Mary.

Below right: Juanita (neck brace), Theresa (right), Roberta (blue), Tandrea in pink. Photo did not list boy's names

Below: John Hyatt & wife, Linda

Juanita died at age 63 and is buried at Resthaven Memory Gardens Fort Collins, Larimer County, Colorado.

www.findagrave.com – Memorial #23643649

Juanita Trascasas *SILVAN* Hansen [Edit Name]

| Memorial | Photos | Flowers | | Share | Edit |

Learn about removing the ads from this memorial...

[Transfer Management] [Edit] [Delet

Birth: Mar. 7, 1918
          San Lorenzo
          Alameda County
          California, USA
Death: Jan. 13, 1981
          Loveland
          Larimer County
          Colorado, USA [Edit Dates]

[Add Bio]
Family links: [Edit]
 Parents:
  Juan Francisco *SILVAN* Hernandez (1875 - 1945)
  Eustoquia Rita Trascasas Marzo Silvan (1880 - 1953)

 Spouse:
  Robert E Hyatt (1919 - 1958)

 Sibling:
  Jose Marzo Silvan (1910 - 1979)*
  Juanita Trascasas *SILVAN* Hansen (1918 - 1981)

*Calculated relationship

[Add Marker Transcription]
[Add Note]

Burial: [Edit]
Resthaven Memory Gardens
Fort Collins
Larimer County
Colorado, USA [Add Plot]

Edit Virtual Cemetery info [?]

Maintained by: Patricia Steele
Originally Created by: MsFoxRider
Record added: Dec 30, 2007
Find A Grave Memorial# 23643649

Added by: Patricia Steele

Added by: MsFoxRider

HUSBAND OF JUANITA SILVÁN TRASCASAS:
ROBERT (Bob) EDGAR HYATT
Estes Park, Larimer County, Colorado, USA
30 July 1919 - 30 April 1958
Married: 24 April, 1946 - Juanita Silván

Bob Hyatt was the oldest of four children born to Carl Hyatt and Bertha E. Kitchen. His siblings were Hazel L. (1921), Dorothy (1924) and Carl, Jr. (1926)

He was a farmer in Estes Park, Colorado as listed on the 1940 Federal Census. While serving in the U.S. Navy, based in California, he met Juanita Silván Watkins Castelar and her daughter, Theresa Marie Watkins where they married before moving to his home state of Colorado. Bob adopted Theresa and they had two children together, Roberta and John.

He and Juanita divorced when the children were young.

He died in Los Angeles, Los Angeles County, California when he was only 38 years old. His burial took place in Loveland, Larimer County, Colorado where he is buried at Lakeside Cemetery. www.findagrave.com – Memorial #42056620

CELESTINO FERNANDEZ SILVÁN
30 June 1919 - 1 July 1973
Married: 1945 – Mary Louise Hutcheson

Celestino Fernandez Silván was the 6th child of Juan Francisco Silván Hernandez and Eustoquia Rita Trascasas after the Silván family emigrated from Spain. He was born in Pittsburg, Contra Costa, California.

While still a young man in California, he married a woman named [91]Frances (last name unknown). There were no children from this marriage. They divorced in the mid 1940s.

After leaving the Navy when WWII ended, he visited his sister, Juanita and her husband, Bob Hyatt, in Colorado. Bob's sister had a small store in Masonville, Colorado. There, he befriended Jack Hutcheson who had a very pretty sister named Mary Louise....

Celestino had the car. Jack wanted to double date. Celestino agreed to drive but only if Mary would be his date. But alas! Mary

---

[91] Photo of Celestino in his Navy uniform is with his first wife, Frances

already had a date and arrived at the same dance to see Jack and Celestino. And it began. Cel and Mary began dating. She was 18 years old.

They married in Reno, Washoe County, Nevada in 1945 while living in Benicia, California near his parents and brothers, August and Joe. Their first child, Celestino Robert, was born a few years later. Soon afterward, they were dismayed to discover Celestino's divorce from Frances had not been finalized as he assumed. (See story about Mary Louise Hutcheson Silván).

Cel worked in Benicia, California, Fair Oaks, California, Fort Collins, Colorado, New Mexico, and Wagner, South Dakota where his second child was born. Christina Silván Vargas laughed reminiscing about living in a tent in June Lake, California. Christina thinks her "chair" was tied from a tree limb. Photo is in collage on next page.

He loved motorcycles and a young man, he wanted one but his father said, "No." But he secretly bought one for $12 a month and slid it through the fence to hide by the barn. John Silvan saw his son through the window, went outside, walked around the barn a few times and shrugged. I wonder if he ever rode it??

Cel and Mary both enjoyed motorcycles. Celestino sometimes took his nieces and nephews for rides; some of their fondest memories were of their adventures, especially remembering Mary had her own leathers.

Nephew, John Hyatt remembers uncles, Gus and Cel, with a thoughtful smile and their love of fishing and the San Francisco Giants. During his teen years, he spent summers in California fishing, fishing and more fishing. He also painted houses to earn money with his uncle Gus. To this day, the guttering sound of motorcycles still reminds him of his Uncle Cel and Aunt Mary Louise.

Celestino was a coal tar enameller and sandblaster. Cel worked with large pipes inside dams and high-rise water tanks, eventually caused his death from Silicosis or Black Lung Disease at the early age of 54. He died July 13, 1973 in Carmichael, Sacramento, California.

His wife, Mary, was quick to tell me that Celestino's nephew, Michael Silván Ruiz (my father), was the first person to show his condolences at the viewing and she never forgot what it meant to her..

Rita and John Silván with Celestino at the
Silván Ranch in Winters, California

Celestino Robert Silván
Born: 11 November 1950, Fort Collins, Larimer, Colorado
Married Kathleen (surname unknown)

Christina Louise Silván
Born: 30 December 1954 Wagner, Charles Mix, S.D.
Married: Daniel Vargas
-Jerry
-Dustin
- Amanda

LuCinda Ann Silván
Born: 20 July 1958, Los Angeles, California
Married: Kenneth Walker
-Rachael Michelle
-Megan Nicole
-Celeste Evette

Mary Kathleen Silván
Born: 27 February 1962, Loveland, Colorado
Married: Scott Tyrone Willis
-Crystal Aleen
-Amber Marie
-Mary Felizia
Makayla Elizabeth-Page

Troy Purl Silván
Born: 18 October 1963, Colorado
Died: 29 May 1995, Forbestown, Butte, CA.
-Thomas J.
-Sean
-Sarah
-Jeremiah,

Troy is buried at Brownsville Cemetery, Brownsville, Yuba, CA. www.findagrave.com –
#77755840

Celestino: www.findagrave.com – Memorial #85030727

Celestino Fernandez "Cel" Silvan [Edit Name]

| Memorial | Photos | Flowers | | Share | Edit |

Learn about upgrading this memorial...

[Transfer Management] [Edit] [Dele

Birth: Jun. 30, 1919
          Pittsburg
          Contra Costa County
          California, USA
Death: Jul. 13, 1973
          Carmichael
          Sacramento County
          California, USA [Edit Dates]

Celestino Fernandez Silvan was the 6th child born to Juan Francisco Silvan Hernandez and Eustoquia Rita Trascasas after the Silvan family emigrated from Spain to the sugar fields of Hawaii and then to California.

Added by: Patricia Steele

Celestino moved to Colorado near his sister, Juanita, where he met Mary Louise Hutchinson in Masonville, Colorado. They married in Reno in 1945 and their first child was born five years later. Their children are Celestino Robert, Christina Louise, LuCinda Ann, Mary Kathleen and Troy Purl.

He was raised as a farmer but chose to earn his living in various ways, living in Fort Collins, CO., South Dakota, New Mexico and California as a Coal Tar Enameler and Sandblaster. He and Mary shared a love for motorcycles and photographs depict the enjoyment they had together.

Added by: SactoGranny

He worked with large pipes inside dams and high rise water tanks. Because of this occupation, he died of Silicosis, or Black Lung Disease.

Mary Louise Silvan survived him by 37 years. [Edit Bio]

Family links: [Edit]
  Spouse:
  Mary Louise *Hutcheson* Silvan (1928 - 2010)*

Chapel of the Chimes
Memorial Park &
Funeral Home
SUNSET LAWN

Cemetery Photo

WIFE OF CELESTINO FERNANDEZ SILVÁN:
MARY LOUISE HUTCHESON

Greeley, Weld County, Colorado
19 December 1928 - 16 September 2010
Married: Celestino Fernandez Silván

Mary Louise was soft-spoken. With a gentle sense of humor, she shared stories of her life with Celestino during our interview in June 2010, just a few weeks before her death. She met her brother's friend, Celestino Silván, and felt an instant camaraderie. They shared love for adventure, which included motorcycle riding, joking and camping. They had five children, Robert Celestino (1950), Christina Louise (1954) LuCinda Ann (1958), Mary Kathleen (1962) and Troy Purl (1963-1995).

She was a fun-loving storyteller with a heart for the underdog. She delighted in sharing one of her stories...I can still hear her laughter.

She and Celestino had been married about six years, Robert was nearing his first birthday and they received documents stating Celestino's divorce from Frances had not been finalized. In essence, their marriage was not legal. Mary flew to the priest to ask him if Robert's birth was legitimate. The minister assured her they had married in good faith and the child was born of that union. Afterward, the documents were finalized and Mary started planning a marriage in the church. What? Celestino said he'd

married her once and that was enough for him. Mary stood her ground even when Celestino took a job away from home.

She knew he hoped she would change her mind. She didn't.

So, Mary (laughing) told me she gave Celestino an ultimatum; if he didn't marry her again, Bob Hyatt was willing to adopt Robert as his son. They were very close to his sister, Juanita, and her husband Bob had already adopted Juanita's daughter, Theresa.

The ruse worked. Celestino, working in Albuquerque, NM, decided marrying Mary again might not be a bad idea…. They remarried in Newton, Iowa May 15, 1956. Mary wondered what the unsuspecting Bob would have said if he ever learned of her trick. Full of laughter, she giggled like a school girl.

Mary Silván purchased most of her appliances from my father, Michael Silván Ruiz, in Carmichael. He offered lifetime guarantees on her appliances from his store and always had a smile for her.

"Whose lifetime," Mary joked, "yours or mine?"

"Both, of course," he'd respond and he held up his end of the bargain.

Celestino died nearly ten years after their last child, Troy, was born. And she proceeded to raise their children alone. She was a widow for 37 years.

Mary Louise moved to Long Beach, California the summer of 2010 to live with her daughter, Mary Kathleen (Kathy) and was giddy about her new adventure. Sadly, within a few weeks of arriving, a heart attack put her in the hospital and she did not survive.

During my interviews with various family members, Mary's conversation stands out because it was filled with so much laughter. To me, she appeared to enjoy life to the fullest even though we both shared the tragedy of losing a child. We spoke about our lost children and she shared so many stories of her abundant and joyful life with her husband, Celestino. I feel privileged to have known just that little part of Mary and so glad I called her that day!

She is buried near her son, Troy Purl Silván, in the Brownsville Cemetery, 8980 La Porte Rd., Brownsville, Yuba County, California.

www.findagrave.com Memorial #113522442

Mary Louise *Hutcheson* Silvan [Edit Name]

| Memorial | Photos | Flowers | | Share | Edi |

Learn about sponsoring this memorial...

[Transfer Management] [Edit] [Dele

Birth: Dec. 19, 1928
          Larimer County
          Colorado, USA
Death: Sep. 16, 2010
          Long Beach
          Los Angeles County
          California, USA [Edit Dates]

Mary Louise was born in Greeley, Colorado to Purl and Berta Hutcheson. She met Celestino Silvan through her brother who was a friend and coworker. She shared Celestino's love for adventure, which included motorcycle riding and camping. They had five children, Robert Celestino (1950), Christina Louise (1954) LuCinda Ann (1958), Mary Kathleen (1962) and Troy Purl (1963-1995).

She was a fun-loving woman with a heart for the underdog and loved to tell stories of her life.

After Celestino died, she raised their children as a widow for 37 years before she moved to Long Beach, California the summer of 2010 to live with her daughter, Mary Kathleen. She was happily looking forward to the new adventure but within a few weeks, she was hospitalized with a heart attack and did not survive. She is buried near her son, Troy Purl Silvan, in the Brownsville Cemetery. [Edit Bio]

Family links: [Edit]
 Spouse:
  Celestino Fernandez Silvan (1919 - 1973)

[Add Marker Transcription]
[Add Note]

Burial: [Edit]
Brownsville Cemetery
Brownsville
Yuba County
California, USA [Add Plot]

Edit Virtual Cemetery info [?]

Created by: Patricia Steele
Record added: Jul 08, 2013
Find A Grave Memorial# 113522442

Added by: Patricia Steele

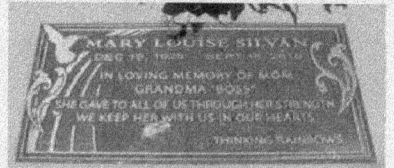

Added by: Stephen Fairman

RAMONA TRASCASAS SILVÁN

Winters, Yolo County, California, USA
9 March 1922 - 22 August 1922
Died: Woodland, Yolo County,, California, USA

Ramona Trascasas Silván was the youngest child of John Francisco Silván Hernandez and Eustoquia Rita Trascasas Marzo. She died at 5 months and 13 days old. Cause of death is unknown. Eustoquia Rita Trascasas Marzo Silvan was forty-two years old.

Ramona Silvan is buried in the Winters Cemetery at Winters, Yolo County, California.

DESCENDANTS OF:

Crescéncia Silván Hernández Gonzales (Weita)
Felix Gonzales Hernandez (Weito)

Back row:
Juan Gonzales, Alejandro Gonzales and
María Gregoria Gonzales

Front row:
Victorina Gonzales, Augustina Gonzales,
Crescencia Silván Hernandez Gonzales (holding Eusebio (Sab) Felix Gonzales),
Felix Gonzales Hernandez (holding Theresa Gonzales) Christina Barceliza
Gonzales and Acension Alfredo Gonzales

ALEJANDRO "RED" SILVÁN GONZALES

Fuentesaúco, Zamora, Spain
9 July 1909 – September 1975
Married: See spousal pages (3)

Alejandro was the first living child of Felix Gonzales and Crescéncia Silván Hernández. He was born in Fuentesaúco, Province of Zamora, Spain 100 miles northwest of Madrid. He inherited red hair and blue eyes from his mother and was called *Red* from an early age. He was also called *Handro*

Before he was two years old, he and his younger brother, Juan, were taken on the adventure of their lives. A train ride, a walk longer than they could have imagined, riding the ocean and living on a big ship. Their long walk was shortened a little because they were plopped into a cart with big trunks periodically during the 12-day trek to get on the SS ORTERIC.

Red learned from an early age that youth was no excuse to avoid working hard. In Hawaii, he learned to cultivate the garden and fish. He learned to watch over his little brother but was delighted when his sister, María, was old enough to take over nanny duties.

Before he was ten, another adventure; another ship, the HERMAN GOVERNOR, headed for California. He would miss the tropical flowers and trees, the easy, slow life, but soon had no time for frivolous daydreaming.   He and his siblings worked with

their parents in the fruit orchards and later enjoyed the camping trips to a place called Putah Creek.

As a young man, he worked with his father on the ranch. Many of his siblings remember him as tender hearted, although he and his brother, John, often teased their younger siblings. They loved locking their sister, Sally, in a closet where she cried and stomped; they would not let the others open the door. She was afraid to tattle on him fearing what he might do next time.

When he was 19 or 20, Red married 16-year-old Adeline *Lena* Fernandez, a Portuguese girl from Oakland. Red and Lena had six children, although their first son, John, died from pneumonia and is buried in the Winters Cemetery, 1925–1928. Felestino was born nine months later, nicknamed "Mac," Felix was nicknamed "Willie", and then came Herman Alejandro. Red's and Lena's daughters were Christina (named after his mother) and Clara Dean (named by Victoria Gonzales).

I have sifted through conflicting stories about Red and Lena. They married as children; she was pregnant and the marriage was doomed from the beginning as it progressively derailed. Unfortunately, the family stories begin to unravel here. One story is she never cared for her children and left them abruptly never to return. And of course, there is always more to the story.

Victorina Gonzales' story: Red's sister remembers the day very well. She said Red took Lena to visit her mother in Oakland, along with the baby, Clara Dean. And then he never went after her. They were extremely poor and she was extremely innocent. Her four children grew up thinking their mother abandoned them and no one saw their little sister, Clara, again.

Theresa Gonzales' story: Her parents, Christina and Felix, saw their son's marriage crumbling and the children kept coming. They drove Lena to her parent's home in Oakland with little Clara, while promising Lena that she could visit her children any time she chose but they would raise the children for her.

Lena's story to her children: She wanted to be part of her children's lives but was denied access to them. This is a story with questions that will probably never be answered.

As a Catholic, my theory is that Red was unable to divorce Lena but fell in love with Edna Letha Flint (from Graton) whom everyone in the Gonzales family grew to love very much. She not only birthed five more children with Red, but also raised Lena's four young children as her own. Edna's children were Edna Jo, Lois May, John Alex, Ralph and Buell William.

Photo: Red and Edna, about 1932, in Winters, CA

A BIT OF HISTORY:

A number of Japanese families were leasing orchard land in Winters, especially in the Olive District. Just before the Gonzales family arrived, there was an anti-Asian restriction such as the **California Alien Land Law of 1913**, which proclaimed aliens ineligible for citizenship or from owning land or property, but permitted three-year leases. It affected the Chinese, Indian, Japanese, and Korean immigrant farmers in California. [92]

With World War II's impact on the Japanese people in America (with internment camps), the Japanese had to inform the government which lands they leased so the government could assign local farmers to work their land during their internments.

---

[92]The law was invalidated in 1952 by the Supreme Court of California as a violation of the equal protection clause of the 14th Amendment to the United States Constitution in the case of Sei Fujii v. California

Red applied for one of the deserted farms. Since he managed his father's ranch and had the experience necessary, the government approved his request and he was assigned four ranches to farm along Central Lane in the Olive District. They were the Tanego Ranch, the Tabushi Ranch, the Susiaki Ranch and the Matsui Ranch.

Eventually, Red was able to buy the Tabushi Ranch in the early 1940s at the end of Central Lane as it joined his property over the hill, the former Bagge property. Red's son, Herman, told his aunt Theresa that his father paid $2,800 for the ranch, which was the total amount of back taxes.

May 14, 1959

The first shipment of apricots from the Winters area left here Sunday for San Francisco markets from the A.R. Gonzales ranch in Olive District. The apricots were seedlings.

Left: Winters Express Newspaper

Photo: 1949

When his father became ill and the ranch was having problems, he purchased a small house in Vacaville where he, Edna and their daughter, Edna Jo lived. Edna was a loving caregiver for Felix Gonzales there until his death in 1963.[93]

By then, Red's personal life was in flux again; he left Edna and Edna Jo in the Vacaville house.

Felix Huckaby, Red's nephew remembers his uncle tenderly. "My knowledge of my uncle Red and aunt Edna was that she was the most loving and kind person on this earth. I had the same feelings about my uncle Red. They both would do anything to help anyone out. They both had very big hearts. I got the feeling that he was a lady's man later in life though. At one point after leaving aunt Edna he was running a fruit packing operation in one city close by this area.

He told my mom (Sally) a story of a young lady who worked for him at the fruit packing place who stared at him whenever he looked up. It made him uneasy. One day, he said the young lady approached him and said "I think you're my father." He said they discussed dates and names and she was his daughter from a woman whom he'd had an affair. This encounter with his long-lost daughter took place in the early 1970's, I think."

---

[93] Source: Theresa Gonzales Sackett

The ranches around Putah Creek differed; some were on very flat land and others were situated on slopes. Many ranchers were able to pump water from Putah Creek to irrigate their farms. Unfortunately that didn't work on the Gonzales Ranch. Red knew that the water situation was indeed a huge problem. He was innovative by laying sprinkler pipes from the farm's well. However, there wasn't enough pressure to sustain an irrigation system even though he tried. Finally giving up, he sold the ranch to a developer because he just couldn't produce enough water to keep the crops alive.

Red's sisters, Theresa and Vic both told me they appreciated Red caring for their parents since all the siblings married and essentially abandoned the ranch and their parents, only coming back for visits now and then. They both asked me to include this important character trait of Red's to counterbalance his personal struggle with relationships between his women and children.

Sally George

In January of 1965, Red married Anna Sandvigen, the widow of his good friend, Carl. Red and Anna had one daughter, Anna Alex.

His picture was taken the same day. The back says Colewood Orchard...no date. Can you imagine how long it would take to cut all the fruit required to fill all those trays. Mom says that anyone that could hold a knife had to be up at dawn, get daily chores done....she milked cows...then to work either picking, cutting, stacking, etc. when I was growing up I had to work in the almond orchard, then the vineyard....so I can understand what they went thru. No play time at all except irrigating time...when everyone got to play in the water.

Alejandro "Red" Silvan Gonzales

View relationship to me

Birth 9 Jul 1908 in Fuentesauco, Province of Zamora, Castilla-Leon, Spain
Death 7 Sep 1975 in Woodland, Yolo Co, California USA

Adeline "Lena" Fernandez

John Gonzales
1926 – 1928

Christina Gonzales
1927 – 2006

Geronimo (Herman) Alejandro Gonzales
1929 – 2005

Felestino "Mac" Gonzales
1930 –

Felix "Willy" Gonzales
1931 –

Clara Dean Gonzales
1932 –

Letha Edna Flint
1914 – 2005

Edna Jo Gonzales
1935 – 2014

John Alex Gonzales
1937 –

Lois May Gonzales
1939 –

Ralph Alfred Gonzales
1940 –

Buell William Gonzales
1951 –

Spouse & Children ▼

Anna Marie Sandvigen
1923 – 2007

Anna Alex Gonzales
1965 –

Special Note: According to his nephew, Felix Huckaby, Red made sure every child had something under the Christmas tree[94].

---

[94] Theresa Gonzales Sackett said she and her siblings celebrated Three Kings Day before "Christmas" touched their Spanish family, their old traditions held firm where Three Kings Day was the gift-giving time, rather than Christmas day. Just as it is common for children to leave cookies for Santa in the U.S., in Spain, it was customary for children to leave their shoes out on the night of Jan. 5, often filling them with hay for the camels, in hopes that the Three Kings would be generous. They awoke on Jan. 6 to find their shoes filled with toys, fruit, gifts or coins.

He taught Spanish as a volunteer at the South Fork Union Elementary School where his daughter, Anna, attended and the students sent thank you notes along with this certificate.

According to his daughter, Anna Gonzales Manley:

"He had lung cancer. We lived in Weldon and he worked in nearby Kernville. Dad came every afternoon to teach Spanish. I remember seeing him walk across the campus to class and the kids would say "here comes Señor Gonzales" or "Anna here comes your dad" I had the biggest smile and so proud...couldn't get my head through the door. He never returned to teach when his cancer was pretty advanced by then. He had surgery in Bakersfield to remove tumors from his lung. Our teacher had all of us write get-well letters and draw pictures for dad. She did the same for me when dad died; all the kids wrote me letters and pictures. Mom tucked all them away and I found them while looking for these pictures."

Three months before Red's death, he and his wife, Anna, lived in Weldon, California where he worked as foreman in a packing company. They moved to Woodland in the early summer before he died in September of throat cancer at age 67. He is buried in the Winters Cemetery, Winters, Yolo County, California.

CERTIFICATE OF DEATH

Alejandro Gonzales

Alejandro "Red" Gonzales, 66, who farmed in Solano county near Winters for 40 years, died Sunday at Woodland Memorial hospital. He was a native of Spain and had lived in Woodland three months.

Funeral services will be held at 1:30 p.m. Wednesday at McNary's chapel in Woodland.

Survivors include his widow, Anna Marie of Woodland, sons Herman and John of Woodland, Mack of El Dorado Hills, Felix of Reno, Nev., Ralph of Winters, Buell of Spray, Ore., and stepsons Ivie and Ross Gelli of Vallejo; daughters, Anna Alex Gonzales of Woodland, Edna Joe Gonzales of Vacaville, Mrs. Lois Mae Foster of Joplin, Mont., Mrs. Christina Borges of Carmichael; brothers Dutch and Felix of Sacramento, sisters Mrs. Sally Huckaby and Mrs. Marie Miller of Sacramento, Mrs. Vic Weber, Woodbridge, Mrs. Thereasa Sackett and Mrs. Augustina Coombs, both of Winters, and 28 grandchildren.

ALEJANDRO GONZALES
"RED"
1909 — 1975

FIRST WIFE OF ALEJANDRO GONZALES:
ADELINA "LENA" F. FERNÁNDEZ
Born about 1910 – life and death information unknown

No information was found during my research. Each clue brought me to a dead end.

~ ~ ~ ~ ~ ~ ~

According to the 1930 US Federal Census, Lena is listed as daughter in law, age 20. Her children listed as Christina (2 years, 7 months and Herman age 11 months).

Lena's parents were born in Portugal. It is unknown whether Lena was born in Portugal, if her family was part of the Hawaiian Portuguese or if she was born in California. Her family lived in Oakland, Alameda County, California.

With those dates in the records, it appears that Lena was about sixteen when her first son, John, was born. He died at age two and is buried in the Winters Cemetery, Winters, Yolo, CA

Several stories swirl around Lena's departure from the family. Nobody knows what happened to her or to the baby (Clara Dean) in her arms when she was taken to her family in Oakland.

SECOND WIFE OF ALEJANDRO GONZALES:
EDNA LETHA FLINT
27 Sep 1914 - 26 March 2005

"Edna had the biggest and kindest heart and sweetest temperament"…were just a few comments from her family and those who knew her.

Edna Letha Flint was born on September 27, 1914 in Galata, Toole County, Montana. She lived ninety years, leaving behind a legacy of love and that special place in everyone's heart that she touched. Edna died on March 26, 2005. She'd been a resident of Winters, California for 47 years.

As a child she moved to Graton, California where she graduated from the eighth grade. Edna met Alejandro "Red" Gonzales and together they farmed and raised their children. In 1961 she moved to Vacaville to care for her father-in-law, Felix Gonzales "Weito", until his death. She remained with her daughter, Edna Jo.

(Excerpt from the Obituary from the "Winters Express," Thursday, April 14, 2005.)

Mrs. Gonzales was a member of the Church of Christ. Favorite pastimes included reading her bible and cleaning her house. She was a great cook making her famous hamburger pie, garbanzo beans, and canned apricot or peach jam. She worked as a housekeeper outside the home and still managed to care for her children. Edna was dearly loved by her children, grandchildren, great grandchildren, great, great grandchildren, church friends and extended family.

Edna was preceded in death by her mother, Artie Mae Dollison Flint, her father, John R. Flint, her sisters, Ruby Bristol and Ruth Webb. She is survived by her sister Elsie Henderson of Silverdale, Washington, her sons Herman Gonzales of Woodland, Willie Gonzales and his wife Vivian of Fairfield, John Gonzales and his wife Virginia of Woodland, Ralph Gonzales and his wife Linda of Winters, and Buell Gonzales and his wife Susie of Drewsey, Oregon. She is also survived by her grandchildren Robbie, Herman, and Tim Gonzales of Woodland, Don and Debi Borges of Sacramento, Carl Borges of Gold River, Richard and Michael Gonzales of Sacramento, Leila Drummond and John Gonzales of Corning, Cathy Ogando, Carole Armstrong and Chery Thomson of Winters, Steve Gonzales and Susie Shoffit of Woodland, Ralph Gonzales Jr. and Della Wharton of Winters, Jack Foster of Helena, Montana, Jeff Foster of Lake Oswela, Oregon, Jana Wolery of Inverness, Montana, Julie Hawkes of Wheatland, Wyoming, Buell Gonzales, Jr. of St. Paul, Oregon, and Josh Gonzales of Vancouver, Washington. In addition, Edna leaves 53 great grandchildren and 17 great, great grandchildren.

The funeral service was Friday, April 1, 2005 at 10 a.m., also at McCune Garden Chapel.

Apricots! Edna and Red on Gonzales Ranch with their children.

Bobbie Gonzales Fortunati shared a memory of her Aunt Edna regarding food.

"It is a dish/soup called tocino (tothino) made with salt pork or bacon (tocino), garbanzo beans, noodles and water. She once asked Aunt Edna what ingredients went into tocino and she answered, "water." The more people at the table, the more water you add! Bobbie says it was an "early hamburger helper" but with bacon for flavor and a little protein, but mostly water." She has never been able to make it like Aunt Edna probably because it's not meant to be made in small batches?

www.findagrave.com Edna's Memorial#28849781
Her daughter, Edna Jo died the second week of June, 2014
Her memorial was June 14, 2014 and was attended by her siblings.
(L-R: Willie, Anna, John, Lois, Buell and Ralph Gonzales)

THIRD WIFE OF ALEJANDRO GONZALES
ANNA MARIE SANDVIGEN
27 October 1923 - 16 February 2007
Married: 23 January 1965

Anna was the youngest of six children per the 1930 US Federal Census of April 15, 1930 in Virginia City, St. Louis County, Minnesota. Her last sister, Clarice, was born the following year. Anna's parents were Theodore Sandvigen and Marie Zacharison, both born in Minnesota. Anna's paternal and maternal grandparents were born in Norway and immigrated to America.

In 1930, the Sandvigen household included Gertrude (17), Melvin (16), Alvin (13), Theodore (11), Elmer (8) and Anna M. (6). Theodore Sandvigen is listed as a watchman in a lumber yard.

After high school, Anna studied nursing and moved to San Antonio, Texas where she worked at Kelly Field Air Force Base. Kelly Field was one of thirty-two Air Service training camps established after the United States' entry into World War I, established in 1917. It was used as a flying field; primary flying school; school for adjutants, supply officers, engineers; mechanics school, and as an aviation general supply depot. And this is where she met her first husband, Albrecht Carl Galle.

Anna and Carl married in 1943 and had two sons, Ross and Albrecht, Jr.. After the war, they moved to Sacramento, California where he worked as an electrician in a poultry plant and became good friends with Red Gonzales.

In 1963, Carl was killed in an automobile accident and Red and Anna's friendship shifted to eventual romance.

Anna Marie was 42 years old when she married Red Gonzales in Reno, Washoe County, Nevada on January 23, 1965. Their only child, Anna Alex, was born September 18, 1965 in Sacramento, Sacramento County, California. They lived in Winters when Anna was a child before moving to Weldon when he got a job in Kernville.

Red was 57 years old when Anna was born. She enjoyed the fruits of his age; her memories bring smiles but an aching loss for a father she lost by the age of nine. She shared many of the photos; some can be seen on Facebook at *Growing Up Gonzales* created by cousin, Sally Weber George.

Young Anna is married to Ron Manley and has twin daughters, Emily and Grace.

Anna Sandvigen Galle Gonzales died at Kaiser Hospital in Vallejo and is buried in a spousal grave with her first husband, Carl, at Sierra Hills Memorial Park in Sacramento, California. www.findagrave.com – Memorial#128114282

JUAN HERNANDEZ GONZALES
31 January 1910 - 11 April 1961
Married: Hazel Spurlock Roginson

John's first breath was on Spanish soil in Fuentesauco, Zamora, Spain, son of Felix Gonzales Hernandez and Crescéncia Silvan Hernandez. His saint's name was *Zenon* (pronounced THAY-known).

He was the second son. Times were poor. People were hungry. The month after he was one year old, he was whisked away from Spain with his parents and older brother to accompany his aunts, uncles and seven cousins to board the SS ORTERIC ship at Gibraltar headed for Hawaii.

John's first memories were probably Hawaiian palms, miles of sugar cane, horses his father worked with at Ewa Plantation on the island of Oahu and later Kauai, fishing, sisters and family gatherings.

He was a prankster and adventurer. As a boy, he loved to show off as all boys do. His father, Felix, had tied a mule at the end of the porch. John ran along the porch, jumped up onto the mules back and rode off. At the time, the story goes that his aunt Rita Silvan saw the antics and slapped at her own son (Gus? Joe?) and asked him why he couldn't do that??

John was a beautiful boy and grew into such a handsome man; girls stared. And he loved it.

His sister, Victorina, said he was their mother's favorite and could do no wrong. Victorina called her brother, "Romeo" because

he always loved the girls. He often contrived ways to avoid work on the ranch and would bribe the younger children with gum. Red didn't get away with much, but John...well, John was another story.

Hazel Spurlock Robinson stopped him in his girl-watching tracks when she caught his eye during his time in the San Francisco area. She was 5' 3" tall, with a great poof of dark hair cradling a face that was usually wreathed in smiles. Her eyes were dark hazel and her lashes long. She made him laugh.

They married shortly afterward and began their married life in San Francisco, San Francisco County, California. The couple later lived in Brisbane, California where their first child, Barbara Jean (Bobbie) was born.

In May of 1939, John applied for and received his Contractor's License while living at 235 San Benito Road in Brisbane, California.

His daughter, Bobbie, was three months old.

John and Hazel loved to dance la jota and the family parties were filled with music besides the food and laughter that followed their hard work. John self-taught himself to play the guitar and sang songs. He listened closely to the radio and mimicked the tunes. When he played the guitar, he used no more than four chords; years later, he told his children to watch his fingers and learn.

This cow has more names than John does. Elsie? Betsy? The best name comes from John's daughter, Bobbie: Oh, the "lullaby" cow. Now that one sticks! Bobbie said her mother, Hazel, called them lullaby cows because her father-in-law, Felix Gonzales, said they were smaller and ate less than standard sized cows, had a high cream content that resulted in better butter and cheese. Maybe that is why he had thirteen dogs on the Gonzales farm? To keep track of the cows? But no, I'm told it was because Christina loved dogs!

Bobbie also shared a story of visiting her grandparent's house at the Gonzales ranch. One night goat was served for dinner and the next morning one of the dogs was missing. Depending on who repeated the story, listeners either gasped or laughed because nobody could ever prove it was the goat or the dog spread out to feed the multitude.

John learned early in his life to farm with precision and care. He could propagate trees by grafting and his children often watched him in the orchards until they fell asleep in the hot sun. He created beautiful and orderly ditches with a shovel; and then, he turned on the water pumps. Water rushed through those ditches to scent the air with wet earth and water poured into the fields, barely cooling the air in the hot orchards enough to breathe.

Orchards meant harvesting. It was during these times the children were usually pulled out of school to help pick and sort the fruit. Everyone worked. Children did not wear shoes in those days, they ran in the dust, tried to make the days slip by… but the work kept them busy and tired.

By the time their second child, John, was born they'd moved to Sebastopol near Santa Rosa, California in an unincorporated area. In 1941, John and Hazel moved to Santa Rosa where they eventually lived on a five-acre farm in the country next to Hazel's mother's prune orchard.

John and his brother, Red, were very close siblings. Every year, Red lent John one of his tractors to plow their pastures in Santa Rosa and his mother-in-law's prune orchard. (Their farm was in the country but has since been built up with tract houses.)

John was cremated and is interred at the Chapel of the Chimes
Santa Rosa, Sonoma County, California. There is no marker.
The Santa Rosa Press Tribune printed an obituary April 12, 1961.

GONZALES—In San Francisco, April 11,
1961, John H. Gonzales, devoted husband
of Hazel Gonzales, Santa Rosa; dearly
beloved father of Bobbie and John Gonzales both of Santa Rosa; beloved son
of Feliz Gonzales, Winters; loving brother of Marie Miller, Santa Rosa, Alexander Gonzales, Tina Coons, Teresa
Sackett all of Winters, Sally Huckaby
and Jerry and Feliz Gonzales, all of
Sacramento., Victorina Webber, Lodi.,
A native of Spain, age 50 years.
    Friends are respectfully invited to
attend the funeral services Friday, April
14, 1961 at 11 a.m. from Welti Chapel of
the Roses.

In Memory of
JOHN H. GONZALES

Born
JANUARY 27, 1910
IN SPAIN

Entered Into Rest
APRIL 11, 1961
IN SAN FRANCISCO, CALIFORNIA

Services At
WELTI CHAPEL OF THE ROSES
FRIDAY, APRIL 14, 1961 AT 11:00 A.M.

Officiating
REV. GILBERT JOHNSON

Organist
WILLIAM THOMPSON

CONCLUDING SERVICES PRIVATE
CHAPEL OF THE CHIMES
SANTA ROSA, CALIFORNIA

WIFE OF JOHN SILVÁN GONZALES

HAZEL SPURLOCK ROBINSON

5 August 1913 – 29 May 2003

Hazel was born in Salt Lake City, Utah to Hamilton Edwin Robinson and Flaura Jean Winona Spurlock (born 12 Dec 1889 in Harlenton, Kentucky, died 25 April 1969 in Sonoma, California). They were married May 27, 1910 in Berea, Madison Co., Kentucky; divorced in 1919 in Salt Lake City, Utah. Hazel grew up estranged from her father; he'd remarried and had a second family. It wasn't until she was an adult, already a mother, that she connected with her father and his second wife, Sylvia.

She was a happy woman whose children remember with love and a smile. She embraced them often; she had a soft voice and shared in many loving conversations. Her sister-in-law, Victorina remembers her as a sweet, beautiful woman.

Although she filed for divorce from John Gonzales in 1961, the divorce was never finalized before his death.

Hazel remained on their ranch property until 1968. She died in Santa Rosa, California just before her ninetieth birthday.

www.findagrave.com – Memorial #128348667

JOHN GONZALES' CHILDREN:

Barbara Joan (Bobbie) Gonzales
6 February 1939

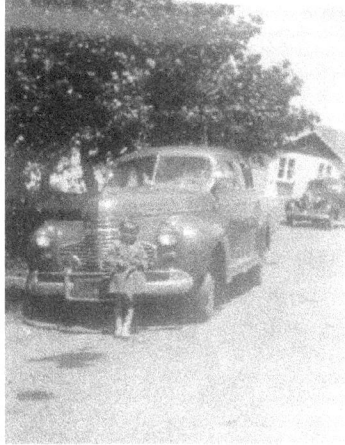

Bobbie says "by 1957, my dad was drinking heavily. We were a good family until alcohol took our father away from us."

He was from the old school; a self-taught man who built homes, not like now, but from scratch. He read blueprints, took his own measurements, ordered building materials, laid foundations, and installed plumbing and electrical cables; nothing was precut.

When the building business in Sonoma County slowed down, a friend suggested he try something new, learning to be a "barge man." Since John had always been a union man, the idea took hold and he went to the Inland Boatman's Union. There, he got a job with the Red Stack Company as an apprentice barge man.

John knew he had a lot to learn. The barges were not self-propelled; as long as a football field, obviously too large to move on their own, they were towed and then maneuvered into position by tug boats with huge marine diesel engines fueled with AV gas (aviation fuel), kerosene, diesel, vehicle fuel, very dangerous and inflammable.

John learned to estimate load capacity from a book of tables and not only worked on the barge but slept and ate aboard. He could not drink alcohol or smoke on the barge and his schedule shifts were 9 days on and 12 days off.

John and Bobbie, 1944

On his off days, he built houses. Bobbie said they should have been rich because the barge job was the best-paying job he'd ever had.

His last building job was for a bar owner. When Bobbie retrieved his personal belongings after his death, the bar owner said her dad owed him money. She was stunned and sad, thinking he drank so much he owed them money? Now, looking back, she is sure they defrauded him and she aches at the disappointing ending for a man with so much promise and potential.

She remembers him as a funny man, a good looking man that sometimes attracted the wrong kind of attention. She felt his time was mostly misspent toward the end of his life but those thoughts are mixed in with the good, funny stuff from her childhood and young-child times saying it was a great place to grow up when they lived in Santa Rosa on the property where she lived until 1959. She currently lives in California near her family.

John Alfred Gonzales
b. 28 January 1943

John's thoughts about his father, seen through his child-eyes were confusing. He said his Mom was a hugger with a soft, loving voice. His dad was the opposite; sometimes invisible, keeping an arms-length distance. "I will never understand why he yelled so much; never making a point I could understand. And so it goes."

.   Not sure who decided I should go to work with dad when I was 9 or 10. I shoveled a lot of mud, ran for tools, extension cords, Skill saws, nails. Dad was a ten in construction, architecture and carpentry, truly a Jack of all trades.

I got these big water blisters. When they popped! Hurt? He told me to pee on them. Sure Dad, thanks for the great info. I smile at the memory now.

Dad built beautiful homes. The downside was the daily celebration after work with his best friend at *The Rhythm Club,* their favorite watering hole. I sat inside the truck two or three hours; the waiting outside the bar was bad. I got hungry or worse.

When I was 12 that summer vacation in 1955, I worked with dad on a ground-up new home in Petaluma for his friend. This was my apprenticeship year at the "Gonzales School of Hard Knocks". When I was 13, I was driving us to job sites while dad napped.

During that time, he took me inside the bar, *Helen and Eddy's*. I saw live drunks buzzing around. Ever see an old lady fall off a bar stool? Bob Basso, the plumber, stopped to talk; never understood him much but he taught me how to fix a flat by patching a tube.

Dad always had me work on the blind side of a house to nail finished siding; all the nails had to be in a straight line….with no hammer marks. It was ugly at first, then got to looking pretty good. I learned later that I was treated like all newbies learning the trades. I definitely learned a lot from my dad.

Dad could also be fun. The best times were summers in Healdsburg when the river was dammed for swimming. Friends from Brisbane rented little cabins for weeks at a time. We had so much fun. Sunburns were bad though. Dad came after work and swam. He had a "wow" build; damn did I lose out.

I felt protected and at times I felt loved. Hotdogs! Dad gave me money to get us each fully-loaded hotdogs at the beach snack bar. I was proud he trusted me to get them by myself.

Then, my maternal grandmother from Brisbane moved in with us. Things changed. Years later, I learned why. He and his partner built a small subdivision and something went wrong; dad's partner ran off and grandmother sold her home in Brisbane to pay off the loans so we could keep our house. I'm sure that led to dad's downfall. He didn't drink much before that time. Dad never saw his partner again; leaving dad to deal with the mess had to be hard on his ego.

Yes, growing up was difficult because my father was distant and then alcohol took over but despite those sad memories, my father was quite smart and passed his good working values onto me. Deep down, he was a good man. I was very proud of him; he was a union man with a contractor's license and a teacher at the SRJC. As I think back, I believe my father was the smartest man I've ever known and I loved him despite the pitfalls of human frailties. John and his wife, Tomi, live in Texas near their family.

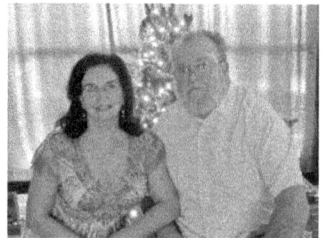

MOTHER OF KRISTIN ANN CHANDLER
BETTY JEAN GALBRAITH
2 Jan 1926 - 9 Jan 2013

Betty Jean Galbraith was the daughter of Donald and Ilene Galbraith, born in Chico, California and the mother of Kristin Ann Chandler.

In spite of the emotional upheaval caused by her liaison with John Gonzales, Betty Galbraith Chandler is included because Kristin is a valued member of the Silván family. Although she hid her daughter's Spanish bloodline for fifty three years, nobody knows the torments and fears she must have endured living a lie.

Despite those fears, she raised four daughters with a loving father named Mac Chandler in Vacaville, California. It was only later that Betty's fears were met when Kristin started questioning a persistent family rumor circulating about the truth of her birth.

Betty's response to her questions challenged Kristin to learn why her mother repeated the mantra, "It's not true." "Move on." "Let's not talk about it." "Let's forget about it." "It's just simply not true."

.   Kristin's Chandler-family genealogical research led her to the 1200s, assuming she followed her father's bloodline. That researching expertise helped her follow the Gonzales trail.

Betty's secret was brought into history.

Kristin found a sister and brother and a large second family.

Some liaisons are not a pretty story and some do not have happy endings. This one, I believe is one of the good ones and we have Kristin to show for it.

Kristin Ann Chandler
24 May, 1947

John's youngest daughter was born to Betty Jean Galbraith in Woodland, California. At 53 years of age, her uncle Mike Papin finally put rumor to fact about her biological father. Her mother, Betty, clutched her secret tightly causing much sadness for her daughter and the family Kristin loves. She'd always felt a piece of herself never quite fit and it wasn't just her eye color. It was a bittersweet thrill to see the first photo of her father while researching his bloodline and she has happily met and been welcomed by her brother and sister as well as the Gonzales cousins. Both her red hair and bright green eyes typify her Spanish genes.

After reading a draft of this biography of her father, she responded with the following note to complete John Gonzales' life for this book:

From Kristin:
"Oh wow, I loved reading all about him. For a long time I felt like a kid looking in a toy store window but not being able to go in. I didn't belong in my birth family (though I didn't know why) and I didn't belong in my biological family. The last reunion (2013) things felt very different for me. I have been

so welcomed and it has meant everything to me. I've

been befriended by so many aunts & cousins. It's just been heartwarming.

My friends have long told me I should put my story on paper. I am doing that; how I found out about my biological father and finally connecting with my biological half sister, Bobbie.

It's not much because I am not the writer you are but you are welcome to use any and or all of it if you want. I couldn't look any more Spanish. Seeing so many photos of John has filled a void for me that very few can understand. It never made sense to me that I looked so different from my birth family and now it does. Thank you much, cousin, for that."

John's sister, Victoria Gonzales Weber, shared her feelings for her brother:

John always had stomach problems and a drinking problem. He was also a heavy smoker. Despite those issues, John was a hard working, intelligent man and I loved him.

John Hernandez Gonzales died of a massive coronary infarction while working as an oil barge master on the Petaluma Branch of the San Francisco Bay Water System in San Francisco. He was transported from his barge to the Leavenworth Hospital in San Francisco where he died.

His brother, Alejandro (Red) went to the county records office in Santa Rosa after his funeral looking for further information.

MARIA "MARIE" GREGORIA SILVÁN GONZALES
11 April 1912 – 9 June 2004
Married Orville Benjamin Miller

María (Marie) Gonzales made her mark during her lifetime and liked being called the Queen of Sheba. She was the third child born to Felix Gonzales and Crescéncia Silván Hernández; the first child born at the Ewa Sugar Cane Plantation in the Territory of Hawaii after her parents immigrated from Spain with her two older brothers, Alejandro and Juan to Hawaii. Surely named for her paternal grandmother, *Gregoria* Hernández, Maria is shown here with baby sister, Barceliza (Sally) at Ewa Plantation on Oahu in the summer of 1915.

As the oldest girl in the Gonzales family, she became the 'nanny' to many younger siblings. Two more children were born in Hawaii within the next five years (Agustína and Victorina); three more in California after they immigrated to America (Alfredo, Theresa and Eusebio).

Maria loved music, loved to dance and is remembered as "always joking and fooling around" to make others laugh. And she, like her sisters, smoked those cigarettes. The ladies stood around in a haze of smoke during their visits, laughter slipping out between the nicotine clouds and fumes. The Gonzales girls had swiped cigarettes from their brothers, Red and John, as teenagers --- using any excuse to get their smokes, even while milking the cows or collecting eggs! A special spot for grabbing a quick smoke was behind the Gonzales hen house while the other sibling kept a lookout for one or both of their parents....

Marie worked on the family ranch alongside her brothers and sisters in the fields; but in between the hard work, she caught the eye of Orville Miller, from Washington state. Her father, Felix, frowned upon the romance but Marie followed her heart and the couple made a plan. Her older brother, Alejandro (Red), knew of the liaison. Life was difficult and they were poor like many families during that time, but he believed in romance. He kept their secret and with their cousin, Augustin (Gus) Silván, clandestinely drove them to Reno, Nevada just after her 22nd birthday where they were married on May 21, 1934.

Felix Gonzales was not happy when he learned she was gone. He sent his sons, Red and John to Reno to bring her home where her brothers pretended to look for the couple. They told their father they couldn't find her. When Marie and Orville returned as husband and wife, Felix resigned himself to the fact his daughter was a married woman and eventually grew fond of Orville.

Marie and her sister, Sally, often dressed alike and tried to keep up with the fashion mode. In this photo,

Marie is on the left, their cousin Felisa Silván Medeiros in the center and Marie's sister, Sally Barceliza on the right. Marie's sister, Victorina (Vic) thinks this photo was taken during the visits back and forth and reminisced about the truck, their brother, the sisters and the fun-loving times they had (see Victorina's chapter).

She loved writing letters; she yearned to make the world a better place and wanted her letters to count for something. Letters went to Eleanor Roosevelt, Social Services for Disabled and Handicapped, movie stars, American presidents and to Democrats in Congress.

During the 1960s, she wrote a letter to President John F. Kennedy asking him if her father was eligible for Naturalization and kept a response from the Solano County in Vallejo, California stating Felix Gonzales had received an Alien Registration Form. She received signed responses from presidents with presidential photos inside and she saved them all.

Marie also played a very large part in the family history. See last chapter regarding Felicidada.

In 1940, Marie and Orville Miller lived in Sonoma County, Analy Judicial Township, Unincorporated area of Graton, California where their three boys were born.

Orville Alexander, March 21, 1935
Charles John, May 22, 1936
James Arthur, January 11, 1938

After the 1940 U.S. Census was taken in April, they moved to Sebastopol,

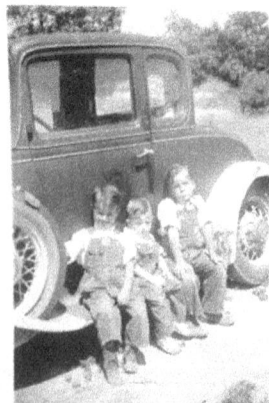

near San Francisco, and their last child, Christina Ann was born November 6, 1941. She was one of several girls in the Silván and Gonzales families named after Christina Silván Gonzales.

April 1940 U.S. Census: Sonoma County, Analy Judicial Township, Unincorporated area of Graton, California. The address is listed as P.O. Graton.

The Millers purchased a house on 331 Eleanor Avenue in Sacramento, California between Norwood and Grove Avenues in their older years, a place they could finally call home.

Red, his wife, Anna, and their daughter also named Anna, took this photo of Orville and Marie at their "ranch". Photo courtesy of Anna Gonzales Manley

Below: Marie Gregoria Gonzales Miller January 6, 1963

Victoria remembers her sister, Marie, unhappy at times possibly due to financial struggles. However, other family members believe her unhappiness was due to a childhood incident that broke her heart; she was the oldest daughter and in those days that meant she was the younger children's caretaker. It was during these adult-like duties as a very young child that she accidentally dropped one of her infant siblings and the baby died. Marie mentioned this sad story to several nieces over the years; she never got over the shock and guilt even though she was entirely too young to have been put in that position in the first place.

Marie loved writing all her life; several articles were published in *Let the Public Speak*. Always interested in her family history, she ordered birth certificates for her mother and father from Spain. Unfortunately, the document she received for her father was for another man and for many years, it was believed his name was Eusebio Gonzales Hidalgo. The mystery of the multiple names is solved; a genealogist sent me proven documents to show his name was Felix Gonzales Hernandez. However, Victoria was adamant he was called Eusebio. The mystery continues.

In July 1998, Marie's enlarged veins were inoperable. Facing mortality, she gave her youngest brother, Sab, the Gonzales family portrait that Felix Gonzales gave to her in 1962. Marie and her daughter, Christina, knew the portrait would be treasured and kept in Sab's family and that is exactly what Linda, Patte and Phillip plan to do. Miraculously, six years later, she was still alive to see the pride Sab and his family showed to have it in their possession. It currently hangs in Phil Gonzales' home as of this writing and was shared on Facebook for all the family to enjoy.

By 2004, Marie's condition worsened. She died June 9th. Marie's ashes currently reside with her daughter, Christina Miller Donovan. Christina will bequeath her mother's cremains to her niece, Linda Miller Rea, a granddaughter whom Marie could count on during her life and whose memories of her grandmother helped me write this biography.

Sally Weber George said her aunt always chuckled when Sally called her outrageous names. Marie's granddaughter, Linda Miller Rea, says Marie loved visiting her grandchildren; a time when everyone laughed together in Santa Rosa, California where Linda lived at that time with her children (Angelina Yukiko, Priscilla Vecenta, Richard Manuel and Chico Vencenta). Marie's daughter, Christina, was also part of those visits.

HUSBAND OF MARÍA GREGORIA GONZALES
ORVILLE BENJAMIN MILLER
24 February 1913 - 11 September 1984

His grandchildren, nieces and nephews remember Orville Benjamin Miller as a gentle, soft-spoken, kind and honest man.

Memories from his nephew, Felix Huckaby: "Uncle Orville was an early riser. When visitors arrived, he prepared us breakfast with eggs, hash-brown potatoes, sausage, bacon and lots of black coffee for the men and boys before taking us on a fishing adventure. The ladies slept in and got leftovers...."

While living in Sebastopol, California, Orville and Marie had a farm with a small orchard and a couple of cows behind the house. Everyone smiled when Orville and Marie invited family to their "cattle ranch."

His mother's maiden name was *Vintors*.

I could not find information on Orville's early life, his parents or any siblings on census listings or public records.

California, Death Index, 1940-1997 about Orville Miller	
Name:	Orville Miller
Social Security #:	572105528
Gender:	Male
Birth Date:	24 Feb 1913
Birth Place:	Washington
Death Date:	11 Sep 1984
Death Place:	Sacramento
Mother's Maiden Name:	Vintors

Orville Miller was born in Washington State and died in Sacramento at 71 years old.

With bittersweet memories, his granddaughter, Linda Miller Rea, explained that although her grandparents were estranged at the time of his death, Marie never stopped loving him. Linda was told sometime during his funeral and subsequent burial, his wedding ring was missing from his finger. Orville and Marie's son, Charles John, noticed it and the family like to think it was Marie's last, loving goodbye to hold his wedding ring in gentle remembrance for the man she loved; the man who fathered her children. They trust it gave her solace in his passing.

Orville is buried near his brother in law, Alvin C. Weber and James Miller in Lodi, California at the Lodi Memorial Cemetery in San Joaquin County. www.findagrave.com – Memorial#120116754

CHRISTINA BARCELIZA "SALLY" GONZALES
31 March, 1915 – 27 February 2003
Married: Allen Elmer Huckaby

She made children feel special and is remembered as the happy and organized aunt. She had several nicknames: Celi which is the literal variation of *Bar-cel-EEZA*, Sally and Silly[95].

"Sally" Gonzales was born in Hawaii at the Ewa Plantation on the island of Oahu and baptized at the Immaculate Conception Church in EWA Plantation. Her parents, Felix Gonzales Hernandez and Crescéncia Silván Hernández, emigrated from Fuentesaúco, Zamora, Spain to the Hawaiian Islands on the SS ORTERIC with other family members and several other villager friends. Each family wanted a life where they could feed their family and earn a

---

[95] These nicknames were given to me by her sister, Theresa Gonzales Sackett

living, something they could no longer do in Spain. Ewa Plantation was the first plantation her father chose to work; his specialty was horses so he was able to avoid the sugar cane farm work for a time.

Sally was the 4th child, the 2nd daughter born in Hawaii. She was light-haired and full of fun. When she was almost three years old, her family sailed to California where she later grew up in Winters, California. She worked on the Gonzales Ranch with her siblings learning to collect eggs, milk cows, pick and slice fruit and any number of other jobs that accompany life on a ranch. She had a special relationship with her siblings.

Sally was the only Gonzales sister to leave home before she married and got away with it. One day, declaring she was tired of working in the dirty fields, she left and started working as a caregiver for Mrs. Newman, an elderly woman in Sacramento who treated her like a daughter. Sally spent her paychecks on clothes for herself and her sisters. When they worked for Red for whole seasons they would be compensated with a pair of shoes from the Sears Roebuck catalogue. Sally's generous gifts to her sisters were well remembered; purses, shoes and clothing far from the farm in Winters.

And then in 1939, Sally's life changed when she fell in love with a man named Allen Elmer Huckaby

Wedding Day - Donner Summit along the old Highway 40 (Pre Interstate 80) February 4, 1939. Allen Elmer Huckaby married Christina Barceliza (Sally) in Reno, Washoe County, Nevada

Sally Gonzales Huckaby and Allen Huckaby - 1942.

Sally and Allen Huckaby had three children:
Christina Rosella Marie Huckaby,
 31 August 1940 – Auburn, Placer, California

Allen Noel "Dutch" Huckaby,
1 July 1942 – Sacramento, Sacramento, California

Felix Victor Huckaby,
11 January 1946 –Sacramento, Sacramento, California

Photo below: Felix Huckaby, Christina Huckaby Lynch and Dutch Huckaby- 2013, Winters, California

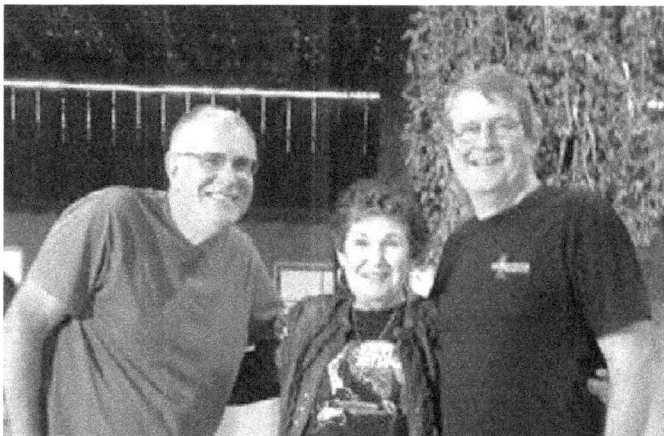

Sally's son, Felix (Fil), visited Hawaii and found the location where the Ewa Sugar Mill stood; where his grandfather, Felix Gonzales, worked before moving to California. He said "the mill was restored into a state park. A few of the original cabins at the mill where the laborers lived are still there and have been restored also. We also visited the Catholic Church, where my mother was baptized, which was just down the street from the mill. We also asked the church for a copy of my mother's baptismal certificate to give to my mother who was still alive at that time. I am unsure who has the certificate now. It was really great to get the feeling of being at the location where my mother was born and my ancestors lived and worked for a short while during their journey to America. We were told the church was moved from its original location on the mill site in 1929 as they needed a larger building. We found the Mill by buying a Map in Honolulu of Oahu. It listed the area of EWA and the Mill's Location. "

Felix also said, "My mother told me my grandfather tended to the horses or mules of the EWA Mill at the stables. I guess that led him to purchasing the apricot ranch in Winters after his short stay working in the General Motors plant after arriving in Oakland."

"Here is a link to the church with a map. If you get to the church, you are near the Old Mill down the street, at the intersection of Park Row and Benton Road. There are two long, white buildings. It has changed a lot because an old building taken down; they had a lot of toxic cleanup done since my visit."
http://www.immaculateconceptionewa.com/about/

Victoria, Allen and Sally
Sally and brother, Sab - 1942, World War II

Late in life she dropped the nickname, Sally, and introduced herself as Christina, when she went to work as a childcare worker for Family Fitness Exercise Facility in Sacramento. Everyone outside the family from that point referred to her as Christina.

Sally did not drive an automobile except on the Gonzales Ranch in Winters when she drove the flat-bed trucks around the orchard picking up the loaded fruit boxes in the harvest. Her brothers let her drive but they may have shifted gears for her? Her children and husband taxied her around until Allen was too ill to drive so her daughter (Tina) and son (Felix) were her chauffeurs once again.

Another story that helped me feel connected to Sally is from her nieces, Patte and Linda, daughters of Sab Gonzales. They have fond memories of their Aunt Sally as a woman who loved having children around her. She made a simple visit into an adventure and their voices warmed in their conversations about her.

Despite her name preference in later years that people should call her Christina, her family still remembers her as their Sally...

Christina B. "Sally" Huckaby
March 31, 1915 – February 27, 2003

Memorial Mass
March 6, 2003, 1:30 pm
St. Philomene Church

HUSBAND OF CHRISTINA BARCELIZA GONZALES

ALLEN ELMER HUCKABY
27 April 1913 - 6 August 2003

Allen Elmer Huckaby was born in Hickory County, Missouri to Elmer Noel Huckaby (b. 6 December 1881, Pittsburg, Hickory County, Missouri) and Rosa Dell Cady.

His father, Elmer, was born in Missouri and his paternal grandparents were born in Kentucky and Tennessee. His mother, Rosa, was born in Missouri and his maternal grandparents were born in Illinois and Indiana).

Prior to Allen's birth, his parents lived in Green, Hickory County, Missouri based on the 1910 Federal Census. He had a baby sister, Nancy Cloren Christina Huckaby, who died of colitis when she was only one year old and before Allen was born.

PHOTO: Elmer Huckaby, Rosa Cady Huckaby and son, Allen Elmer Huckaby

About 1922, Allen's family moved to Auburn, Placer County, California where his father began working at the Auburn Lumber Company. Allen was about 9 years old at that time. They lived at 263 Center Street in Auburn, where Allen attended grade school, and later graduated from San Jose State College. He later moved to Sacramento.

The 1930 Federal Census lists Elmer Huckaby's occupation as a laborer in a lumber yard. Rosa is a waitress in a restaurant.

1930 United States Federal Census about Allen E Huckaby

Name:	**Allen E Huckaby**
Gender:	Male
Birth Year:	abt 1914
Birthplace:	Missouri
Race:	White
Home in 1930:	Auburn, Placer, California
Map of Home:	View map
Marital Status:	Single
Relation to Head of House:	Son
Father's Name:	Elmer Huckaby
Father's Birthplace:	Missouri
Mother's Name:	Rosa Huckaby
Mother's Birthplace:	Missouri
Occupation:	
Education:	
Military Service:	View Image
Rent/home value:	
Age at first marriage:	
Parents' birthplace:	
Neighbors:	View others on page

Household Members:	Name	Age
	Elmer Huckaby	48
	Rosa Huckaby	39
	Allen E Huckaby	16
	Clay A Huckaby	13

During World War II he served the government working as a civilian at McClellan Air Force Base in the North Highlands area of Sacramento County, 7 miles northeast of Sacramento, California. After the war he remained on the Base and retired with over 40 years of government service.

From left to right: Dutch Huckaby, Christina Huckaby, Felix Huckaby, James Herman Weber and baby Sally Weber 1948 Woodbridge, California

Below: Victoria and Theresa with niece, Tina Huckaby

Allen became ill as he neared his eighty-fifth birthday and died in Sacramento, Sacramento County, California five years later. Allen and Christina (Sally) were married 64 years and died within six months of one another in 2003.

Both Sally and Allen's wishes were to have their ashes strewn over Hawaii, the place of her birth. As of this writing, both of their ashes reside at their daughter's home for a memorial once Dutch Huckaby completes the home he is building in Hawaii. This memorial will bring Sally full circle back to Hawaii.

AGUSTÍNA "TINA" GONZALES
27 September 1916 – 10 February 2005
Married: Robert Charles Coombs

Agustína was born in Kilauea, Hawaii on the island of Kauai to Felix and Crescéncia Gonzales during their sugar plantation years after they emigrated from Fuentesaúco, Zamora Spain. She was the 5th living child; the 3rd child born in Hawaii. Her older siblings were Alejandro, John, Maria and Christina Barceliza.

She grew up in Winters, California where she attended Olive School and completed the eighth grade. She worked in the fields on the Gonzales Ranch with her siblings and in other orchards.

Excerpt from "Growing up Gonzales" as told by Tina's sister, Victoria to her daughter, Sally Weber George:

Sally George

1936 Colewood Orchard

Victoria and Augustina Tina and family dog Brownie.

This cabin is future home to Tina and Bob Coombs when they were first married. The table at the far end on the porch is where Weito and the boys would gather after a day of work. Father always had his wine handy. There were always chickens running around, the dog would be barking...no one in a hurry to head back to the ranch for evening chores. The chickens drove the kids crazy as it was their job to hunt down the eggs. The older girls, Marie and Sally would go straight home to help Mother prepare the evening meal.

Colewood Orchard was one of several ranches along Putah Creek.

~ Tina and Bob Coombs ~

Just after Tina's 21st birthday, she married Charles Robert "Bob" Coombs on October 24, 1937.

Photo: Tina with her mother, Christina Silvan Gonzales

This photo is one of the few photos of Tina at this age that the family can find in their mementos. It has been noted that by then, Crescéncia's ongoing discomforts due to her Diabetes showed she wore soft slippers even outside of the house because of her tender feet, a symptom of the disease.

It appears to be the same day the photo of Tina and Bob was taken.

According to the 1940 U.S. federal census in Winters, Yolo County, California, Bob and Tina rented their residence on Grant Avenue with their only child, Judith Fay Coombs who was age two at that time (born May 5, 1939). They lived a short distance from Dick and Mary (Munoz) Ruiz.

In 1995, Bob and Tina Coombs' residence was listed as 312 Abbey Street in Winters, California.

Augustina Gonzales Coombs died quietly in her home on February 10, 2005 surrounded by her family. At the time of her death, she was survived by her daughter, Judy, and her husband, Jim Correia of Arbuckle, grandsons Kevin Correia of Arbuckle, Craig and wife Lisa Correia of College City, granddaughter Tammy Haynie of Moses Lake, WA., seven great grandchildren and one great, great grandson. Tina was known as the sunshine of the family. Graveside services were held February 16, 2005 at the Winters Cemetery.

Judy lost her mother just three months after her father.

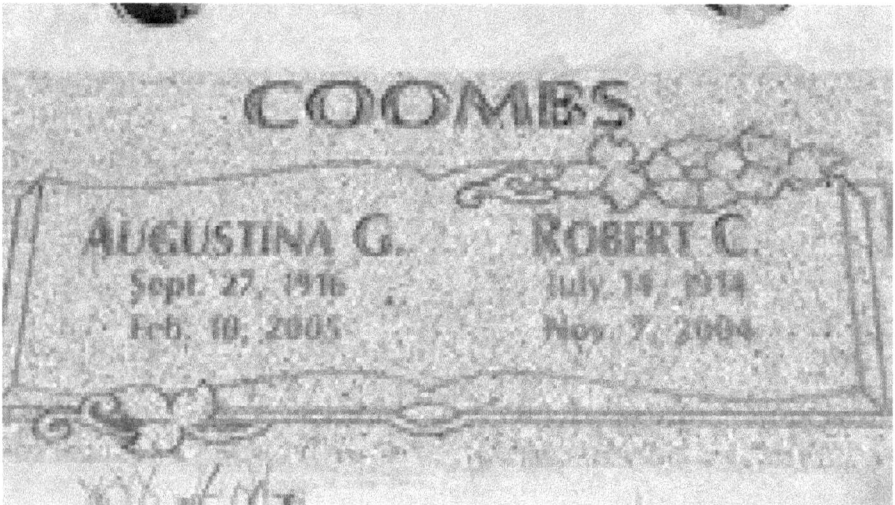

www.findagrave.com - Memorial# 27578761

Augustina G "Tina" *Gonzales* Coombs

Memorial | Photos | Flowers   Share | Edi

Learn about sponsoring this memorial...

Birth: Sep. 27, 1916
Death: Feb. 10, 2005

Augustina was born in Kilauea, Hawaii to Felix and Crescéncia Gonzales during their sugar plantation years after they emigrated from Fuentesaúco, Zamora Spain. Her siblings were Alejandro, John, Maria and Barceliza Christina (Sally).

She grew up in Winters, California where she attended Olive School, helping in the family orchards before marrying Robert Coombs in 1937. They had one daughter, Judy Fay.

She died February 10, 2005 survived by her daughter and grandchildren. Tina was known as the sunshine of the family. Graveside services were held February 16, 2005 at the Winters Cemetery. She died three months after her husband, Bob.

* Bio written by Patricia Steele member #47551507 on Sept. 9, 2013

Added by: Patricia Steele

Family links:
 Spouse:
  Robert C Coombs (1914 - 2004)

Burial:
Winters Cemetery
Winters
Yolo County
California, USA

Edit Virtual Cemetery info [?]

Added by: KG

Created by: KG
Record added: Jun 15, 2008
Find A Grave Memorial# 27578761

HUSBAND OF AUGUSTINA F. GONZALES

ROBERT CHARLES "BOB" COOMBS

14 July 1914 - 7 November 2004

Bob Coombs was born in California, the son of Robert Fulton Coombs (18 March 1866 - 3 July 1952) and Stella Coombs (16 August 1879 - 21 October 1960) (maiden name unknown). His father, Robert Coombs, was a rancher who lived in Winters, Yolo County, California during the 1896 Voter Registration notices. He had blue eyes and dark hair and stood 5' 7.5" tall.

Listed on the Silveyville, Solano, California Federal Census of 1920, Bob had two brothers (Howard 1916) and Melvin Albert (1917). By the 1930 Federal Census, they were listed in Winters with three sons, Robert, Howard and Melvin.

Bob completed the first year of high school. By the 1940 U.S. federal census, he and Tina lived in Winters. At that time, he was a stenographer for the U.S. Government. Robert Charles Coombs, passed away peacefully on Nov. 7, 2004, three months and three days before Tina's death. He was 90 years old. Graveside services were held, November 10th at the Winters Cemetery.

www.findagrave.com - Memorial# 27578902

Robert C Coombs

Memorial | Photos | Flowers   Share | Ed

Learn about removing the ads from this memorial...

Birth: Jul. 14, 1914
Death: Nov. 7, 2004

Bob Coombs was the son of Robert Fulton
Coombs (18 March 1866-3 July 1952) and
Stella Coombs (16 August 1879-21 October
1960) (maiden name unknown). His father,
Robert Coombs, was a rancher who lived in
Winters, Yolo County, California during the
1896 Voter Registration notices. He had blue
eyes and dark hair and was 5' 7.5" tall.

Added by: Patricia Steele

Listed on the Silveyville, Solano, California
Federal Census of 1920, Bob had two brothers
(Howard 1916) and Melvin Albert (1917). By
the 1930 Federal Census, they were in
Winters and included their three sons, Robert,
Howard and Melvin.

Added by: KG

They are both buried in the Winters Cemetery,
Winters, Yolo, California. Robert C. Coombs
passed away peacefully on Nov. 7, 2004,
three months and three days before Tina's
death. He was 90 years old. Graveside
services were held, November 10. at the
Winters Cemetery.

***Bio written by Patricia Steele member
#47551507

Family links:
 Parents:
  Robert Fulton Coombs (1866 - 1952)
  Stella F Coombs (1879 - 1960)

 Spouse:
  Augustina G Gonzales Coombs (1916 - 2005)*

*Calculated relationship

Burial:
Winters Cemetery
Winters
Yolo County
California, USA

Added by: KG

Add a photo
for this person

Request
A Photo

There is 1 more photo not showing...
Click here to view all images...

Photos may be scaled.
Click on image for full size.

VICTORINA "VIC" SILVÁN GONZALES
3 October 1917 –
Married: Albert Carl Weber

Victorina was the 6th living child out of nine when she was born; the fourth and last child born in Kilauea, Kauai, Hawaii to Felix Gonzales and Crescéncia Silván Hernández as they finished their sixth year in the sugar plantation fields before re-emigrating from Hawaii to California.

Victorina, also called Victoria, Vicky or Vic was three months old when her parents and siblings, Alejandro, John, Maria, Sally and Tina boarded the HERMAN GOVERNOR in Honolulu to sail into San Francisco with her Aunt Rita, Uncle John and cousins, Manuela, Agustin, Joe and Maria.

Vic attended grade school in Winters with her siblings, cousins and many Japanese children in a one room classroom at Olive School.

(Right) Victoria Gonzales - 16th birthday photo in 1933. This color-tinted portrait was displayed prominently in the photography studio's window when the sisters went to pick up the photos. Felix Gonzales was very proud of its spot in that window and drove by purposely to view it until one day it was gone! Someone had stolen her portrait out of the display window and the mystery was never solved. The story made me smile as I imagine some young man staring at the beautiful face in the portrait and wanting it for himself.

Three years later, on her 19th birthday – October 3, 1936, a celebration: to town to dinner and a movie.

Victoria is on the far left wearing dark lipstick mimicking her favorite movie star, Greta Garbo, who played in *Camille* with Robert Taylor. She wore a navy-blue skirt, red sweater vest and white saddle shoes. Her sister, Tina, had her hair cut short and wore brown saddles shoes. Theresa was barefoot? Sally's flowery dress had ruffles. Hazel, John's wife, often wore white and her shoes always had tassels. Her trademark hair was brightly colored henna. Sab's pants look like hand-me-down jeans; the bottom cuffs are worn and frayed. And as tall as Dutch was, his jeans are still rolled up.

Everyone was ready to pile into the truck while waiting for Felix and Crescéncia. On Saturdays, special occasions rarely slipped by without going to Sacramento or Vacaville, dinner or movie or both. Crescéncia loved movies; her favorite actors were Gary Cooper and Lionel Barrymore. John Gonzales took the photo; Red and Marie were missing, already married.

Left to Right: Vic 19, Tina 20, Theresa 15, Sally 21, Hazel 23, Fred, Sab 13, Dutch 17

As Victoria grew up, she worked alongside her siblings on the family ranch; she learned at an early age to pick, cut, de-seed and layer fruit in trays. She remembers the white, powdery sulphur sprinkled on the fruit before placing them into drying shacks. The sulphur kept insects from chewing the fruit. Then, she placed the tray in the sun to dry for a couple of weeks. It was hard work and later --- as an adult, she only worked in the fruit three months during the summer.

She remembers her mother, Crescéncia, receiving letters from her Uncle Gerónimo Silván, who lived in Spain and later in Cuba. Vic helped translate the letters until her mother met a Spaniard who replaced her in the translation department. She said her mother asked Gerónimo many times to come to America but he never arrived.

Vic shared fond memories of her tio Juan (Juan Francisco Silván Hernández) and his wife, tia Rita, although she said her aunt was very ornery. She loved the music her tio Juan made with his drum, "el bombo" and says the big family get-togethers were always full of fun and good food.

Her cousins, Felisa (Alice) and Theodora (Dora) Silván were visitors as well. She loved watching Alice and her husband, Joe, (whom they called Saa) dance. She laughed as she remembered Alice jumping up, putting out her hand to her husband and say, "Come on, Saa, let's show everyone how it's done." Victorino Silván was Alice's father and Victoria's godfather.

Victoria's favorite cousin was Celestino Fernandez Silvan, son of tio Juan and tia Rita. She lost track of Cel when they became adults and was delighted to see a photo of a grown-up Celestino with his family after our initial interview.

Victorina Gonzales Birth Certificate
(The document incorrectly lists name as Vitrina Gonsules)

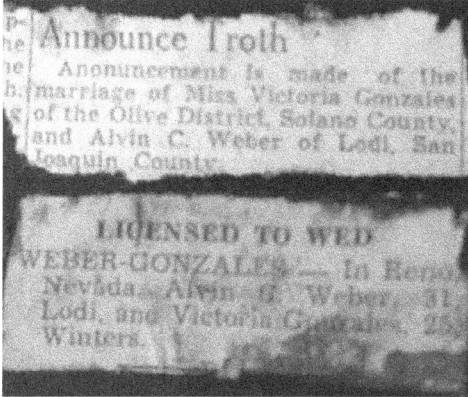

Vic fell in love with Alvin Weber (who was the foreman at the Garrison Ranch) from Woodbridge, California when she was twenty one years old.

They drove to Carson City, Nevada to get married on November 11, 1942. She remembers how grumpy she was when she learned it was a holiday and the stores were closed. She'd planned a shopping trip!

But, the Gonzales family made up for it with a cake, laughter and celebration four days later at Sally and Allen Huckaby's house. I loved the look on Crescéncia's face in this photo and the beautiful laughter Victorina shared with her sisters in the photo on the next page.

Al had a son named Walter from a prior marriage; a ready-made family. The Weber home was in Woodbridge, California, not far from Sacramento and the Winters Ranch.

Their first child, James Herman Weber was born July 23, 1945 and daughter, Sally Victoria Weber, September 11, 1948.

Victorina, Theresa and Buel Sackett in Winters, California between the years 1946-1950.

Right: Eusebio (Sab) and Victorina

Sadly, their son, Jimmy, died when he was twenty five years old, in April 1971. Grief rocked them and was still fresh when Vic was devastated again when her husband, Alvin, died less than two years later, January 20, 1973. He was only 62.

Jimmy Weber was survived by his wife, Darlene Twitty Weber and their little son, James Wayne Weber who was born September 19, 1968. He was 2 ½ years old when his father died.

Victoria took solace with her daughter, Sally Weber George and her husband, Bob in Aiea, Hawaii where she remained and currently lives at the time of this writing.

Despite living in Hawaii, she traveled to California to visit her siblings and Montana to visit her daughter-in-law and grandson until the last few years. She loves living in Hawaii and perks up when her grandchildren and great grandchildren are around and every time the phone rings....

She shared a wealth of information regarding the Gonzales family history through her daughter's (Sally) Facebook page with shared photographs and stories that have piqued other Gonzales memories in Facebook/*Growing Up Gonzales*.

Four Generation* photo at EWA Plantation near the area where the Gonzales family's Aloha life began.

Four generations: Back L to R: Marcia, Sally, Bob, Lee holding Taylor and Wendy George

Front: Ethan, Maya, Victoria Gonzales Weber holding Megan. *Todd, Sally's oldest son, is missing from the photo because of a traffic jam on the freeway near the Aloha Stadium. – See next photo

Left: My son and daughter-in-law, Frank and Reimi Zaccone who were my proxies to meet Victoria in Hawaii during 2011.

Bob George, Todd George, Victorina Weber, Lee George and Sally Weber George in Oahu, Hawaii

HUSBAND OF VICTORINA GONZALES:
ALVIN CARL WEBER[96]
12 December 1910 - 20 January 1973

From Shieldsville, Rice, Minnesota, Alvin was the oldest of eight children born to John Karl Weber and Bertha E Schmitke. His parents were born in Minnesota; his grandfathers in Germany and grandmothers in Germany (grandmother Schmitke) and Iowa (grandmother Oehler). He moved from Minnesota, where he was born along with Edwin, Lucille and Leona to San José, California, between 1920 and 1922 where the last four children, Edna, Leslie, Laverne and Charlotte were born.

A June 14, 1905 - 5th Decennial CENSUS of Minnesota shows John Weber living in Morristown, Rice County, Minnesota, and age 24. (A bit of mystery surrounds John Weber; first, he is shown born August 26, 1881 in Minnesota and second, there is documented evidence that he was born in Mackenbach B A Homburg Bay, Germany on August 26, 1881. His parents are both from Germany. Could the advent of World War I have anything to

---

[96] Possible meaning of the surname Weber - German and Jewish (Ashkenazic): occupational name for a weaver, Middle High German Wëber, German Weber, an agent derivative of weben 'to weave'. JXE, AB This name is widespread throughout central and eastern Europe, being found for example as a Czech, Polish, Slovenian, and Hungarian name. Oxford University Press. Dictionary of American Family Names

do with the inconsistency? Karl Weber, Bavaria, Germany, WWI Personnel Rosters, 1914-1918.) The 1930[97] Elkhorn, San Joaquin, California U.S. Federal CENSUS lists Alvin Weber at age 19 years old along with his parents and siblings.

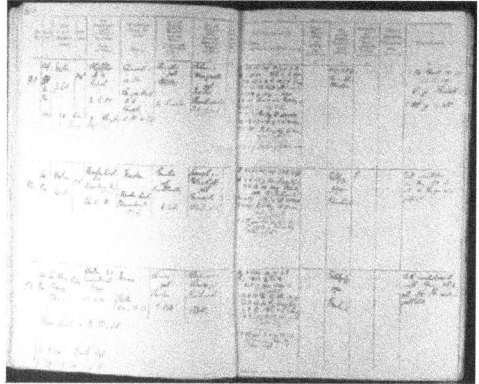

The 1940 U.S. Federal CENSUS shows Alvin Weber as "head of household" at age 29, listed as a foreman on a fruit farm, the Garrison Ranch. Two years later he married Victorina Gonzales. He was 31 and she was 25.

1930 United States Federal Census	Alvin C Weber	
Name:	Alvin C Weber	
Gender:	Male	
Birth Year:	abt 1911	
Birthplace:	Minnesota	
Race:	White	
Home in 1930:	Elkhorn, San Joaquin, California	
Map of Home:	View map	
Marital Status:	Single	
Relation to Head of House:	Son	
Father's Name:	John K Weber	
Father's Birthplace:	Minnesota	
Mother's Name:	Bertha E Weber	
Mother's Birthplace:	Minnesota	
Occupation:		
Education:		
Military Service:	View Image	
Rent/Home value:		
Age at first marriage:		
Parents' birthplace:		
Neighbors:	View others on page	
Household Members:	Name	Age
	John K Weber	49
	Bertha E Weber	37
	Alvin C Weber	19
	Edwin J G Weber	18
	Lucille A E Weber	14
	Leona A H Weber	12
	Edna H Weber	8
	Leslie I Weber	0
	Laverne M Weber	6
	Charlotte A Weber	1
		01
		7/121

___

[97] Copy of 1930 and 1940 Census available upon request.

The couple made their home in Woodbridge, California and had two children, James (Jimmy) and Sally to make a family with his son, Walter, from his previous marriage.

Al Weber's interest in guns was noteworthy; he was a gunsmith for twenty-five years in Woodbridge and a member of the NRA, National Riflemen's Association. A magazine feature article credits him with creating the "world's most powerful rifle," with 12,000 foot pounds of muzzle energy blasting out at each shot. It was the biggest of all 'big fifties' using the .50.calibre machine gun cartridge.

The children grew and their lives flourished. There were chickens, roosters, a vegetable garden, lots of grass to mow, a chicken coop. Jimmy had a little building behind the house that his cousins called a *bungalow*. And there were almond trees to be cared for, harvested and eaten.

Felix Huckaby said the rooster was vicious. Every time he was on chicken-pen detail, that rooster bit him every time. He also remembers his Uncle Alvin going to the chicken coop to pick out dinner. He saw him pick up a hen, grab it by the neck and spin it around in circles. Sometimes he had to use a hatchet if the hen wouldn't die easily!

Alvin's daughter, Sally, said she was a slave (smiling) growing up… One particular memory was when it was time to harvest the chickens, ducks, turkeys and pigeons, she was the one chosen to stretch their necks over the tree stump. She was happy she never saw her father spin the birds like Felix did. After the head was chopped off, the bird was placed into a huge tub of boiling water to soak and loosen the feathers. Then, she and her mother, Victoria, pulled all the feathers out. Her mom and dad shared "gutting duty" and Sally's job was to clean the gizzards. She happily ate them later. She said her brother always disappeared to go fishing or …….

Al's oldest son, Walter, moved to Fresno, California where he married and gave them a grandchild to love named Charles Chuck Weber.

Their son, James (Jimmy) became ill and died at age twenty-five in 1971.

Two years later, just after the New Year in 1973, Alvin died. His funeral services were held in the chapel of the Lodi Funeral Home and he is buried at the Lodi Memorial Cemetery.

Victoria Gonzales Weber lost a son and became a widow within two years of one another.

"California, Death Index, 1940-1997,"

index, *FamilySearch* (https://family search.org/pal:/MM9.1.1/VPHK-B4L : accessed 11 Nov 2013), Alvin C Weber, 1973.

Alfred C. Weber

Alfred Carl Weber, 62, of 715 E. Mokelumne St., Woodbridge, a noted gunsmith, died Saturday in a Palo Alto hospital after a long illness.

Born in Shieldville, Minn., he lived there until moving to San Jose at the age of 10. He completed his education in Lodi schools and later served as foreman on the Garrison Ranch near here. He was married to Victoria Gonzales in 1942.

For the past 25 years he had been a gunsmith in Woodbridge, and was a member of the American Emanuel Lutheran Church and of the National Riflemen's Association.

A magazine feature article credits him with creating the "world's most powerful rifle,", with 12,000 foot pounds of muzzle energy blasting out at each shot. It is the biggest of all 'big fifties' using the .50 calibre machine gun cartridge.

He is survived by his wife, Mrs. Victoria Weber of Woodbridge; two children, Walter Weber of Fresno and Sally Weber of Long Beach; one brother, Harold Weber of Lodi; five sisters, Mrs. Lucille Maxisdent of Concord, Mrs. Charlotte Henry of San Pablo, Mrs. Edna Plines of Lodi, LaVerne Weber of San Pablo and Mrs. Leona Silveria of Stockton; and five grandchildren.

Funeral services will be held at 2 p.m. Wednesday in the chapel of the Lodi Funeral Home.

At the request of the family, friends who desire to do so may send memorial contributions to the building fund of the American Emanuel Lutheran Church.

Page 14

CA death index
WEBER ALVIN C
dob 1910 12 12 MN
county of death SANTA CLARA
dod 1973 01 20
ss# 550468698 age 62

www.findagrave.com – Memorial #120160188

Alvin Carl Weber [Edit Name]

| Memorial | Photos | Flowers | | Share | Ed |

Learn about sponsoring this memorial...

[Transfer Management] [Edit] [Dele

Birth: Dec. 12, 1910
         Morristown
         Rice County
         Minnesota, USA
Death: Jan. 20, 1973
         Lodi
         San Joaquin County
         California, USA [Edit Dates]

Alvin was the first of eight children to John
Karl Weber and Bertha E Schmitke. His parents
were both born in Minnesota, but his
grandfathers were born in Germany. His
grandmothers, were born in Germany
(grandmother Schmitke) and Iowa
(grandmother Oehler). His siblings were Edwin,
Lucille, Leona, Edna, Leslie, Laverne and
Charlotte.

Added by: Patricia Steele

The Weber family lived in Minnesota where
Alvin, Edwin, Lucille and Leona were born and
moved to California sometime between 1918
and 1922 where the last four children, Edna,
Leslie, Laverne and Charlotte were born.

Alvin married Victorina Gonzales, from Winters,
Yolo County, California in November, 1942.
They had two children, James and Sally. They
made their home in Woodbridge, California. He
is buried in the Lodi Memorial Cemetery, Lodi,
California.
[Edit Bio]
[Link family members]

Added by: Joy

[Add Marker Transcription]
[Add Note]

Burial: [Edit]
Lodi Memorial Cemetery
Lodi
San Joaquin County
California, USA
Plot: Pioneer II, S, 324 [Edit Plot]

Cemetery Photo
Don't show cemetery photos
on this memorial [?]
Added by: Tim Cook

ASCENSIÓN "DUTCH" GONZALES
9 August 1919 – 1 November 1999
Married: Cecelia LeLuc
Married: Sarah Ann Brown

He did not have a middle name, so he gave himself one when he enlisted – when "Jerry" was born.

Ascensión's American name was Alfred. His nickname was "Dutch," the first child born in America after his parents sailed from Hawaii to California on the ship, HERMAN GOVERNOR, January 1918.

Dutch was born in Oakland, Alameda County, California, where his parents settled before moving to Putah Creek. They'd camped in the area of Putah Creek and purchased land nearby. His father built a house on what would be called the Gonzales Ranch near Winters, California, more appropriately listed as Silveyville, Solano County, California.

The first photograph I found of Dutch was found in "Images of America: WINTERS" where he sat on a bicycle beside two of his siblings, Theresa and Eusebio. He was a fair-haired child with blue eyes, hence the nickname, "Dutch".

This photo was donated by his daughter, Alicia, who thought he was about 8 years old sitting on the fender of the truck his father drove to deliver fruit from their ranch.

Dutch attended the Olive School with his siblings but like many children in that time, he had to quit school in the sixth grade to work on the family ranch. He later earned his GED.

As World War II loomed, Ascensión "J" Dutch volunteered in the United States Marines.

His sister, Theresa, reminisced about her brother, Dutch. She told me he did not have a middle name so he gave himself one: Jerry. So, his military records show A. J. Gonzales – Alfred Jerry Gonzales. Ascension was the Spanish name for Alfred and I have used both names for clarity. I believe he was named after his paternal grandfather, Ascension Gonzales. However, some cousins remember him being called Alfred Geronimo. No documents show this name.

Dutch was close to his oldest brother, Red, and often became misty eyed when he remembered how poor their family was says his daughter, Alicia. He shared fond memories with his daughter, Alicia, saying his brother (Red) gave him his first rifle. With eleven years between them, Dutch felt Red was more of a father figure than a brother and always remembered him with kindness.

In the early 1950s, Dutch married Cecelia LaLuc from Brisbane, California. They had one daughter, Theresa Joanne Gonzales on April 4, 1954 in Sacramento, California. It was with great sadness when they divorced around 1966 because Cecelia was well loved by the Gonzales family. She and their daughter, Theresa, remained friends with the family and attended family functions for a time. Sadly, due to the divorce, Dutch and his daughter, Theresa, became estranged and never reconciled. She did not respond to my request for copies of her father's military papers, photographs and any other memorabilia that was retained by her mother after their divorce. It is my understanding that Theresa Joanne Gonzales has never married.

Shortly after the divorce, Dutch remarried Sarah Ann (Sallie) Brown about 1966 or 1967. She had three boys named Ryan, Gary and Kelly from her previous marriage. In 1968, they had a daughter named Alicia J. who was born in Sacramento, 29 October, 1967. Alicia shared heartwarming stories and photographs for this biography.

During the July 1977 Gonzales reunion, Dutch and Sallie lived at 2337 Catalina Dr., Sacramento, California. Dutch was a carpenter by trade but during the war, he worked at McClellan Air Force Base in California and remained employed there for many years.

He began volunteering with his brother, Sab, at the California State Railroad Museum. Close in age, they shared many of the same likes and dislikes. One special bond they enjoyed together was traveling to Spain in later years, where they walked through the village of our ancestors in Fuentesaúco, Zamora, Spain.

His daughter, Alicia, shared a special memory of her father; she accompanied him to Putah Creek where the Gonzales Ranch stood many years ago. The locals still refer to the patch of land by the Gonzales name. She said a new home is now built on the flat portion of the property. She and her father had permission from the new owners to walk around the property and were delighted to find the remains of the Gonzales' old brick oven where Christina baked bread. The landowner allowed them to take some of the bricks, which she still keeps as a memento.

That same day, they continued down the road to find the ranch his brother, Red, owned and it was still there, although of course, new owners.

In 1992, Dutch attended the last Gonzales family reunion. Missing were Red and John who had died prior to the reunion.

Dutch became very ill in the fall of 1999 and he asked his sister, Victorina, to fly from Hawaii to California and stay with him a few days, because they were very close. She came. Then, he rallied and she returned home to the islands. When he fell ill again, she returned to his side. He rallied once again.

Dutch died in November 1, 1999 of congestive heart failure in Sacramento, Sacramento, California. According to his sister, Theresa, he died due to complications from malaria from World War II.

He is buried in the San Joaquin Valley National Cemetery, 32053 West McCabe Road, Santa Nella Village, Merced County, California.

www.findagrave.com - Memorial# 86334821

PFC Alfred Jerry "Dutch" Gonzales [Edit Name]

Memorial | Photos | Flowers   Share | Edit

Learn about sponsoring this memorial...

[Transfer Management] [Edit] [Dele

Birth: Aug. 9, 1919
         Oakland
         Alameda County
         California, USA
Death: Nov. 1, 1999
         Sacramento
         Sacramento County
         California, USA [Edit Dates]

Added by: Patricia Steele

Ascensión "Dutch" was the first child born in America after his parents sailed from Hawaii to California on the SS Herman Governor early 1918. His parents were Felix Gonzales and Crescencia Silvan Gonzales, both from Spain. Though born in Oakland, he was raised at his family ranch near Winters, CA.

Dutch attended the Olive School until he quit school in the sixth grade to work on the family ranch, later earning a GED.
He enlisted in the U.S. Marines, March 5, 1946. One of his sisters stated Alfred did not have a middle name so he gave himself one: Alfred Jerry Gonzales.

Added by: William Tatum

One of 8 children, his surviving daughters are Theresa and Alicia. Granddaughters, Alejandra and Sophia.

He died of congestive heart failure believed to have been caused due to complications from malaria contracted in WWII while fighting in Guadalcanal and Iwo Jima.
[Edit Bio]
[Link family members]
[Add Marker Transcription]
[Add Note]

SAN JOAQUIN VALLEY NATIONAL CEMETERY

Burial: [Edit]
San Joaquin Valley National Cemetery
Santa Nella Village
Merced County
California, USA
Plot: Section C-5 Site 767 [Edit Plot]

Cemetery Photo
Don't show cemetery photos on this memorial [?]
Added by: David Olson

Edit Virtual Cemetery info [?]

Created by: Patricia Steele
Record added: Mar 06, 2012
Find A Grave Memorial# 86334788

Add a photo for this person   Request A Photo

Change Photo Order

THERESA "TEET" GONZALES
Birth: 31 January 1921
Married: Buel Arthur Sackett

Theresa Gonzales is the mainland's matriarch as of this writing. She was the second of the three Gonzales children born in America to Crescéncia Silván and Felix Gonzales Hernández after they emigrated from Hawaii. She was born in Oakland, Alameda, California, inherited the reddish-blond hair of her ancestors as a result of the Irish emigrating into Northern Spain and intermarrying with the Spanish. She grew up with a large family and shared her memories of the camping trips to Putah Creek where Diversion Dam now stands, near Winters, California…her paradise. Her first memory of Putah Creek was standing at the water's edge on clean wet sand. She watched her mother, Christina, place soapy dishtowels on small boulders to bleach in the sun. She remembers the glistening water flowing and what her mother wore: a long bleached cotton skirt. Her mother's red-gold hair was knotted at the back of her head and small tendrils lay on her temples. She remembered thinking how pretty her

mother was and her voice softened over the phone at the memory.

Theresa learned from an early age to work hard; the ranch taught her about apricots, plums, growing, harvesting, canning, storing and competition between other fruit farms as well as how her father shipped the harvests. Then there was picking, cutting, and best of all, the eating.

Life wasn't always good. Business was often slow. She remembered when their truck was nearly repossessed, but saved by her typically-quiet mother. An emotional Christina Gonzales tried to remove the spare tire from the underside of the truck before it would have been hauled away. The dumbfounded owners could not take it.

Overall, they had a good life. Warm milk right out of their cow, chorizo, blood sausage and bacon from their animals and the full Matanza ran full speed ahead at the Gonzales ranch. Her tia Rita Silván's job was to stir the blood as it drained from the pigs to avoid curdling. It was horrible to watch but Theresa assured me the finished product was delicious, never enough.

Then, there was bread making and baking in the outdoor ovens as the scent of freshly baking bread wafted through the air. Several siblings helped with the weekly chore; it was a long process. Their bread was reminiscent of what we now know as French bread with a harder crust.

She remembers walking with tin cans pressed to her feet and rolling rubber tires. It was a wonderful place for children as they could run free in an uncomplicated world. In and around the playtimes, there were the Tokay grapes and her father's wonderful home-made wine. She loved helping! Crushing those grapes with her bare feet in a huge wooden tank and all the fermenting, pressing that was to follow. If it soured in the heat, her mother got vinegar…and her father got "White Mule" which was similar to clear vodka. Adding cherries to the brew was a Christmas treat. Theresa told me their bare feet were remarkably clean afterward….

Theresa attended Olive School with her siblings and a mixture of Spanish and Japanese students. After school, they walked to the Ansel Pleasants Ranch for catechism once a week.

During her childhood, there were always the family gatherings. She remembered how her tio Juan Silván would arrive with his wife, Rita, and their children to visit. He played his drum as everyone sang and danced --- a Spanish tradition that still makes her smile.

By the early 1940s, romance was in the air. Buel Arthur Sackett lived on the Golden Star Ranch and was drafted into what later became World War II. She hadn't known him well but when he wrote to her, she responded.

She said he was the most eligible bachelor in Winters and their romance bloomed when he returned to town. They danced at Veteran's Halls and later, the postman recognized romance; to avoid delivery delays between the ranches, he scribbled on their stamps and personally delivered each letter. And he smiled a lot. Theresa and Buel Sackett were married in Reno, Nevada on June 25, 1946, just two days after the fruit harvest. Theresa wore a two-piece turquoise suit and open-toed pumps.

Their married life began in a small wood-framed house on a ranch along Sacketts Lane at the mouth of Putah Canyon. She loved the peace of the ranch life. Buel milked the cow and she churned butter with wooden paddles. She kept busy on the ranch and managed to keep track of their accounting as well.

When her mother died within six months of her marriage, it was an emotionally crippling time for her. She was glad she could stay busy with her ranch life.

Photo: Alejandro (Red), Victorina (Vic), Allen Huckaby and Theresa

Theresa Gonzales Sackett and her niece, Kristen Ann Chandler (daughter of John Gonzales), at the Silvan Family Reunion in Winters in August of 2013 – The Gonzales resemblance is amazing.

THERESA GONZALES SACKETT'S CHILDREN

Buel Arthur Sackett, Jr.
2 December 1955

He graduated from California State University Sacramento in 1995 and teaches Social Studies at Cache Creek High School in the Woodland School He is married to Elena Obrego Sackett

Chester "Chet" Hiram Sackett II
March 31, 1959
Chet attended MTI, a computer school in Sacramento and the Mechanic Institute in Freemont, California. He later worked at a firm that fabricated building materials. He is married to Pamela Dubois Sackett.

Both boys attended Olive School, rode horses and helped on the ranch. Both of her boys graduated from Winters High School.

1959 – Chet Sackett with his cousin Tina Huckaby.

In 2000, Theresa was interviewed by Jacqueline Avellar for a paper titled, *Winter's Tales* that summarized her life in Winters, California.

This photo shows Theresa's intrinsic *style* for me. I smiled when I read her words on the backside of the photo (in her handwriting): "Attire by Liz Claiborne, Glasses by Lauren Bacall, and Makeup by Lancôme.

A cousin visited Theresa in 2011 and I smiled to read her note regarding the reception she received as follows: "She is 90 years old and sharp as a tack. She was very gracious, even with her beer, which she enjoys daily at 10 am. Only one she has all day!! She insisted we have one together; after all it was nearly one in the afternoon by the time I got there. She assured me it was the Gonzales way. She is a real kick in the pants!"

As of this writing, Theresa Gonzales Sackett resides in Winters, California and remains in close contact with her only surviving sibling, Victorina aka "Vic" in Aeia, Oahu, Hawaii.

HUSBAND OF THERESA GONZALES:
BUEL ARTHUR SACKETT, SR.
12 March 1915 - 28 February 1995

Buel Arthur Sackett learned to farm at a young age on his parent's farm, the Golden Star Ranch, which was located upstream on Putah Creek. Born in Winters, he was drafted into the U.S. Army in 1944 where he earned the rank of Sergeant in World War II. He was in the 76th Division Co L, 417th Regt. They were part of the 3d Battalion in General George Patton's Third Army.

Information was received from a military historian to explain the warfare that earned Buel Sackett a Purple Heart as follows: *The unit had been rushed to the front in response to the German offensive in December 1944 known as the Battle of the Bulge. By the time Co L reached the front, the Germans had been thrown back into Germany in their sector and the 417th had been selected to participate in the invasion of Germany from Echternach, Luxembourg.*

The attack was poorly planned, poorly led and poorly executed because of the inexperience of the officers involved and the rush to go on the offensive. Some units were sent across on 7 Feb and additional attacks were

launched on a night so dark, one could not see his own hand in front of his face. It was a night like this that Buel and his company raced toward foxholes with the Germans in pursuit. He fell into the hole unevenly and was injured as shrapnel caught him in the jaw.

He was shipped to Modesto, California where he healed at the Hammond Military Hospital where he remained for one month before returning to Winters on leave where romance bloomed with Theresa Gonzales as they danced to the music of Lloyd Adams Band and Harry James.

From there, he proposed and they married in June 1946. Buel managed his uncle's apricot ranch on Sackett Lane on Putah Creek at the mouth of Putah Canyon. It was a beautiful area to raise their boys in between horses, milking cows and apricots. Theresa's husband, Buel Arthur Sackett, died February 28, 1995. His ashes are interred at the Winters Cemetery, Yolo County, California, USA, Plot: Sec 6 Lot 28 East

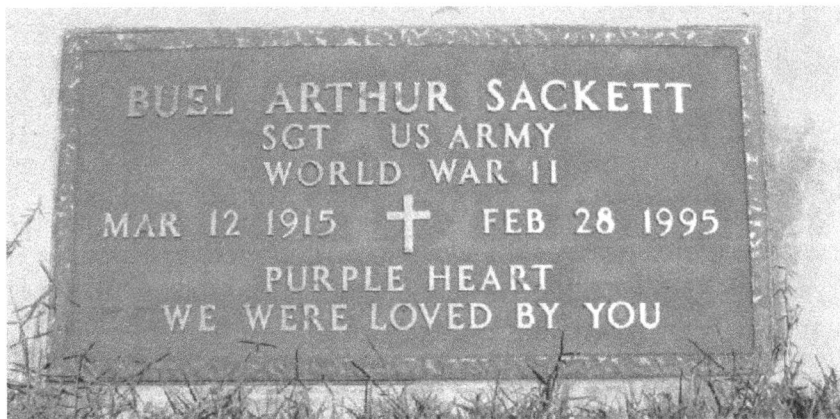

www.findagrave.com - Memorial# 32751200

EUSEBIO FELIX "SAB" GONZALES
18 May 1923 - 11 June 2004
Married: Phyllis Hall Yankee

He had a great sense of humor and well remembered as the well-loved baby brother who grew to be 6' 4" tall.

Eusebio Felix Gonzales was the last and ninth living child of Crescéncia and Felix Gonzales born in Oakland, Alameda, California. He grew up on the Gonzales ranch at Putah Creek and went to school in Winters, California where he graduated and later joined the United States Marines.

Eusebio was called Sab and as the youngest Gonzales child, found himself on a busy ranch and worked alongside his older siblings. It was during those times when the music that surrounded him from his uncle John Silván and brothers, that he learned to love the guitar. You can see the ease with which he played; His leg slung over the top of the steps as he serenades his mother and those that looked up from below.

This photo was taken at the Gonzales ranch. It was a two story house where Felix and Crescéncia lived upstairs and Red and Edna lived on the ground floor with their children. It was a home the Gonzales family remembers filled with food, laughter and

yes, always the ever-present work in the orchard. But Sab always found time to play his guitar.

During his military service for the United States of America, he earned a Purple Heart while serving on Iwo Jima, Guam and in China. He also returned from the Philippines with a Dobro stainless steel guitar. It had a unique sound; its facade was etched with palm trees. The guitar's name has a long and involved history that is interwoven with that of the resonator guitar[98].

A newspaper article in the Winters Express states: "E. F. Gonzales, son of Mr. and Mrs. F. Gonzales, arrived last week from San Diego, where he received his discharge from the Third Marine Division. Gonzales had been stationed at Tientsin, China.

Crescéncia, young Eusebio (Sab) and Felix Gonzales - 1942

---

[98] His son, Phil, has his father's guitar as a memento.

When Sab was 26, he met and romanced Phyllis Hall Yankee, a young woman who worked at Dean Witter & Co. in Sacramento, California.

A July 1949 wedding

BACK ROW: The bride, with a small veil on her head is Phyllis Yankee. To her left is the tall dark-haired groom, Eusebio Gonzales. To the groom's left is Felix Gonzales, his father.
FRONT ROW: Crescéncia and Felix's eldest child, Alejandro (Red), second from left.

Red's eldest child, Christina (Borges) is over his right shoulder in a knee length white dress wearing a white choker. Standing to her left is her (very handsome) brother, Herman, named after Uncle Gerónimo who remained in Spain, brother of Crescéncia Silván Gonzales.

In 1951, the couple's first child, Linda Alicia Gonzales, was born. Following her birth was Patricia Ann (aka Patte) in 1956 and a son, Philip Gale the year afterward in 1957. Two grandchildren, daughters of Linda and Scott (Rhoades): Sydney and Whitney.

He was employed at Walker Pre-Cast, where he retired at age 62 in 1985. At that time, with their children already adults, he and his wife, Phyllis, volunteered many hours at Amtrak, the California State Railroad Museum and SPCA. They also loved to travel. Upon retirement, they set their sights on seeing the world and visited Asia, Europe, North and South America and his parent's birthplace in Fuentesaúco, Zamora, Spain. They created memories and snapped photographs that fill several photo albums that their children still enjoy.

Eusebio was an avid gardener and he also liked to fish and hunt. Although closest to his younger sisters and brothers, he enjoyed the camaraderie of them all. He and his brother, Dutch, traveled to Spain together with their wives to Fuentesaúco, the village their parents emigrated from in 1911. During their visit, the Santa Maria del Castillo Iglesia (church) was being renovated and chunks of the wall littered the ground. They were delighted when the priest allowed them to gather pieces of stone to carry home to family members.

Their children carried these chunks....a 'piece of Fuentesaúco' down the aisle during their weddings. The chunks are now encapsulated into glass-framed memory boxes. It still warms my heart to visualize Eusebio and Dutch holding those precious stone pieces all the way home to California.

Over the years, Eusebio was called many names, such as Sab, Felix, Sabito and Eusebio.

In 1992, Johnny Gonzales asked him to give a brief history of the Gonzales family at the family reunion organized by Sab, Johnny Gonzales, Ralph Gonzales and Christina Borges. His speech was humorous, as always...stating being retired felt like "floating on a cloud." He remembered being bopped in the back of the head by his father if he opened his mouth and told "you don't know anything". But they were fond memories and he loved his family.

Phyllis, Phil, Linda, Patte and Sab

Linda with daughters, Sydney and Whitney beside Patte, Phyllis and Sab

Linda married Scott Rhodes (Elk Grove, CA), Patte married Everett "Butch" Kronlund (Big Sur, CA) and Phil married Marsha (Oregon).

Sab became very ill in Elk Grove, he was hospitalized in Sacramento and died at age 81, with his family surrounding him. He died four years before his wife, Phyllis.

At his request, he was cremated and no services were held.

99   Eusebio Felix "Sab" Gonzales   Sign Guest Book

GONZALES, Eusebio Felix "Sab"
Born May 18, 1923 in Oakland, CA. Passed away on June 11, 2004, in Elk Grove, CA. Survived by loving wife Phyllis Yankee Gonzales; daughters Linda G. Rhoades (Scott) and Patte G. Kronlund (Butch); son Phil G. Gonzales; and granddaughters Whitney and Sydney Rhoades. Also survived by sisters Tina Coombs, Vic Weber and Theresa Sackett and sister-in-law Edna Gonzales; and many well-thought-of nieces and nephews. He earned The Purple Heart while serving as a Marine on Iwo Jima, Guam and in China. He was a member of SIRS #50 and United Commercial Travelers. He volunteered over 3500 hours at the California State Railroad Museum and on Amtrak. He was an avid gardener, fisherman and hunter and traveled the world after retiring from Walker Pre-Cast in 1985. He had a great sense of humor and was well-liked and admired by all who came in contact with him. He will be sorely missed. At his request, no services will be held. Donations may be made to Sacramento SPCA, 6201 Florin-Perkins Rd., Sacramento, CA 95828.

99 Photo: Theresa, Eusebio (Sab), Sally, Tina, Dutch and Marie Gonzales – 1992 Gonzales Reunion

WIFE OF EUSEBIO GONZALES
PHYLLIS H. YANKEE GONZALES
19 December 1924 - 20 March 2008
Oakland, Alameda County, California

Phyllis H. Yankee was called "the voice of Dean Witter from KFBK Radio". She was the daughter of Rendle Bourne Yankee and Alice M. Dumas.

FATHER: Rendle Bourne Yankee was born in Salt Lake City, Utah on 16 February 1893. He died 20 May 1976 in Sacramento, Sacramento County, California at age 83. His father was Elgin Stowell Yankee, born in Missouri in 1862 and died in 1951. His mother was Georgina Adelaide Hall, born in Canada in 1863 and died in 1948.

Rendle Yankee registered between1917-1918 for the Civilian Draft in Esmeralda, Nevada. In 1920 he is shown as single on the Federal Census in Sacramento living with his parents, at age 26, and an older brother (Elgin S. age 33) and a younger sister (Ella age 14). By 1925, he lived in Oakland and Berkeley California and moved to Sacramento area by the 1930 Federal Census. He registered again in 1942 for the World War II Draft in Sacramento. He was listed as a salesman but later became a baker and lived in the Sacramento area until his death in 1976.

Her mother was Alice Dumas, born in Chicago, Cook County, Illinois on 9 September 1892 and died March 26, 1946 in

Sacramento, Sacramento County, California at age 53. Her father was Henry Dumas (dates unknown) and Henrietta S. Higley (some records show "Highley") born in 1857 and died in 1940. Her parents were both born in England according to the 1910 Federal Census in Chicago, Cook County, Illinois.

Alice M. Dumas had six sisters (Elizabeth, Henrietta, Agnes, Mildred, Winifred and Grace) and one brother (Henry A.). Her siblings were born between 1881 and 1896. Alice was next to the youngest child. Alice moved to the Oakland, California area from Chicago with her family between 1920 and 1925 and married Rendle Yankee in the early 1920s.

The 1930 Federal Census in Sacramento, California lists Alice and Rendle Yankee, age 31 and age 37 with their 5-year old daughter, Phyllis Yankee. No other siblings are listed.

Phyllis attended school in Sacramento and eventually lettered in archery and was a member of the Equestrian Riding Club and Rally Club at Sacramento High School. After graduating, she attended secretarial school and at age 19, she began working for Dean Witter & Co. in Sacramento where she worked for 44 years until she retired in 1987. She manually updated stock market prices on a stock board and became the voice of Dean Witter for more than twenty years on KFBK radio from a microphone at her desk, updating investors on current stock prices.

The Sacramento Bee's obituary stated she was a community volunteer. Also, as railroad enthusiasts, she and her husband, Eusebio, donated over 3,500 hours as California Railroad Museum docents. The couple also raised a puppy for Guide Dogs for the Blind and volunteered at annual SPCA book sales; she was a past president of the SPCA Guild.

Phyllis Yankee Gonzales also volunteered at the *Casa de los Niño's Restaurant* of the Sacramento Children's Home where she also tested their recipes. She experimented with new recipes. No TV dinners or store-bought desserts for Phyllis; she proudly cooked meals from scratch and was an excellent cook.

They raised three children, Patricia (Patte) Kronlund, Linda Rhoades and Phil Gonzales. She had two granddaughters, Whitney and Sydney Rhoades.

She and her husband, Sab, were world travelers. They saw Asia, Australia, and Europe, North and South America and Fuentesaúco, Spain. She is remembered as warm, gracious, kind and always smiling.

Phyllis died of respiratory failure in Sacramento, California at age 83. Eusebio and Phyllis' asked to be cremated and scattered across the world. Respecting their parent's wishes, their children, Linda, Patte and Phil, have indeed scattered some of the ashes on their world-wide trips. Their children are considering burial for the remaining ashes at the new veterans cemetery in Dixon, California.[100]

---

[100] Source: Linda Alicia Gonzales Rhoades

PART 5

The OTHER Silván Family

FELISIDAD ~ "FELISIDADA" ~ FELICIDADA

I call Felisidada a shadowy "cousin" as I have made a lot of assumptions; her name has risen in conversations, oral memories at interviews and letters. She was indeed part of our family --- through marriage.

Crescéncia corresponded with her brother, Gerónimo in Spain, often begging him to join the Silván family in California. Her daughter, Theresa Gonzales Sackett, remembers listening to her parent's conversation during the 1930s as they discussed their worry about Felicidada's welfare. Theresa thought maybe someone's parents had died --- in Spain? She did not know Felicidada. After our interview, I found the ship manifest in 1930 listing both Gerónimo and his wife, Joaquina, on a ship leaving Cuba and returning to Spain. It was my first clue.

Assumption #1 is Gerónimo and Joaquina sailed from Spain to Cuba to work in the sugar plantations (?) when Felicidada was young. She may have stayed behind with relatives as her parents earned money for the family during that starving time. Crescéncia and Felix Gonzales were worried about Felicidada due to her parent's temporary emigration, not due to their death.

In October of 1969, my father, Michael Silván Ruiz made his first pilgrimage to Spain and the villages our family left behind. He wrote a letter to his sister, Rose Ruiz Gobert, to say he found "Uncle Gerónimo Silván's adopted daughter, Felicidada." It was after this letter that her name began to bud and bloom during conversations with other family members so many years later. My father's letter continued, *"The poverty was something that made me feel bad. With eight or nine children, the father had no education and no job. Together the family lived in a two-room house, along with a pig, chickens and some rabbits. With the combination of all this, it is quite different to describe the various odors into one. Hiding my feelings, I spent the night.*

I was afraid to find out if four or five kids were in the same bed with me or the pig. The warmth was still there. I closed my eyes and prayed for dawn. That was a long time coming."

"With the priest the following day, we located more Silván family members. Only to find that they would not acknowledge me or admit they were from the same family. Having acquired a large wealth, they did not want it known that Felicidada was related and permitted to live as such. The priest scolded them soundly in a religious way and we left. I firmly believe there was more love in the house of poverty than in all the wealthy homes of our relatives combined."

In another letter dated August 27, 1976 sent to the attention of Marie Gonzalez Miller, a Señor Manuel Zapatero Garcia (administrator of Correos, the universal postal union) responded to her request to find people who might be related to her parents. His letter stated there was a cousin to Crescéncia Silván named Clara Silván (Felicidada) who had 5 or 6 sons living in Fuentesaúco. The letter also stated he could not document her father, Eusebio Gonzales Hernandez born June 12, 1880. (We know this was because her father's name was not Eusebio, but Felix Gonzales Hernandez – a fact that caused confusion for years, right up to the inscription on his headstone.)

Assumption #2 is that Felicidada grew to adulthood, married Segundo **Sánchez** Arias and had a large family who remained in Fuentesaúco.

Manuel Zapatero García

ADMINISTRADOR DE CORREOS

Teléfono 90.01.02

FUENTESAÚCO

(Zamora)

27 de
agosto
1976.-

Sr. Dª. Marie González Miller.

331 Eleanor Ave.- SACRAMENTO 95815.-
CALIFORNIA USA.-

Muy Sra. mia:

En nuestro poder su atta. carta de 22 junio ppado. y en relación con
la misma hemos tenido la gentileza de extremar la búsqueda de cuantos datos
interesa, infirmándole lo siguiente.

En primer lugar, no aparece como nacido en 12 junio de 1880 su querido
padre D. EUSEBIO HERNANDEZ GONZALEZ ó GONZALEZ HERNANDEZ, toda vez que tanto
en los libros de archivo del Registro Civil ni en los de la Parroquia como bautizado no figura registrado su nombre en los años 1879-1880 y 1881.-

En virtud de ello hemos indagado de personas que aún viven en la localidad y que aproximadamente tiene la edad de sus padres, habiendo sacado los
siguientes informes.-

Que Doña Cristencia Silvan era hija de Pedro y Agustina.Su esposo, o
sea su padre de V. estuvo trabajando en casa de una familia llamada SAMANIEGOS.
Que recuerdan el nombre de las siguientes hijas del matrimonio y hermanas de
V. que fueron: Pascuala, que se casó en un pueblo cerca de aquí llamado ARCENI-
LLAS. Otra, llamada Rosa, se caso, al parecer en el exterior. Otra, llamada
Angeles se casó aquí con un señor llamado Pedro (de apodo) el tio Petaco. Esta
Angeles tenía una hija que se casó aquí con un Herrador. Otro hermano, llamado
Jeromo: después viven unas nietas que suelen llamarlas de Maria la Silvana y
se llaman Natividad que fué casada con un Sr. llamado de apodo Ñaña y del que
viven sus hijos llamados Marcelino, Nemesio y Fernando.

Por ultimo tenemos una prima carnal de Dª. Cristencia Silvan que
se llamaba Clara Silvan (fallecida) pero existen 5 o 6 hijos que todos viven
aquí en Fuentesaúco.

No hemos preguntado nada a ningún nieto de los que le menciono sin
antes informarle a V. de todo por si tiene alguna idea de cuanto se le indica

no obstante si continua V. interesada en que sigamos interesando informes hasta encontrar su verdadera familia, puede V. volver a escribirme que muy gustoso le atenderé, pués estoy seguro que le servirá de satisfacción y de alegría en virtud de los deseos que tiene de saber notícias de los suyos.

No obstante, debe recordar antes algún detalle más exacto, como por ejemplo las fechas de nacimiento de sus padres y sus hermanos, en especial el año que nacieron, ya que como le indico al principio no nació su padre el dia 12 junio 1880. Tambien es necesario saber si su madre Cristencia nació aquí en Fuentesaúco o nació en Zamora.-

Me indicaron tambien que su madre Cristencia era casi seguro que tuviera ahora 94 años por ser amiga íntima de una señora de aquí de su misma edad.

Si me aclara algunos datos más, es probable que le podamos dar datos concretos y reales, que le sirvan de base para encontrar a su familia.

Sin otro particular, le saluda muy atto. affmo. y ss. ss.

NOTA.-

Si no tiene inconveniente, le ruego escriba en español ya que en esta localidad nadie sabia traducir el inglés de su carta y he tenido que ser yo quien desinteresadamente he tenido el gusto de traducirla y contestarle a V. No obstante, no es bueno mi inglés.

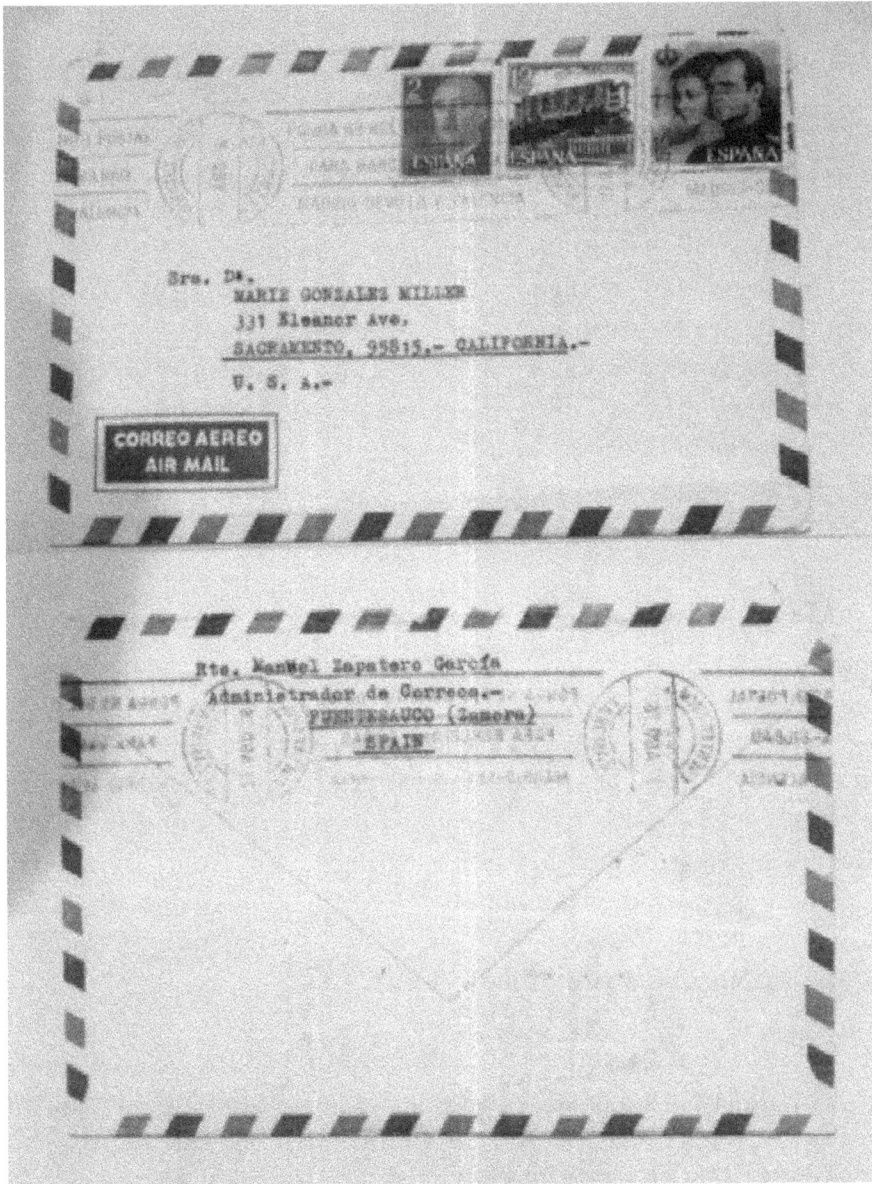

MARIE GONZALES MILLER NEVER GAVE UP! SHE KEPT WRITING THOSE LETTERS and she eventually received answers that helped so much in the gathering of this elusive information about Felicidad, or Felicidada as she was sometimes called. I applaud her tenacity and curiosity because I have the same genes!

Five years later, a letter dated November 21, 1981 was received by María Gonzales Miller written by Cecelia, the granddaughter of Joaquina Bragado Vicente, who was the wife of Gerónimo Silván. The letter basically states they had no knowledge of cousins of Uncle Gerónimo. She also shared that her mother died thirty years ago "shortly after Uncle Geronimo." Cecelia said she had been in contact with Eusebio and Phyllis Gonzales and sent a photo to them. Evidently, Marie Gonzales Miller asked if any letters written from Crescéncia to her brother, Gerónimo, still existed. No, was Cecelia's answer as it had been many years past. I have posted a copy of the 2-page letter from Cecelia in the next pages.

Assumption #3: Cecelia calls Gerónimo "uncle" so it confirms he was not her grandfather. A step-grandfather might be called uncle out of respect. It also tells us Gerónimo and Joaquina both died in the 1950s.

Summary: Felicidad was the stepdaughter of Gerónimo Silván Hernandez. Her mother was his wife, Joaquina Bragado Vicente and she was a child from a prior marriage. Felicidad married a man named Segundo Sánchez Arias and they lived at Calle Benjamin Martin, numero 3, in Fuentesaúco, Zamora, Spain. Felicidada's daughter was named Cecelia.

Question: Michael Silván Ruiz visited Fuentesaúco twelve years before Cecelia wrote the letter above. He slept in the home of Felicidada and Segundo, so it was surprising that the family did not know cousins of Gerónimo existed and lived in America. It could be that Cecelia was very young and had not heard about his visit from her elders.

Fuentesauco - 21 - 11 - 1981

Estimada Prima Maria y familia
Maria por el Señor Manuel el de correos
emos sabido buestras notisias que -
hasia muchos años que no sabia
nada de bosotros el Tio Geronimo
murio hase muchos años y no tubo
familia con mi Madre Guaquina
mi Madre hase unos 30 años que
murio poco despues que el Tio.
Geronimo yo siempre fui quien es_
cribia a buestros Padres en las
fechas que pones en tu carta tus
hermanos felis y Eusebio estubie_
ron haqui hase unos años y te_
mando una foto que esta tu
hermano Eusebio para que nos
conoscas!
Maria temando las fes de nasi_
miento de tus Padres que nos
acostado bastante en conseguirlas
por que nasieron en otra fecha
a la que tu nos dises en tu carta

taubien nos dises que si haj alguma
carta haquí de buestros Padres pues
oscine que hase tautos años que
murieron mis Padres que lla no
queda nada sin mas nos alegramos
mucho de buestras noticias j espero
que entendais mi carta porque el
ingles haquí no sesabe.
sedes piden con cariño buestros
primos

Segundo y felisidad

una felir Navidad j un prospero
año nuevo

os escribe una j ija de buestra
prima felicidad mi nonbre es
Cecilia

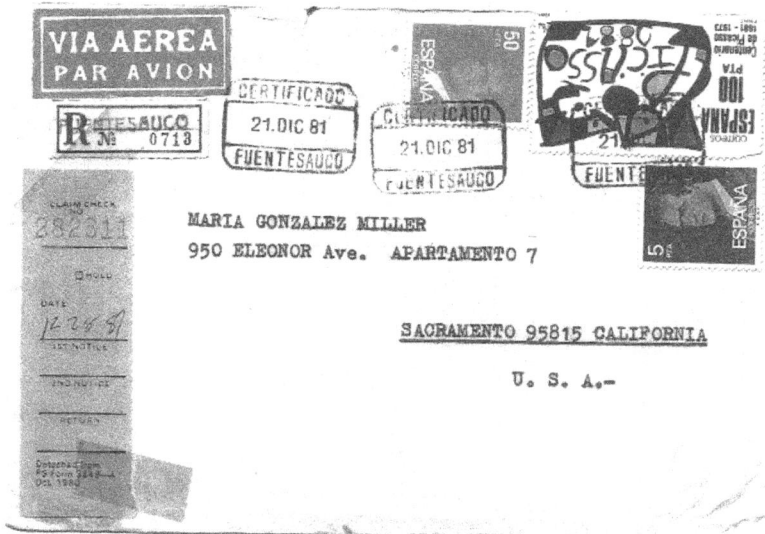

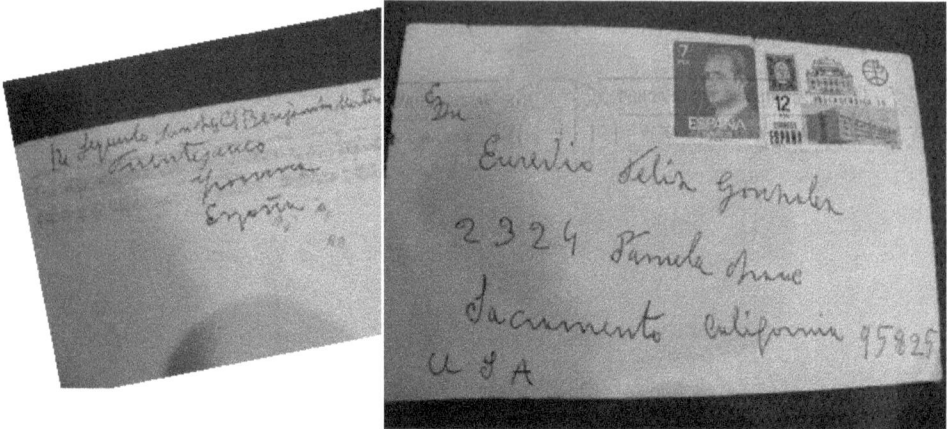

This photo was taken in Fuentesaúco, Zamora, Spain during a visit by brothers, Eusebio (Sab) and Alfred (Dutch) Gonzales. They and their wives made a pilgrimage to the Silván ancestral village. After their visit, they corresponded with people from the village. I can only surmise this couple might be Felicidad and her husband, Segundo.

Photo courtesy of Patte Gonzales
Kronlund and Linda Gonzales
Rhoades

The Silván Family Tree continues to grow new leaves on this genealogical tree as new generations are born each year.

So many members had never met one another, so I hosted the SILVÁN FAMILY REUNION on August 11, 2014 at Lake Solano Park on Pleasants Valley Road in Winters, California. The family names were Silván, Souza, Martin, Medeiros, Gonzales, Ruiz, Cuellar, Hyatt and many others. There were nearly 250 attendees.

This area is where the Silván families settled and where I lived two years of my young life. It was an overwhelming pleasure to introduce so many cousins and hear the stories and meet the families --- and share The Girl Immigrant, their ancestor's immigration story at that time. It has been an amazing journey.

Karen Souza brought the cake and my brothers and several cousins brought the music.

Patricia Steele researched, interviewed family and found documents to continue the Silván history. She also created many of their memorials on www.findagrave.com if they were interred in cemeteries. As a volunteer for the Find-A-Grave organization, she enjoys sharing the excitement she felt when she "found" an ancestor's gravestone photo on the site some years ago. She photographs gravestones for family historians looking for their own family gravestones.

Patricia has been helping transcribe the immigrant ship manifests sailing from Spain to Hawaii between 1907-1913 with the vigorous and steadfast input from Steven Alonzo and Cristobal Navas Perez.

She is also one of the administrators for the Hawaiian Spaniards Facebook page whose site often helps other Spanish descendants find and connect with cousins they were unaware of.

Besides writing a column for the Facebook site, her own books, researching and finding new cousins, she also attends book-signing events. She's a speaker for the Arizona Genealogy Society and presents talks on genealogy and her book, *The Girl Immigrant.*

"I want all of our future grandchildren to know the people they came from," she says, "through the eyes of their ancestors." *Silván Leaves* has biographies inspired by the author's Spanish ancestors' immigration story…from *Fuentesaúco*, Spain to the Hawaiian sugar cane fields, and later to America and life afterward. Once she published their immigration story, she hoped to define each family member and this book strives to do this in biographical memoirs.

Steele includes tales from Silván descendants, photographs and documents and is now writing the third book in her Spanish Pearls Series titled, *Ruiz Legacies*, the other half of her Spanish heritage.

She lives in the low desert of Arizona with her husband.

www.ingramcontent.com/pod-product-compliance
Lightning Source LLC
Chambersburg PA
CBHW021613270326
41931CB00008B/676